THE EAST INDIA VOYAGER

THE EAST INDIA VOYAGER

EMMA ROBERTS

GYAN

Published by

Gyan Publishing House
5, Ansari Road
Daryaganj, New Delhi-110002
Phone: 011-47034999, 9811692060
E-mail: books@gyanbooks.com

Distribution Network
gyanbooks.com
India, USA, Canada, UK, Australia

ISBN: 978-93-7169-208-3 (PB)

First Published, 1839

2nd Impression 2025

Printed at: Gyan Press, Delhi.

THE EAST INDIA VOYAGER
Author: EMMA ROBERTS

ROBERTS'S

EAST INDIA VOYAGER.

THE

EAST INDIA VOYAGER,

OR THE

OUTWARD BOUND.

BY EMMA ROBERTS,

AUTHOR OF

"MEMOIRS OF THE RIVAL HOUSES OF YORK AND LANCASTER," "SCENES AND CHARACTERISTICS OF HINDOSTAN," &c. &c.

London:

J. MADDEN & CO., LEADENHALL STREET.

1845.

DEDICATED

TO

ROBERT GILLIES, Esq.,

COMMANDANT OF THE ASIA.

My dear Sir,

The Dedication of this little volume will I hope be acceptable to you, as affording an assurance that the kindness and attention which I experienced during my voyage home from India, as a passenger on board a ship which you commanded, were not unappreciated at the time, and can never be forgotten. In offering you this tribute of esteem, I know that I am doing that which will be most pleasing to the companions who shared in the enjoyments of the voyage; and feeling that all who could avail themselves of a similar opportunity of recording their opinions of your friendly and liberal conduct, would express the same sentiments. I remain with the greatest respect and regard,

Most gratefully Yours,

EMMA ROBERTS.

London, July 1*st*,
1839.

CONTENTS.

Page

Preface v

CHAPTER I.

Choice of a Cabin 1

II.

Ladies' Outfit 11

III.

Desultory Remarks 21

IV.

Domestic Economy, Diet, Clothing, Etc. 35

V.

The Civil Service 49

VI.

The Civil Service Continued 65

VII.

Cadets 85

VIII.

Cadets Continued 104

IX.

Cadets Continued 118

Page

CHAPTER X.

CADETS CONTINUED 132

XI.

THE MEDICAL SERVICE 147

XII.

THE MEDICAL SERVICE CONTINUED 160

XIII.

THE MEDICAL SERVICE CONTINUED 177

XIV.

DESULTORY REMARKS UPON THE OFFICE OF CHAPLAIN, ETC. 191

XV.

THE OVERLAND JOURNEY 209

JOURNEY FROM LONDON TO BOMBAY, ETC. 223

EXPENDITURE ON JOURNEY TO BOMBAY, ETC. 226

APPENDIX 229

PREFACE.

WHILE Hand-books, Guides, Itineraries, and Directions of every description are afforded to tourists who may desire to repair to any part of Europe; the large and most important territory belonging to Great Britain in the East, is comparatively neglected; only one work having hitherto appeared which professes to furnish instruction to those who meditate a visit to British India.

No one can be more anxious to do justice to the value and excellence of the General East India Guide and Vade Mecum, than the author of the present volume. It is a work of the most interesting and important character, and one which no person desiring to become acquainted with topics intimately connected with the advantages to be derived from a residence in British India, should neglect to purchase. It may be justly said, that numerous highly gifted people might spend the greater portion of their lives in India, without having, themselves, the opportunity of obtaining half the information supplied by Dr. Gilchrist in his comprehensive volume. Nevertheless there is room for a new work more exclusively addressed to individuals at home, who in going out to India require instructions contained in a small compass, relative to the best methods which they should pursue in order to secure the highest degree of comfort to themselves in their settlement in a foreign country. The various alterations which have taken place in the different departments of the public service, and the condition of India generally, since the last edition of the Vade Mecum, seem to call for farther information; while the main objects of the two works are so dissimilar, that the present may be said to have borrowed little or nothing from its predecessor.

The establishment by Captain Melville Grindlay of a House of Agency, upon a plan so liberal, advantageous, and comprehensive, as to merit all the praise that can be given to exertions having some of the highest objects in view, has proved of the greatest possible utility to the Anglo-Indian public; encouraging the formation of other establishments of the same nature, and thus increasing the facilities of those who are about to proceed to India. All who require information and advice upon every subject connected with a visit to Oriental countries, may avail themselves of the fruits of an experience acquired by Captain Grindlay, during a long and actively employed residence in the East, with the advantage also of those widely spreading connexions which have enabled him to carry out the plans of an undertaking of the most extensive and beneficial description. The difficulty, or it may be said the impossibility of obtaining admittance to a club composed of members well acquainted with our Asiatic possessions, renders Captain Grindlay's establishments in the City and at Charing Cross, peculiarly advantageous to young men going out to, or returning from India, who without incurring the expence of a club, will have the opportunity of meeting with gentlemen belonging to the three Presidencies, whose acquaintance cannot fail to be of infinite service to them. Great however, as the assistance assuredly is, that may be derived by subscribing to the various houses of Agency, which the success of Captain Grindlay's establishments have produced, a work of the present nature seemed necessary for the purpose of enabling travellers to prepare themselves for their journey, and to become acquainted with the prospects opening before them ; and the expectations of advantage and profit which they may reasonably entertain in pursuing a career of adventure in the Honourable Company's territories.

NOTICE.

The Publishers of this Work, with a view to render it as complete as possible, have added the Regulations established by the Court of Directors for appointments to the East-India Company's Service. The "EAST-INDIA VOYAGER," *whether proceeding in a Civil, Ecclesiastical, Military, Medical, or Marine capacity, will, on reference to this Work, acquire all the preliminary information connected with his Appointment, and which, derived from authentic sources, is now, through a popular medium, made extensively available.*

REGULATIONS AS TO THE NOMINATION OF STUDENTS FOR THE EAST-INDIA COLLEGE.

No Candidate for the College can be nominated thereto, until he has completed the sixteenth year of his age: And no person who has been dismissed the Army or Navy, or has been expelled from any place of public education, will be nominated to the College.

No Student can be appointed a Writer to India whose age is less than eighteen or more than twenty-three years, nor until he shall have resided four Terms at least in the College, and shall have obtained a certificate, signed by the Principal, of his having conformed himself to the statutes and regulations of the College.

The Parent or Guardian of every Candidate for the College will be required to address the following letter to the Nominating Director:

"Sir:—I beg to assure you, on my honour, that my...., "to whom you have been so good as to give a nomination "to the College, has not been dismissed the Army or the "Navy, and that he never was expelled from any place of "public education.

"I have the honour to be, &c."

Candidates for the College must produce the under-mentioned Documents, previous to their being nominated as Students.

An Extract from the Parish Register of their Birth or Baptism, properly signed by the Minister, Churchwarden, or Elders; and, in addition thereto,

A Certificate, agreeably to the following form, must be written, signed, and produced by the Parent, Guardian, or near Relation:

"I do hereby certify, that the foregoing Extract from "the Register of Baptisms of the Parish of ——— in the "County ———, contains the date of the Birth of my "———, who is the Bearer of this, and presented for a "Nomination as a Student at the East India College, by "———; and I do further declare, that I received the "said Presentation for my ——— gratuitously, and that no "Money or other valuable Consideration has been or is to "be paid, either directly or indirectly, for the same; and "that I will not pay or cause to be paid, either by myself, "by my ———, or by the Hands of any other person, any "pecuniary or valuable consideration whatsoever, to any "Person or Persons who have interested themselves in "procuring the said Presentation for my ——— from the "Director above-mentioned.

"Witness my Hand, this —— Day of ——, in the year "of our Lord ——."

In the event of no Parish Register existing, or to be found, a Declaration must be made of such circumstances before a Magistrate, to the following effect, viz.

"I, C. D., presented as a Student for the East-India "College by ————, do declare that I have caused search "to be made for a Parish Register, whereby to ascertain "my age, but am unable to produce the same, there being "none to be found; and further I declare, that from the

"Information of my Parents and other Relations (which "Information I verily believe to be true), I was born in the "Parish of ——, in the County of ——, on ——, "in the year ——.

"Declared before me
"this————
"Day of ————

"Witness my Hand, this —— Day of ——,
"in the Year of our Lord ——
"C. D."

The Parent, Guardian, or near Relation, must then add their Certificate as to the truth of the Declaration, made applicable thereto, and in conformity with that ordered to be annexed to the Extract from the Parish Register.

The above-mentioned Certificate (and Declaration, in cases where a Declaration shall be required) are to be annexed to the Petition to be written by the Candidates (*which Petition is to be agreeable to the form hereafter given*), and they are to sign a Declaration thereon, that they have read these printed Instructions. The same Declaration is to be signed by the Parent, Guardian, or near Relation of the Candidates respectively. Every Candidate for the College, and his Parent or Guardian, will be required to make the following Declarations, in writing, to the Director who nominated him.

"Sir:—While I offer you my acknowledgments for the "appointment to which you have been pleased to recom- "mend my —— of a Student at the East-India College, "in order that, if he should in all respects conduct himself "properly there, he may be appointed a Writer in the "service of the Company in India, I am at the same time "to assure you, that he accepts of this favour with grati- "tude, and that it is his own free choice and liking to go "to the College, and subsequently to his destination in "India, if he shall be found qualified."

Declaration to be made by the Student on his Nomination to the College.

"SIR:—In conformity with the preceding letter from "my ——, I beg leave to assure you that I accept of the "appointment to the East-India College, and the destina- "tion to a Writership, which you have been pleased to "give me, with gratitude, and that it is with my own free "consent that I go to the College, and ultimately to India, "if I shall be found qualified."

Candidates will be interrogated in an open Committee as to their character, connexions, and qualifications, conformably to the General Court's Resolution of the 6th July, 1809. The nature of this Interrogation may be known on application to the Clerk of the College Department, East-India House.

On a Student's appointment to be a Writer, *after he has quitted the College*, a legal instrument is to be entered into by some one Person (to be approved by the Court of Directors), binding himself to pay the sum of £3,000 as liquidated damages to the Company for breach of a covenant to be entered into, that the Student's Nomination hath not been in any way bought, or sold, or exchanged for any thing convertible into a pecuniary benefit.

A Student publicly expelled the College shall not be admitted into the Company's Military Seminary, or into the Company's Civil or Military Service in India.

AT A COURT OF DIRECTORS, HELD ON WEDNESDAY, AUGUST 9, 1809:

Resolved,—That any Person who shall, in future, be nominated to a situation, either civil or military, in the service of this Company, and who shall have obtained such nomination in consequence of purchase, or agreement to purchase, or of any corrupt practice whatever, either direct or indirect, by himself or by any other Person, with or without his privity, shall be rejected from the service of the Company, and ordered back to England, if he shall have proceeded to India before a discovery of such corrupt practice be made: and if such situation shall have been so corruptly procured by himself, or with his privity, he shall be rendered incapable of holding that, or any other situation whatever, in the said service. Provided always, that if a fair disclosure of any corrupt transaction or practice of the nature before described, wherein any Director has been concerned, shall be voluntarily made by the Party or Parties engaged in the same with such Director, the appointment thereby procured shall be confirmed by the Court.

FORM OF THE PETITION.

To the Honourable Court of Directors of the East-India Company.

The humble Petition of

SHEWETH:

That your Petitioner has received the rudiments of a commercial and classical Education, and is desirous to devote himself to the Civil Service of the Honourable Company in India, and with that view to qualify himself by further improvement in liberal and suitable Learning.

He therefore humbly prays, that the Honourable Court will be pleased to place him in the East-India College, in order that, if his Behaviour and Attainments there should prove satisfactory to the Honourable Court, he may be appointed a Writer on the ——— Establishment.

And your Petitioner will ever pray.

I do hereby acknowledge to have read a printed Paper,

entitled, "Regulations as to the Nomination of Students, for the East-India College."

[*To be signed by the Petitioner, and by his Parent, Guardian, or near Relation.*]

Additional Declaration to be written and signed by the Petitioner, and addressed to the Honourable Finance and Home Committee.

Honourable Sirs;—The practice of keeping Dogs, and Shooting and Sporting upon the Manors of Gentlemen in the neighbourhood of the College or elsewhere, without their consent previously obtained, being injurious to the discipline of the Institution, I hereby respectfully assure the Honourable Committee, upon my honour, that I will abstain from the said practices during my residence at the College.

RULES AND REGULATIONS TO BE OBSERVED WITH RESPECT TO THE EXAMINATION OF CANDIDATES.

Each Candidate shall produce testimonials of good moral conduct under the hand of the Principal or superior authority of the College or Public Institution in which he may have been educated, or under the hand of the private instructor to whose care he may have been confided, and the said testimonials shall have reference to his conduct during the two years immediately preceding his presentation for admission.

Each Candidate shall be examined in the four Gospels of the Greek Testament, and shall not be deemed duly qualified for admission into Haileybury College unless he be found to possess a competent knowledge thereof; nor unless he be able to render into English some portion of the works of one of the following Greek authors: Homer, Herodotus, Xenophon, Thucydides, Sophocles; and Euripides; nor unless he can render into English some portion of the works of one of the following Latin authors: Livy, Terence, Cicero, Tacitus,

Virgil, and Horace. And this part of the examination will include questions in Ancient History, Geography, and Philosophy.

Each Candidate shall also be examined in Modern History and Geography, and in the Elements of Mathematical Science, including the common rules of Arithmetic, Vulgar and Decimal Fractions, and the first four books of Euclid.

He shall also be examined in Moral Philosophy, and in the Evidences of the Christian religion, as set forth in the works of Paley.

It is, however, to be understood, that superior attainments in one of the departments of Literature or Science, comprised in the foregoing plan of Examination, shall, at the discretion of the Examiners, be considered to compensate for comparative deficiency in other qualifications; and also that the examination shall be so conducted as to give to each Candidate reasonable time to prepare himself for the said examination.

Terms of Admission.

One hundred guineas per annum for each student; a moiety whereof to be paid at the commencement of each term, there being two in the year; besides the expense of books and Stationery.

Students to provide themselves with a table-spoon, tea-spoon, knife and fork, half a dozen towels, tea equipage, and a looking-glass; also, with not less than two pair of sheets, two pillow-cases, and two breakfast cloths.

Ten Guineas to be paid on leaving the college by each student, for the use of the philosophical apparatus and library.

COLLEGE TERMS.

First commences 19th January and ends 30th June; second commences 10th September and ends 15th December in each year.

N. B.—The students are to provide themselves with proper academical habits.

The days for receiving petitions at the East-India House from Candidates for admission into the College, are the two Wednesdays immediately preceding the 10th January and 1st September in each year.

Observations on the personal expenses of the students at the East-India College.

Unnecessary and extravagant expense, unless effectually checked, is likely to prove a great and serious evil to the East-India College. It has already, in various instances, produced pernicious effects: it is immediately connected with, and promotive of, disposition to idleness, dissipation, and other immoralities.

This is an evil which the discipline of any public institution can with difficulty and but imperfectly combat.

Regulations have been made for the counteraction of it, and might be, in a great measure, effectual, if the parents and relatives of the students would heartily join their endeavours to promote the observance and efficacy of them. But, unfortunately, they too often act in a direct opposition to the letter and spirit of those regulations; and the evil in question originates too much from the ill-judged indulgence and liberality of those very parents and relatives themselves, who, by furnishing their children or connexions with sums of money, far beyond what the regulations prescribe, or are in any way necessary, teach them to disregard the regulations, place in their hands at once a temptation to improper gratifications, and the means of procuring them.

But the mischief does not rest here. The taste once indulged for expense, is not limited to the pocket-money, even profusely furnished. Debts are contracted, sometimes to an enormous amount; tradesmen dishonourably ministering to the extravagance of youth, and trusting, perhaps, to what they often find true, that parents will silently submit to pay these improper debts, rather than suffer their children to be exposed.

But neither is this the limit of the evil. Example is infectious :—the dissipation of one produces imitation in others ; and even sober youths, who desire to practise economy, become ashamed of it, when they see so many glory in overleaping its bounds.

It need hardly be observed, that in proportion as this temper prevails, the love of study and virtuous habits, subordination to the rules of the college and to the governors of it, must decline.

Thus the very end and design of the institution is counteracted, and, so far as these evil tendencies prevail, frustrated.

It is lamentable, that such baneful effects should be produced by the error and imprudence, to use no stronger term, of parents and relatives, those most interested in the good conduct and proficiency of the student ; and who, as they would, in promoting the welfare of those who ought to be most dear to them, promote also the success of the institution, do, by their injudicious indulgence, counteract the one and the other.

It is not sufficient to say, that such evils prevail in all colleges and great seminaries, where numbers of the young are congregated. This may be true ; and that the evils fall less under observation there than in the confined institution at Haileybury, where irregularities come more immediately under the eye. But the inference to be drawn from any such statement is, that discipline and regulation ought to be excited in every possible way (especially iu a place, from its smallness, so open to minute inspection as Haileybury College is), to prevent what all must acknowledge to be highly prejudicial to good education. To the Parents, Guardians, and Relatives, therefore, of young men placed at that college, an appeal must be now made. They will see, from this short statement, of what importance it is to their children, that they should be subjected to habits of frugality and economy, and therefore restricted to what is necessary in respect of pocket-money, and absolutely prohibited from the contraction of any debt at college to which the principal or registrar shall not give a previous assent.

Not only do the proficiency and good conduct of young men, whilst at the college, materially depend on the observance of such regulations, but their progress through life will usually take much of its character from the habits they form there.

If they are sober and studious, their future career will probably be honourable and successful: if they are led into the paths of prodigality and dissipation, with which idleness and other evils are closely allied, their principles and practices are tainted at the outset of life, and are likely to become more vitiated, as time and opportunities afford new means of indulgence; especially in such a country as India, where the means of dissipation are too easily furnished by the Natives to young men in the service.

The credit, the comfort, and perhaps the support of parents, families, and relatives, are deeply concerned in this subject. Every man of right feeling will also consider, that the interest of the Company, which the parents of those whom they adopt into their service ought to desire, and indeed the interest of the public at large, which all ought to regard, are here materially concerned. There is, likewise, yet another consideration, which ought peculiarly to affect both the parents of youths elected to the college, and the youths themselves, namely, the situation in which the director, who bestows so valuable a patronage, is placed, when the object of his patronage behaves unworthily. What must be his mortification: to what a painful conflict may he be exposed, between his public duty and his private feelings? How unsuitably is he dealt with, for the liberal favour he has conferred? Students, it is to be feared, have too often presumed upon his patronage, to encourage themselves in disregarding the college regulations; but it will be no less a justice to the director than to the service, to save him from the painful office of interfering in cases of delinquency, and to make him, when about to present a student for the college, the medium of communicating the regulations of that establishment to the parents or guardians of the student, and exacting from them a solemn promise of co-operation, in inculcating them upon the youth, and especially those which relate to pocket-money and the incurring of debt: so that if those parents or guardians afterwards fail to observe the promise, they will have themselves to blame for the consequences, which may perhaps involve (as in such case it undoubtedly ought) the loss of the service: and if the friends of young men will, from a most unnecessary indiscretion and false kindness, expose their protégés to ruin, and so important an establishment as the Company's College to serious counteraction and injury, they deserve to feel the effects of such conduct.

In order to prevent these evils, this admonition is addressed to parents and relatives, with the following regulations respecting the scale of allowances to students for pocket-money, and the declaration to be made on the subject by the parent or recommending friend of the student to the nominating director.

Pocket-money to be given to the Students in the East-India College.

In the course of the first two Terms, not exceeding five guineas in the whole of each Term.

For the following Terms, not exceeding eight guineas in the whole of each Term.

Letter to be addressed by the Parent or recommending Friend of the Student, to the Director nominating him, to be by him laid before the Court of Directors.

Sir,

I have perused the "*Observations*" circulated by order of the Court "*on the Personal Expenses of the Students at the East-India College.*" I approve of them, and hereby promise to conform to them, and to use my utmost endeavours that the rules proposed in them, respecting the scale of pocket-money, and not contracting debt without the previous assent of the Principal or Registrar, shall be strictly observed by my . . . .

College Department,
East-India House,
1839.

Wm. T. HOOPER,
Clerk of the College Department.

East-India Company's Military Seminary, Addiscombe House, near Croydon, Surrey.

General Caution.

Notice is hereby given, that should it be discovered at the time the cadet is appointed, or at any subsequent period, that his appointment has been obtained by purchase, or agreement to pay any pecuniary or valuable consideration whatsoever, either directly or indirectly, when the appointment is completed, the cadet will not only be dismissed from, and rendered ineligible to hold any situation in, the East-India Company's Service, under the Court's Resolution of the 9th August, 1809, but all the parties concerned in procuring the appointment surreptitiously, or in disposing of, or receiving the same under such circumstances, will subject themselves individually and collectively to a criminal prosecution for a misdemeanour, under the Act of the 49th of

George the Third, cap. 126; and the Court of Directors of the East India Company do hereby further declare, that they will prosecute any person or persons who shall hereafter be detected in such illicit traffic.

The candidates are desired to present themselves to Mr. T. R. Clarke, clerk for passing cadets and assistant surgeons, at the East-India House, with their certificates properly filled up and signed, by 10 o'clock in the morning, or as soon after as possible, in order that they may have their nominations prepared against the committee meet, or the nominating director arrives; in failure of which they may have to wait for several hours, or to come another day.

Terms of Admission.

1. No candidate can be admitted under the age of fourteen, or above the age of eighteen years.

2. Every candidate must produce a certificate of his birth, taken from the parish register, and signed by the minister, and countersigned by the churchwardens, or, if born in Scotland, by the sessions' clerk and two elders, accompanied by a declaration from his father, mother, or nearest of kin, the forms of which may be had at the Cadet office. In the event of there being no register of his birth or baptism, the candidate will be furnished with the form of a declaration, to be taken by him previously to his being appointed.

3. No candidate will be admitted without a certificate that he has had the small-pox, or has been vaccinated; nor without a certificate, in the prescribed form, to be given by two practising surgeons, that he has no mental or bodily defect whatever to disqualify him for military service.

4. Every candidate must produce a certificate of good conduct from the master under whom he has last studied.

5. Every candidate must deliver the names and addresses

of two persons residing in London, or its vicinity, who engage to receive him if he shall be dismissed from the seminary, or removed from sickness or any other cause.

6. It is an indispensable qualification that the candidate write a good legible hand. He will be required to write down a sentence from dictation by the head master; and if he should be found deficient in his handwriting, or in his orthography, his reception into the institution will be deferred for such length of time as the head master shall report to be necessary.

7. No candidate will be admitted who cannot read and construe Cæsar's Commentaries, and who is not expert in vulgar and decimal fractions.

8. Every cadet upon his admission is considered a *probationary* pupil for the first six months, at the end of which period the public examiner will be required to report to the military committee, on the probability of the cadet being able to pass for the artillery or infantry in the required period of four terms. Should this appear improbable, either from want of talent or diligence, the cadet will then be returned to his friends.

PAYMENTS, &c.

1. The parents or guardians of the gentleman cadet are required to pay £50. per term towards defraying the expense of his board, lodging, and education, also an entrance subscription of £2. 2s. to the public library; which payments include every charge except for uniform clothes, books, and pocket-money as hereafter specified.

2. Such articles of uniform dress* as may be considered by the military committee to be necessary, shall be provided

* Viz. jackets, waistcoats, stocks, foraging caps, trousers, shoes, gloves, together with a proportionate share of the expense of any other periodical supplies, and the repairs of the same. The average cost is £6. 6s. per term.

at the cost of the cadet. The amount of pocket-money issued to him at the rates* fixed by the rules of the seminary is also to be defrayed by his parents or guardians.

3. The following class books will be provided at the public expense, the mutilation or destruction of which to be chargeable to the cadets, viz.

Hindustani Dictionary; Latin ditto; Woodhouse's Spherical Trigonometry; Inman's Nautical Astronomy; Ditto Nautical Tables.

4. The cadets will, on their first joining Addiscombe, be supplied with the following books, the cost of which will be charged to their parents or guardians, viz.

Cape's Mathematics; Straith's Treatise on Fortification; Shakespeare's Hindustani Grammar; First Vol. Hindu Selections; Fielding's Perspective; French Grammar; Ditto Dictionary; De la Voye's French Instructions; Cæsar's Commentaries.

Any books not included in the above enumeration, or which may be hereafter required at the seminary, to be paid for by the cadets.

5. A cadet entering in a term, at whatever part of it, must pay the regulated sum for the whole term in which he enters, which will count as one of the four terms of his residence; and no return of any portion of the advance will be made in the event of a cadet's quitting the seminary.

6. Previous to the cadet's admission, his parents or guardians shall furnish him with the following articles, viz.

Twelve shirts, (including three night-shirts;) Eight pairs of cotton stockings; Six ditto worsted ditto; Six towels; Six night-caps; Eight pocket-handkerchiefs; One pair of white trousers; Two combs and a brush; A tooth brush; A Bible and Prayer-book; A case of mathematical instruments of an approved pattern, to be seen at the shop of Mr.

* Viz. 2s. 6d. a week, with 1s. additional to censors, and 2s. 6d. additional to corporals.

Gilbert, Optician, 97, Leadenhall Street; or at Mr. Jones's, 62, Charing Cross: To be repaired, or, if necessary, to be renewed by the parents or guardians at the vacation.

7. The payment of the fixed charges for each term is to be made in advance; and the payment for clothes, pocket-money, and books for the preceding term, is to be made previous to the cadet's return to the seminary.

Prohibition.

The cadet must not join the seminary with a greater sum in his possession than one guinea, and a further supply from any of his relations during the term may subject him to dismissal from the seminary.

Vacations.

Midsummer commences about the middle of June, ends 31st July; Christmas commences about the middle of December, ends 31st January.

At the close of every vacation, the cadet must apply at the Cadet Department, East India House, for an order for his re-admission, and all sums then due to the Company must be paid up. This order will express that he is only to be re-admitted upon his returning with the same number of books and instruments which he took home with him, that his linen is put into proper repair, and that he is in a fit state of health to renew his studies.

Notice to Parents and Guardians.

The friends of every cadet are hereby informed, that provision being made for furnishing him with every requisite, he cannot really want a supply of money to be placed at his disposal while at the seminary; and if they do notwithstanding think proper to furnish him with money, they put it in his power to commit irregularities, which must always retard his studies, and may eventually lead to his removal from the institution.

The parents and friends are further particularly desired not to attend to any application from the cadet for money, under the pretence of his having incurred any debts at Croydon, or elsewhere, or for the purpose of subscribing to public charities, or on any other pretence whatever.

It having become known that cadets have been in the habit of writing to their friends for money, under the pretence that there were so many stoppages from their weekly allowance that they had scarcely any money left, the committee have ascertained that these stoppages have arisen, not only from wilful and wanton destruction of public property, but in a considerable degree from the postage of letters and the carriage of parcels addressed to the cadets. It has in consequence been ordered, that no letter or parcel shall be admitted into the seminary unless the postage or carriage of such letter or parcel shall have been previously fully paid for by the person sending the same. It has also been ordered, that every parcel shall be opened in the presence of one of the orderly officers and the cadet to whom it is sent; that should it contain wine, or any thing prohibited by the regulations, the parcel, upon the first offence, will be returned to the person sending the same; and that upon the second offence, the cadet will be ordered home, and will not be re-admitted until a written apology has been sent to the committee by the person who has committed a breach of this regulation.

Extract from the Standing Regulations of the Seminary,
SEC. 1, CLAUSE 1.

"No professor, master, or other person in the institution, "shall receive from the cadet, or the parents or friends of "any cadet, any pecuniary present or consideration, on any "pretence whatever."

Extract Resolution of Court of 12*th March*, 1823, *and Military Letter to Bengal, dated* 30*th August*, 1826.

"That all persons nominated in future as cadets, be re-"quired, as a condition to their appointment, to subscribe "to the military funds of their respective Presidencies."

MEMORANDA.

The gentlemen cadets educated at the Military Seminary are eligible for the corps of engineers, artillery, and infantry. Admission to the two first of these branches, viz. the engineers and artillery, is only to be obtained by these cadets, none others being eligible. Those who are most distinguished are selected for the engineers, according to the vacancies in that branch. Those immediately following in order of succession, are promoted to the corps of horse and foot artillery.

Those cadets for whom there is no room in the engineers, but who are reported to have attained to a high degree of qualification, receive honorary certificates, and their names are announced to the Governments in India, and published in general orders to the army, as meriting particular notice. They have the privilege of choosing the Presidency in India to which they shall be stationed. The cadets not appointed to the engineers or artillery, are, when reported qualified, posted to the infantry, and rank together according to the rank which they obtained at the Seminary.

The gentlemen cadets may pass through the Seminary as rapidly as their attainments and qualifications will enable them to pass after a year's residence, provided that they are of the age of sixteen years on or before the day of their final examination. Their stay at the institution is limited to four terms.

The cadets educated at this institution take rank in the army above all other cadets who are appointed from the commencement of three months previously to the date of the Seminary cadets being reported qualified; and all the time passed by them at the institution after they attain the age of sixteen, counts as so much time passed in India in calculating their period of service for retiring pensions on full pay.

Preparatory Instructions to Persons who may be nominated direct Cadets in the Service of the Honourable East-India Company.

Resolutions of the Court of Directors.

Dec. 7, 1808.—Resolved, *That the age of FIFTEEN, at which period young men have hitherto been eligible for Appointments as Cadets for the Infantry and Cavalry in the Company's Service in India, is too early an age, and therefore in future, the age of SIXTEEN years be the earliest period at which Cadets for those Corps may be appointed.*

August 9, 1809.—Resolved, That any Person who shall in future be nominated to a Situation, either Civil or Military, in the Service of this Company, and who shall have obtained such Nomination in consequence of Purchase or Agreement to Purchase, or of any corrupt practice whatever, either direct or indirect, by himself or any other Person, with or without his Privity, shall be rejected from the Service of the Company, and ordered back to England, if he shall have proceeded to India before a discovery of such corrupt practice be made; and if such Situation shall have been so corruptly procured by himself, or with his privity, he shall be rendered incapable of holding that, or any other Situation whatever in the said Service. Provided always, that if a fair Disclosure of any corrupt Transaction or Practice, of the nature before described, wherein any Director has been concerned, shall be voluntarily made by the Party or Parties engaged in the same with such Director, the Appointment thereby procured shall be confirmed by the Court.

May 21, 1828.—Resolved by the Ballot, That it be a standing order of the court in future, that all cavalry and infantry cadets and assistant surgeons who shall fail to apply at the Cadet Office for their orders for embarkation within three months from the date of their being passed and sworn before the committee, or shall not actually proceed under such orders, be considered as having forfeited their appointments, unless special circumstances shall justify the court's departure from this regulation.

June 19, 1833.—Resolved, That no person who has been dismissed or obliged to retire from the Army or Navy, the Royal Military College at Sandhurst, the Royal Military Academy at Woolwich, or from any other public institution, on account of immoral or ungentlemanly conduct, be in future appointed a cadet direct for India.

Dec. 4, 1833.—Resolved, That all direct cadets appointed or sworn in before the committee for passing military appointments between the 10th March and 10th of June, or between the 10th September and 10th December (or the days which may be fixed on for the public examination of the Seminary cadets), do rank after the Seminary cadets who may pass their said examinations, provided the latter sail for their respective destinations within *three months* after passing their said examinations.

Jan. 11, 1837.—Resolved, That no person be in future appointed a cadet direct for India, without the production of a certificate, signed by two practising surgeons, that he has no mental or bodily defect whatever, to disqualify him for military service.

N.B.—All cadets who may be appointed between the dates of public examination at Addiscombe and the 10th of March or 10th September, will be allowed to rank from the date of their sailing, provided this takes place within three months after their being passed and sworn.

The certificates required to be produced by the Act of Parliament, and the Court's several Resolutions, accompany this.

Unless the whole of the said certificates are delivered in by the cadet he will not be passed.

In the event of no parish register existing, or to be found, the before-mentioned Act of Parliament provides as follows, *viz.*

> "That if no such register can be found, a declaration, "pursuant to the Act passed in the 5th and 6th year of his "late Majesty William the Fourth, of that circumstance "shall be made by the party himself, with his in- "formation and belief, that his age is not under sixteen "years, and doth not exceed twenty-two years."

Forms of the declaration may be had on application to the clerk for passing cadets, &c., at the East-India House.

It is here necessary to remark, in consequence of several persons having been detected in attempting to pass under false certificates, when they have either been under or above the age prescribed, that all persons who may in future be nominated as cadets, if there is any cause to suspect their certificate has been forged, or alteration made therein, or collusion made use of in obtaining the same, they will, on detection, be immediately dismissed the Company's Service, and rendered for ever ineligible to hold any situation or employment in the Company's Civil, Military, or Marine Service, either abroad or at home.

Where the person to be appointed a cadet has held a commission in Her Majesty's Service, for the term of one year at least, or in the Militia or Fencible Corps when embodied, and shall have joined his regiment, and been called into actual service, or shall have been in the Company of Cadets of the Royal Regiment of Artillery, such person is eligible for the appointment of cadet in the Company's Service, provided his age does not exceed twenty-five years: of which circumstance he must, nevertheless, produce the several certificates before-mentioned, as also his commission, together with a certificate from the War Office, or commanding officer of his regiment, of his having actually joined and done duty with the regiment for the full term of one year, or upwards; and that he was neither dismissed nor resigned his regiment in consequence of any misconduct.

When the cadet is ready to embark, he must apply to Mr. T. R. Clarke, Clerk for passing Cadets, &c., for a certificate of his having passed, which certificate will direct him to the Secretary's Office, where he will obtain the certificate of his appointment. He will then hold himself in readiness to embark, either previous to the ship's departure from Gravesend, or at the last Port from whence the ship shall be ordered to take her departure from England.

Cadets' Certificates.

General Cautions.—First. Notice is hereby given, that should it be discovered at the time the cadet is appointed, or at any subsequent period, that his appointment has been obtained by purchase, or agreement to pay any pecuniary or valuable consideration whatsoever, either directly or indirectly when the appointment is completed, the cadet will not only be dismissed, and rendered ineligible to hold any situation in the East-India Company's Service, under the Court's Resolution of the 9th August 1809, but all the parties concerned in procuring the appointment surreptitiously, or in disposing of, or receiving the same under such circumstances, will subject themselves individually and collectively to a criminal prosecution for a misdemeanour, under the Act of the 49th of George the Third, Cap. 126; and the Court of

Directors of the East-India Company do hereby declare, that they will prosecute any person or persons who shall hereafter be detected in such illicit traffic.

Secondly. The candidates are desired to present themselves to Mr. T. R. CLARKE, at the Cadet Department, with their certificates as underneath, properly filled up and signed, by ten o'clock in the morning, or as soon after as possible, in order that they may have their nominations prepared against the Committee meet, or the nominating Director arrives—in failure of which they may have to wait for several hours, or to come another day.

N.B. The following forms are printed expressly for the purpose of the blanks being properly filled up and signed previously to the cadet being nominated.

FIRST.

The BLANKS in this LETTER to be filled up and signed by the person who procures the nomination from the Director for the party to be appointed.

GENTLEMEN,

I do hereby declare, upon my honour, that I received the nomination of a cadet for the (A.) __________ from (B.) __________ Esq., gratuitously and expressly for Mr. (C.) __________ and to whom I have given it gratuitously, being well acquainted with his character, family, and connexions.

I am, GENTLEMEN,

Your most obedient Servant,

To the Honourable Court of Directors
of the East-India Company.

The person recommending to sign at full length, and to insert his address. } __________

(A.) Insert the Presidency, whether for Bengal, Madras, or Bombay, as also whether for Infantry or Cavalry.

(B.) Insert the Director's name from whom the appointment is procured.

(C.) Insert the Christian and Surname of the person to be appointed a cadet.

SECOND.

If a cadet produces a false certificate, or the dates are found to have been altered for the purpose of making him appear to be of a proper age, he is rendered ineligible to hold any situation in the Company's Service.

Extract from the Register Book*

of the Parish of
in the County of

Resident Clergyman's or Sessions' Clerk's Signature ________________

Churchwardens' or Elders' Signatures ________________
____

N.B.—The above Extract must be signed by the RESIDENT CLERGYMAN, and countersigned by the CHURCHWARDENS; or, if in Scotland, by the SESSIONS' CLERK and TWO ELDERS.

* If there is no Register of Birth and Baptism to be found, the *cadet himself* must then make a declaration of the circumstance, and of the date of his Birth, the printed forms of which may be had in the Cadet Office, for the purpose of being filled up by him previous to his appearing before a Magistrate for that purpose.

THIRD.

The Blanks in this Certificate must be filled up to correspond with the Certificate of Birth.

The Parent's or Guardian's Certificate.

I do hereby certify, that the foregoing Extract from the Register of Births and Baptisms of the Parish of ____________________ in the County of __________ contains the Date of the __________ of my ____________________ who is the bearer of this, and nominated a Cadet, on the ________ Establishment, by ____________________ and I do further declare, that I received the said appointment for my ____________________ through the gratuitous solicitation of ________________ ________________ and that no money or other valuable consideration has been or is to be paid, either directly or indirectly, for the same; and that I will not pay or cause to be paid, either now or hereafter, by myself, by my ________________ or by the hands of any other person, any pecuniary or valuable consideration whatsoever, to any person or persons who have interested themselves in procuring the said nomination for my ____________ from the Director above-mentioned: and I do declare I am fully aware, that if it should be discovered hereafter that the said appointment has been obtained by purchase, or by any other unlawful means, he will be subject to dismission from the East-India Company's Service, and rendered ineligible to hold any situation whatever in the Company's Service again.

Witness my hand, this ______ day of ________________

in the Year of our Lord ________________

The Parent, or nearest of Kin alive, or Guardian, to sign at full length. } ____________________

FOURTH.

To be signed by two practising Surgeons.

MEDICAL CERTIFICATE.

I have this day carefully examined ____________________ and certify that his eye-sight and hearing are perfect; that he is without deformity, and has the perfect use of all his limbs; that he has no appearance of any constitutional disposition or tendency to disease; and that he does not appear to have any mental or bodily defect whatever to disqualify him for Military Service.

____

____

To be signed by the Parent or Guardian.

This is to certify, that my ____________________ has had the Small Pox, or has been vaccinated.

____

The candidate will likewise be required to produce a certificate from the master under whom he last studied, of his good conduct and attainments.

DIRECTOR'S AUTHORITY.

MR. T. R. CLARKE, (Clerk for passing Cadets and Assistant Surgeons, &c.)

You are hereby authorised to permit the bearer, Mr. ____ to fill up his petition for a Cadetship in the ___________________________ upon my nomination to ________________________________

____

ADDISCOMBE—CADETS' CERTIFICATES.

General Cautions.—First. Notice is hereby given, that should it be discovered at the time the cadet is appointed, or at any subsequent period, that his appointment has been obtained by purchase, or agreement to pay any pecuniary or valuable consideration whatsoever, either directly or indirectly, when the appointment is completed, the cadet will not only be dismissed, and rendered ineligible to hold any situation in the East-India Company's Service, under the Court's Resolution of the 9th August 1809, but all the parties concerned in procuring the appointment surreptitiously, or in disposing of, or receiving the same under such circumstances, will subject themselves individually and collectively to a criminal prosecution for a misdemeanor, under the Act of the 49th of George the Third, Cap. 126; and the Court of Directors of the East-India Company do hereby declare, that they will prosecute any person or persons who shall hereafter be detected in such illicit traffic.

Secondly. The candidates are desired to present themselves to Mr. T. R. Clarke, at the Cadet Department, with their certificates as underneath, properly filled up and signed, by ten o'clock in the morning, or as soon after as possible, in order that they may have their nominations prepared against the Committee meet, or the nominating Director arrives—in failure of which they may have to wait for several hours, or to come another day.

N.B.—The following forms are printed expressly for the purpose of the blanks being properly filled up and signed previously to the cadet being nominated.

FIRST.

The Blanks in this Letter to be filled up and signed by the person who procures the nomination from the Director for the party to be appointed a cadet.

Gentlemen,

I do hereby declare, upon my honour, that I received the nomination of a cadet for the Military Seminary from (A.) ______________________________ Esq., gratuitously and expressly for Mr. (B.) ______________________________

and to whom I have given it gratuitously, being well acquainted with his character, family, and connexions.

I am, Gentlemen,

Your most obedient Servant,

To the Honourable Court of Directors
of the East-India Company.

The person recommending to sign at full length, and to insert his address. } ____________

(A.) Insert the Director's name from whom the appointment is procured.

(B.) Insert the Christian and Surname of the person to be appointed a cadet.

SECOND.

If a cadet produces a false certificate, or the dates are found to have been altered for the purpose of making him appear to be of a proper age, he is rendered ineligible to hold any situation in the Company's Service.

Extract from the Register Book*
of the Parish of————
in the County of————

Resident Clergyman's or Sessions' Clerk's Signature. } ____________

Churchwardens' or Elders' Signatures. { ____________
____

* If there is no Register of Birth and Baptism to be found, the *cadet himself* must then make a declaration of the circumstance, and of the date of his Birth, the printed forms of which may be had in the Cadet Office, for the purpose of being filled up by him previous to his appearing before a Magistrate for that purpose.

N.B.—The above Extract must be signed by the RESIDENT CLERGYMAN, and countersigned by the CHURCHWARDENS; or, if in Scotland, by the SESSIONS' CLERK and TWO ELDERS.

THIRD.

The Blanks in this Certificate must be filled up to correspond with the Certificate of Birth.

THE PARENT'S OR GUARDIAN'S CERTIFICATE.

I do hereby certify, that the foregoing Extract from the Register of Births and Baptisms of the Parish of ______________________________ in the County of ______________ contains the date of the ____________ of my ______________________________ who is the bearer of this, and nominated a Cadet, on the ____________ Establishment, by ______________________________ and I do further declare, that I received the said appointment for my ______________________________ through the gratuitous solicitation of ______________________ and that no money or other valuable consideration has been or is to be paid, either directly or indirectly, for the same; and that I will not pay or cause to be paid, either now or hereafter, by myself, by my ____________ or by the hands of any other person, any pecuniary or valuable consideration whatsoever, to any person or persons who have interested themselves in procuring the said nomination for my ________ from the Director above-mentioned; and I do declare I am fully aware, that if it should be discovered hereafter that the said appointment has been obtained by purchase, or by any other unlawful means, he will be subject to dismission from the East-India Company's Service, and rendered ineligible to hold any situation whatever in the Company's Service again.

Witness my hand, this ________ day of __________

in the Year of our Lord ______________

The Parent, or nearest of Kin alive, or Guardian, to sign at full length. } ________________

FOURTH.

To be signed by two practising Surgeons.

MEDICAL CERTIFICATE.

I have this day carefully examined ________________ and certify that his eye-sight and hearing are perfect; that he is without deformity, and has the perfect use of all his limbs; that he has no appearance of any constitutional disposition or tendency to disease; and that he does not appear to have any mental or bodily defect whatever to disqualify him for Military Service.

____

____

To be signed by the Parent or Guardian.

This is to certify, that my ________________ has had the Small Pox, or has been vaccinated.

____

The candidate will likewise be required to produce a certificate from the master under whom he last studied, of his good conduct and attainments.

Regulations for the Admission of Medical Gentlemen into the East-India Company's Service as Assistant Surgeons for India.

Age.—The Assistant Surgeon must not be under Twenty-two Years, in proof of which he must produce an Extract from the Register of the Parish in which he was born, or his own Declaration, and other Certificates, agreeably to Forms to be obtained in the Office for Cadets and Assistant Surgeons.

Qualification in Surgery.—The Assistant Surgeon, upon receiving a Nomination, will be furnished with a Letter to the Court of Examiners of the Royal College of Surgeons, to be examined in Surgery, and their Certificate will be deemed a satisfactory testimonial of his qualification : but should the Assistant Surgeon be previously in possession of a Diploma from the Royal College of Surgeons of London, or of the Colleges of Surgeons of Dublin or Edinburgh, or of the College and University of Glasgow, or of the Faculty of Physicians and Surgeons of Glasgow, either of them will be deemed satisfactory as to his knowledge of Surgery, without any further examination.

Qualification in Physic.—The Assistant Surgeon will also be required to pass an Examination by the Company's Examining Physician in the practice of Physic, in which examination will be included as much Anatomy and Physiology as is necessary for understanding the causes and treatment of internal diseases, as well as the art of prescribing and compounding medicines ; and Dr. Hume will then require him to produce satisfactory proof of his having attended at least two courses of Lectures on the practice of Physic ; and above all that he should produce a Certificate of having attended diligently the practice of the Physicians at some general *Hospital* in London for six months ; or at some general Hospital in the Country (within the United Kingdom) for six months, provided such provincial Hospital contain at least, on an average, one hundred in-Patients, and have attached to it a regular establishment of Physicians as well as Surgeons. No attendance on the practice of a Physician at any *Dispensary* will be admitted.

The Assistant Surgeon is also required, as a condition to his Appointment, to subscribe to the Military or Medical and Medical Retiring Fund at his respective Presidency.

The Assistant Surgeon is required, by Resolution of Court of the 21st May 1828, to apply at the Office for Cadets and Assistant Surgeons for his orders for Embarkation, and actually proceed under such orders within three months from the date of being passed and sworn before the Committee for passing Military Appointments; he will then be furnished with an order to obtain the Certificate of his Appointment, signed by the Secretary, for which he will pay a fee of £5 in the Secretary's Office.

Assistant Surgeons' Certificates.

General Cautions.—First. Notice is hereby given, that should it be discovered at the time the Assistant Surgeon is appointed, or at any subsequent period, that his Appointment has been obtained by purchase, or agreement to pay any pecuniary or valuable Consideration whatsoever, either directly or indirectly, when the Appointment is completed, the Assistant Surgeon will not only be dismissed, and rendered ineligible to hold any Situation in the East-India Company's Service, under the Court's Resolution of the 9th August 1809, but all the Parties concerned in procuring the Appointment surreptitiously, or in disposing of, or receiving the same under such circumstances, will subject themselves individually and collectively to a criminal prosecution for a misdemeanor, under the Act of the 49th of George the Third, Cap. 126; and the Court of Directors of the East-India Company do hereby declare, that they will prosecute any Person or Persons who shall hereafter be detected in such illicit traffic.

Secondly. The Assistant Surgeons are desired to present themselves to Mr. T. R. Clarke, Clerk for passing Cadets and Assistant Surgeons, with their Certificates as underneath, properly filled up and signed, by Ten o'Clock in the Morning, or as soon after as possible, in order that they may have their Nominations prepared against the Committee meet, or the nominating Director arrives—in failure of which they may have to wait for several hours. or to come another day.

N. B. The following Forms are printed expressly for the purpose of the Blanks being properly filled up and signed previously to the assistant surgeon's being nominated.

First.—The Blanks in this Letter to be filled up and signed by the person who procures the nomination from the director of the party to be appointed.

Gentlemen,

I do hereby declare, upon my honour, that I received the Nomination of an Assistant Surgeon for (A.) ———— from (B.)———— Esq., gratuitously and expressly for Mr. (C.)————and to whom I have given it gratuitously, being well acquainted with his character, family, and connexions.

I am, Gentlemen,

Your most obedient Servant,

To the Honourable Court of Directors of the East-India Company.

The Person recommending to sign at full length, and to insert his address. } ————

(A.) Insert the Presidency, whether for Bengal, Madras, or Bombay.

(B.) Insert the Director's name from whom the Appointment is procured.

(C.) Insert the Christian and Surname of the Person to be appointed an Assistant Surgeon.

Second.—Extract from the Register Book *

of the Parish of———————
in the County of———————

Resident Clergyman's, or Sessions' Clerk's Signature. ———————

Churchwardens' or Elders' Signature ———————
———————

If an Assistant Surgeon produces a false Certificate, or the dates are found to have been altered for the purpose of making him appear to be of a proper age, he is rendered ineligible to hold any situation in the Company's Service.

N. B.—The above extract must be signed by the resident clergyman, and countersigned by the churchwardens; or, if in Scotland, by the sessions' clerk and two elders.

Third.—The Parent's or Guardian's Certificate.

I do hereby certify, that the foregoing Extract from the Register of Births and Baptisms of the Parish of ——————— in the County of ——————— contains the Date of the ——————— of my ——————— who is the bearer of this, and nominated an Assistant Surgeon, on the———Establishment, by———————and I do further declare, that I received the said appointment for my———————through the gra-

* If there is no register of Birth or Baptism to be found, the *Assistant Surgeon himself* must then make a declaration of that circumstance, and of the date of his Birth, the printed forms of which may be had in the Cadet Office, for the purpose of being filled up by him previous to his appearing before a magistrate for that purpose.

tuitous solicitation of——and that no money or other valuable consideration has been or is to be paid, either directly or indirectly, for the same; and that I will not pay or cause to be paid, either now or hereafter, by myself, by my —— or by the hands of any other person, any pecuniary or valuable consideration whatsoever, to any person or persons who have interested themselves in procuring the said nomination for my——from the director above mentioned; and I do deelare I am fully aware, that if it should be discovered hereafter that the said appointment has been obtained by purchase, or by any other unlawful means, he will be subject to dismission from the East-India Compauy's Service, and rendered ineligible to hold any situation whatever in the Company's Service again.

Witness my hand, this——Day of——
in the Year of our Lord——

The Parent, or nearest of Kin alive, or Guardian, to sign at full length. } ——

The blanks in this Certificate must be filled up to correspond with the Certificate of Birth.

Fourth.—Medical Certificate.

I have this day carefully examined——and certify that his eye-sight and hearing are perfect; that he is without deformity, and has the perfect use of all his limbs; that he has no appearance of any constitutional disposition or tendency to disease; and that he does not appear to have any mental or bodily defect whatever to disqualify him for Military Service.

——

——

To be signed by two practising Surgeons.

Regulations having reference to the Medical Care of Troops on the Voyage.

That it form a condition in the engagement of ships for the conveyance of Military, that the Court reserve to themselves the power of appointment to the Medical charge of the Troops to be embarked.

That should the said appointments be made on the part of the Company, a preference be given to surgeons belonging to the establishments in India, who may be in Europe on furlough, or sick leave, and who are about to rejoin their corps, and may be desirous of undertaking the charge, or to any assistant surgeon who may have been recently nominated for the Indian establishment, provided he has the qualifications hereafter stated. That should two or more persons be desirous of the appointment, the senior in rank and service have a preference. That the appointment shall continue open to the Court till within three weeks of the period fixed for the embarkation of the troops, and in the event of the Court declining to nominate, that the owners shall then be bound to present a person qualified according to the following Regulations.

That in no case shall an individual be appointed, who has not obtained a Diploma from the College of Surgeons of London, Edinburgh, Dublin, or Glasgow, and who moreover has not been a voyage to the East or West Indies, or who has not served in His Majesty's, or in the East-India Company's Service for at least six months, or in some other situation of equal responsibility for the like period.

That in addition to the qualifications abovementioned, the parties shall severally be subject to the approval of the Company's examining physician.

That medicines sufficient for the number of military to be embarked, be provided from Apothecaries' Hall, at the expense of the surgeon, from the allowance made to him for this purpose and for his personal services.*

* For men and women 15*s.* each; for children, 7*s.* 6*d.* each.

That a "capital set," and a "pocket case," of instruments be supplied by the Company, for the use of the surgeon on the voyage, which instruments the surgeon shall deliver in good order into the care of the Secretary of the Medical Board at the Presidency for which he is destined, in order that they may be received into the general store, or reshipped with troops or invalids returning to England.

That the allowances for the performance of the duty in question, and the conditions on which the same are to be paid, do remain as at present.

That the several Governments in India be made acquainted with the foregoing Regulations, and directed not to intrust an individual with the medical charge of military destined for Europe, who is not qualified in the same manner.

That a journal be delivered in India to the surgeon, on taking charge of the troops, and that such journal, as heretofore, be examined and approved by the Company's Examining Physician before the Surgeon's allowance is issued.

Regulations for the Appointment of Volunteers to the Indian Navy.

That nominees shall not be under 15 years or above 18 years of age unless they shall have served on board a steam vessel or under an engineer in a factory or foundry from the completion of their 18th year up to the time of their being put in nomination; and that in such case the nominees shall not exceed 19 years, and shall produce a certificate of their having been so employed.

That nominees shall produce a certificate that they have undergone an examination in arithmetic and the elementary branches of nautical education, so far as to satisfy the court, or any committee thereof, that they are qualified to enter upon the service.

That nominees shall produce a certificate from a respectable engineer that they have acquired such a knowledge of marine engineering as to afford promise of efficient service on board a steam vessel.

That every person nominated for the Indian navy be required to produce a certificate from two practising surgeons that he has no mental or bodily defect that may disqualify him for the service.

That no person who has been dismissed the army or navy, or who has been obliged to quit any school or institution for immoral or ungentlemanly conduct, will be appointed to the Indian navy.

That volunteers for the Indian navy be required to proceed to India within three months after their appointment shall be completed, or their appointment will be considered as forfeited:—and that they be ranked from the date of sailing from Gravesend (by Lloyd's List) of the ships on which they may embark for the purpose of joinlng the Service in India; that those who may embark at an out port be likewise ranked upon the same principle from the date of the ship's departure from such out port (by Lloyd's List); and that in the event of more than one volunteer proceeding on the same ship they take rank with each other according to the seniority of the nominating director. The date and place of embarkation being certified under the hand of the officer in command of the ship.

That all volunteers appointed to the Indian navy subscribe to the Indian navy fund.

Regulations for the Appointmenf of Volunteers to the Bengal Pilot Service.

That all persons nominated for the Bengal Pilot Service produce, previous to appointment, an eztract from the Parish Register of their Birth or Baptism,properly signed by the Minister, Churchwardens, or Elders, or in lieu thereof a solemn declaration of his age made by either of the parents in the presence of a magistrate.

That no lad be appointed who is under 15, or past 17 years of age, unless he has already been at sea; in which case, provided his age do not exceed 19 years he shall be eligible upon producing a Certificate of having served at sea for as many years or months as his age shall at the time of appointment exceed seventeen years.

That no lad be appointed who is not of a strong, robust constitution, and who has not produced a certificate signed by two practising surgeons to the effect that his eyesight and hearing are perfect, that he is without deformity, and has the perfect use of all his limbs; that he has no appearance of a constitutional disposition or tendency to disease, and that he does not appear to have any mental or bodily defect whatever to disqualify him for the Pilot Service.

That volunteers for the Bengal Pilot Service be required to proceed to India within three months after their appointment shall be completed, or such appointment will be considered as forfeited.

VETERINARY SURGEONS.

At a Court of Directors, 27th September, 1826.

Resolved:—That adverting to the Military Dispatch, dated the 6th instant, wherein the Court have apprized the Governments of Bengal, Madras, and Bombay, of their intention to appoint veterinary surgeons for the mounted corps in India, and to the Regulations transmittted with such Dispatch. The veterinary surgeons so to be appointed be not under twenty. nor above twenty-five years of age, and that they produce, as evidence of their qualifications, a Diploma from the Veterinary College of London, and a certificate from the Professor, of their general fitness for the Service.

At a Court of Directors held on Wednesday, the 11th January, 1837.

Resolved, by the Ballot:—That such part of the Court's Standing Order of the 27th September, 1826, for the admission of veterinary surgeons into the Company's Army, as fixes a maximum of twenty-five years, beyond which age they are declared ineligible for the Company's Service, be rescinded, any rule to that effect being found unnecessary with respect to the superior appointment of Assistant Surgeons. The sum of £95. is allowed by the Company, as Passage-money to the Veterinary Surgeon.

Veterinary Surgeon's Declaration.

I ——— do hereby declare, that I have received the appointment of Veterinary Surgeon gratuitously, and that no money, or other valuable consideration, has been, or is to be paid, either directly or indirectly for the same; and that I will not pay or cause to be paid, either by myself or by the hands of any other Person, any pecuniary or valuable consideration whatsoever, to any Person or Persons who have interested themselves in procuring the said appointment; and that I am aware that if it should be hereafter discovered that my appointment has been obtained by improper means, I shall be dismissed. and rendered ineligible to hold any situation in the Company's Service again.

To be signed in the office for Cadets and Assistant Surgeons, East-india House. } ———

ERRATA.

Page 161 and 167, Chap. xii.

Covenants, as regards the appointment of Assistant Surgeon, have been long abolished.

Copies of the Regulations of the Service are given to the Candidate for the appointment preparatory to his being passed and sworn, by the officer to whom this duty is especially intrusted. *See* page 160.

Appointment of Chaplain.

The Court of Directors require of every Gentleman appointed Chaplain, a testimonial in the form subjoined, and his Letters of Orders, Deacon, and Priest.

" We, whose names are hereunder written, declare and " testify from our personal knowledge of the life and behaviour " of ———, for the space of Three Years last past, that he hath " during that time lived piously, soberly and honestly, nor hath he " at any time (as far as we know or believe) written, taught, or " held anything contrary to the doctrine or discipline of the Chnrch " of England.

" In Witness whereof, we have hereunto set our hands " the ————."

This testimonial must be signed by Three Beneficed Clergymen.

Chaplains must attend the Political and Military Committee, with their Letters of Ordination as Deacon and Priest, and testimonials as above, previous to appointment.

The Bishop of London requires a testimonial, in a form differing somewhat from the above, which form may be obtained upon application to the Bishop's Secretary.

When sworn, the sum of £150. is paid to them to defray the expenses of their passage and outfit.

Chaplains must proceed to their destination within Six Months from the date of the Conrt's Resolution, by which they were nominated, (unless with Courts' leave) otherwise their appointments will lapse.

Salaries of the Chaplains in India, together with their Pay on Retirement from the Service.

	No. of Chaplains	Per Month Company's Rs.	Per Annum at 1s. 10½d. per Rs. £ Sterling
Bengal.			
Senior Presidency Chaplain	1	1,226 1 0	1,379 6 6
Junior ditto ditto....	1	1,149 7 0	1,293 2 0
Chaplains..................	17	800 0 0	900 0 0
Assistant Chaplains	30	500 0 0	562 10 0
	49		
Madras.			
Senior Presidency Chaplain	1	1,200 0 0	1,350 0 0
Junior ditto ditto....	1	980 0 0	1,102 10 0
Chaplains..................	9	700 0 0	787 10 0
Assistant Chaplains	18	500 0 0	562 10 0
	29		
Bombay.			
Senior Presidency Chaplain	1	1,200 0 0	1,350 0 0
Junior ditto ditto....	1	980 0 0	1,102 10 0
Chaplains..................	5	670 0 0	753 15 0
Assistant Chaplains	10	500 0 0	562 10 0
	17		

Retiring Pay.

After 18 Years' service, including 3 Years on Furlough, Per Ann. £292 0 0
If compelled through ill health to retire after 10 years " 173 7 6
———————————— 7 years " 127 15 0

Furlough.

After 7 Years' service .... " £191 12 6
Before 7 Years' service, if compelled by ill health to come to Europe, he is entitled to.................... " 127 15 0

MEMOIR

OF THE

EAST-INDIA COMPANY'S MILITARY SEMINARY.

Addiscombe Place, near Croydon, which was purchased in 1809, of E. H. D. Radcliffe, Esq., had been successively the residence of the Lord Chancellor Talbot, who died here, of Lord Grantham, and of the late Earl of Liverpool, who improved the house, and added to the plantations, before the property came into the possession of the East-India Company. The land consists of sixty-three acres freehold (including five acres purchased in 1823), and twenty-four rent-hold.

In the History and Antiquities of Croydon, by the Rev. D. W. Garrow, B. D., mention is thus made of the place, at page 40:—

"Addscomb, Addiscombe, Edgecomb, is situated about a mile from the town on the Shirley road. This noble mansion, in the time of Henry VIII., was in the possession of a family of the name of Heron.* Thomas Heron died here in 1518. William, his son, a very distinguished justice of the peace

* "The male issue of this family failed; in that of Sir Nicholas, the representation was continued through the second daughter, who married Thomas Barham, of Barham Court, in the county of Kent, by whom she had one child, Anne, who married Sir Oliver Boleter, of Sharnbrook, Bedfordshire, Knt. The issue of this marriage was Sir William Boleter, of Teston, who, having raised a regiment for the King's service, at his own expense, was slain at Cropeday Bridge, in Oxfordshire, June 29, 1644 The family of the Boleters occasionally resided at Croydon."

for the county of Surrey, died here in 1562; Nicholas Heron, Knt., brother to William, died here in 1562" (an apparent error). "It was afterwards in the possession of a gentleman named Tunstall, from a respectable family in the county of Durham; he was gentleman-usher and esquire to Queen Anne, consort of James I. Through an heiress of the Drapers, the estate became, by marriage, the property of Charles Clarke, Esq., of Oakely, one of whose descendants, Charles John, being at Paris, at the conclusion of the Peace of Amiens, there lost his life by the fall of a scaffold, at a public show. Ann Melicant Clarke, his sister and heiress, married Emilius Henry Delme, Esq., who has taken the additional name of Radcliffe. The late (first) Earl of Liverpool had a lease of Addiscombe House for life, and made it his ordinary residence. Upon his death, it was sold to the Hon. the East-India Company, by whom it has been improved by the addition of many commodious buildings, for the purpose of converting it into a military academy for cadets. On the east front of the house is the following inscription, in Roman capitals, '*Non faciam vitio culpâve minorem*,' thus translated: 'I will not diminish the value of the estate by any vice or folly of mine.'"

The present mansion* is a brick edifice, built by W. Draper,

* Relative to the origin of this building, the following passages occur in Evelyn's Memoirs:

"27th June, 1702. I went to Wotton, with my family, for the rest of the summer; and my son-in-law, Draper, with his family, came to stay with us, his house at Adscomb being now building.

"11th July, 1703. I went to Adscombe, sixteen miles from Wotton, to see my son-in-law's new house. The outside to the covering, being such excellent brick-work, based with Portland stone, with the pilasters, windows, and within, that I pronounced it, in all points of solid and good architecture, to be one of the very best gentlemen's houses in Surrey, when finished."

Mr. Vanbrugh is said to have been appointed secretary to the commissioners for building Greenwich Hospital, in consequence of being mentioned by Mr. Evelyn.

Esq. (the architect being, probably, Vanbrugh), in a fanciful style of architecture, bordering upon the Elizabethan; and consists of a basement, two state stories, and an attic. The entrance is in the east or public front, by a flight of steps, which leads into the great hall; over the central windows of this front, and above the attic, is the inscription, in Roman characters, already quoted from Garrow's work. To the west or garden front, there is a handsome brick portico and loggia.

The entrance hall leads to the grand staircase, by which there is an ascent to the saloon, which is very magnificent; the walls and ceilings of the grand staircase and saloon are decorated with paintings, chiefly by Sir James Thornhill, from the heathen mythology, finished in a masterly manner. The circular compartment of the ceiling represents the feast of Bacchus.

The corners and smaller compartments of the plafond consist entirely of trophies painted in brown chiaro-scuro. There are five doors leading out of the saloon, over which are as many allegorical subjects in brown chiaro-scuro, or mezzo-tinto. The subject of the one over the folding-doors is Vertumnus and Pomona; above the door, to the left of the fire-place, is Diana visiting Endymion sleeping; over the door, to the right of the fire-place, is Danaë and the golden shower. The fire-place is chastely embellished with the arms of the East-India Company, above which is Britannia leading by the hand the Goddess of Justice towards our Eastern territories, represented under the figure of an elephant. These two last subjects are of comparatively recent date. Over another door is the god Pan surprising the nymph Syrinx.

In the Rev. D. Lysons' "Environs of London," Sir John Vanbrugh is stated to have been the architect.

The death of Inigo Jones, which happened in 1652, destroys the supposition that he designed this edifice.

Over the remaining door is Flora, seated on the ground, and reclining against Zephyrus.

There are some landscapes on the walls of the room, which have become faded, and consist of heathen temples, aquatic pieces, trees, &c., which certainly must not be attributed to Sir James Thornhill.

On the ceiling of the great staircase is an assemblage of gods and goddesses celebrating the festal marriage of Peleus and Thetis. Jupiter holds in his hand the apple thrown amongst them by the goddess Discord, which he is delivering to Mercury, who appears descending from the ceiling, and in a lower compartment on the side wall of the stairs, is seen giving the present to the shepherd Ida. Paris delivers this prize of beauty to Venus. The two subjects are in chiaro-scuro.

Higher up the staircase there is a young girl caressing an Italian greyhound, amidst a profusion of fruit. This and the ceiling are doubtless the work of Sir James Thornhill. Opposite these is a boy, fruit, and a peacock, seen through a colonnade, but inferior to its companion piece. Trophies, busts, statues, &c. occupy the remaining spaces.

From the south front there is also an entrance through a handsome porch, that conducts to the grand staircase.

The cadets' dining-hall is situate in those parts of the building to the north of the mansion, and is a grand room, about forty-three feet square, having windows on the north and south sides, decorated with scagliola pilasters, of the Corinthian order, and the centre part having columns and entablature supporting the roof, all in the Grecian style, designed by Mr. Wilkins, the late architect and surveyor to the East-India Company.

The various outbuildings consist of the public lecture-hall and chapel, with arcade under, leading from the study-court to the parade-ground, the armoury, model-room, library, and fortification-hall, the class-studies, professors' rooms, gentlemen-cadets' dormitories, and kitchen buildings. These were very much improved by alterations and additional buildings, about thirteen years since, according to the designs of Mr. Wilkins, in which the grand dining-hall was then included; and in this state * they remain to the present time: such extensive alterations were found necessary to meet the objects of the existing institution.

The whole of the buildings are considered ample and convenient. The mansion is an elegant residence, and now in the occupation of Major-General Sir Ephraim Stannus, C.B., the lieut.-governor of the institution, who has assigned a portion as quarters for the staff-captain, &c.

The character of the design of the east front, or public entrance, is not so imposing as its extent of frontage might have admitted; but the garden-front, which is scarcely seen, produces a more pleasing effect.

Previous to its conversion into a military seminary, the education of the Company's cadets was conducted partly at the Royal Military College, Marlow, partly at the Royal Military Academy, Woolwich, or in part privately. The number of cadets at Woolwich was limited to forty-six, and the average expense was £250 each. The Company allowed two hundred guineas to each cadet educated privately, and forty-five guineas, or half the yearly expense, to each cadet educated at Marlow.

The estimated expense for two years of each cadet educated in their own seminary was £188. 16s. The seminary was originally confined to the education of officers for the artillery or engineer corps, and the regulations for its establishment were framed in conformity to the forty-fourth clause of the

* A small barrack for the detachment of Sappers and Miners, including a work-shop for the tailors of the Institution, a room for the construction of models, and a projected ward for infectious patients in the Hospital; the latter being a detached building, comprise the more recent additions to the conveniences of the Seminary.

Act 53rd George III. cap. 155. The establishment and object of the institution were sanctioned by a resolution of the General Court of the 7th April 1809. It was placed under the superintendence of Dr. Andrew, who was paid at the rate of £80. each per annum for sixty pupils. When the seminary was first established, the cadets' subscriptions were at the rate of £30. a year, and they also paid for certain articles of military clothing, at an expense of £13. 16s. 5d. The successive augmentations which have taken place are,

1st. April 1821, from £30. to £40. a year, in addition to the sum of £13. 16s. 5d. for clothing.

2nd. March 1829. First year £65, inclusive of military outfit; second year £50. There has been also, since 18th March, 1825, an entrance-subscription of £2. 2s., payable by each cadet for the use of the public library.

On the 16th January, 1828, the seminary was opened for the education of cadets for *general service*, exclusive of cavalry, the maximum number of students being 150.

3rd. On the 14th October, 1835, the Court of Directors, considering that the payments of the cadets were disproportioned to the value of their education, fixed them at their present rate, which, all expenses included, may be taken at £61. 18s. per term, or about £240. for the two years' residence.

The annual total expense of the seminary, upon an average of the six years ending Midsummer, 1835, may be taken at about £20,000, of which the Company's proportion was between £11,000 and £12,000.

The number of cadets qualified during this period was, engineers 58, artillery 80, infantry 242.

The age for admission to the institution is from fourteen to eighteen years, subject also to a preliminary examination in arithmetic and Latin of the candidates, who are nominated by the members of the Court of Directors, and by the President of the Board of Control.

The plan for the seminary, according to a report of the 11th April, 1809, " was first submitted to the Chairman and Deputy-Chairman, by Mr. Abington, of the India House, under whose direction the system has been digested and arranged, with a zeal, attention, and vigilance, deserving the Court's liberal encouragement," &c. &c.

On the 22nd November, 1837, the Court of Directors resolved, that all the time during which cadets actually continue at the seminary, after attaining the age of sixteen, and before they pass their public examination (provided they pass within the fixed period of *four* terms), shall count as a portion of the period which may eventually entitle them to retire upon *full pay*, under the regulations as now established.

The establishment of the seminary consists of a public examiner, an oriental examiner, a lieutenant-governor, staff-captain, two orderly officers, a broad-sword master, fifteen professors and masters (one of whom, being in orders, officiates as chaplain), six non-commissioned officers, a bugler, and a proportionate number of public domestic servants.

The course of studies consists of mathematics, fortification, military drawing, military surveying, Hindustani, civil and lithographic drawing, French and Latin. Lectures, moreover, on experimental philosophy, chemistry, and geology, are delivered at stated periods.

Since June, 1836, an occasional detachment of sappers and miners has been employed in throwing up field and other works, which, in their gradual progress, afford most useful lessons of instruction.

Those cadets for whom there is no room in the engineers, but who are reported to have attained to a high degree of qualification, receive *honorary certificates*, and their names are announced to the Governments in India, and published in general orders to the army, as meriting particular notice.

They have the privilege of choosing the Presidency in India, at which they shall be stationed.

The infantry cadets educated at this institution take rank in the Company's army above all other cadets who receive *direct* appointments, from the commencement of three months previously to the date of the seminary cadets passing their public examinations.

There are two public examinations held at the East-India Company's Military Seminary in the course of the year, in the presence of the members of the Court of Directors, when a selection is made of those duly qualified for the engineers, artillery, and infantry. Those who may be chosen for the *engineers*, proceed to Colonel Pasley's establishment, at Chatham, for the purpose of studying a course of the field duties of engineer officers, and of practical architecture. This course occupies ten or twelve months, the expense of which is borne by the East-India Company. The cadets have temporary commissions, and local rank as ensigns in her Majesty's army, whilst doing duty at the establishment for field instruction.

The cadets selected for the corps of engineers were, previously to the year 1820-21, sent on the trigonometrical survey prosecuted in Wales, under the authority of the Board of Ordnance. At this date, arrangements were made, at the suggestion of Major-General Sir Howard Douglas (the public examiner), for instructing the cadets at the Company's Military Seminary in practical surveying. On the 8th February, 1837, another arrangement took place for giving increased efficiency to the separate branches of military drawing and military surveying taught at the Addiscombe institution.

Since April, 1838, the course of surveying and military reconnoissance, previously practised at Addiscombe, has been continued at Chatham, upon an extended scale; and the engineer cadets are made fully conversant in the knowledge and application of all geodesical and astronomical problems of general and practical utility.

In his evidence, taken before the select committee of the House of Commons, in 1832,* preparatory to the renewal of the Charter, Sir John Malcolm described the education given to the *engineers* at Addiscombe, and completed at Chatham, as excellent; and stated that officers of the *artillery*, who require science, are also well-educated at the same institution. Major-General Sir James Limond bore similar testimony to the very able manner in which the artillery cadets are here educated.

In an address delivered by Sir James Rivett Carnac, Bart., M.P., on the occasion of his presiding, as chairman of the Court of Directors, at the public examination on the 11th December, 1837, are the following sensible observations:

The Directors of the East-India Company view this seminary and its pupils with parental regard: they look to it with confidence to furnish a constant succession of officers qualified to perform the duties and uphold the character of the Indian army—well instructed in those branches of liberal learning which are the most useful and important—well grounded in the principles of those sciences upon which the military art depends—well versed in the elements of the *native languages*—and trained to the love and practice of every moral duty, and every honourable obligation. Not one of these can be neglected with impunity; each of them is necessary alike for your own benefit, and for that of the service in which you are to be engaged. A certain degree of general knowledge is indispensable to all who are to bear the character of gentlemen. The military sciences, of course, must occupy a large portion of the attention of those who are preparing for a military life; and, though this species of knowledge is more

* Since the end of this year, forty engineer cadets, and forty-seven artillery cadets, have proceeded to India.

necessary to some branches of the service than to others, yet to whatever branch it may be your fortune to be attached, you will derive advantage from the possession of scientific information; you will find that it will enable you to discharge your duty more beneficially to those whom you serve—more beneficially to those whom you command—and more satisfactorily to yourselves.

These observations are equally applicable to the study of the native languages. I have, on former occasions, endeavoured to impress you with a sense of their value and importance, and I avail myself of the present opportunity of again adverting to them, because I feel that I cannot direct your notice to any subject which better deserves your serious attention.

On the necessity for forming the character upon high moral principles, it must be quite unnecessary for me to dwell. There are certain moral habits, indeed, which have peculiar reference to a soldier's station, and which you here have especial opportunities of forming. A soldier, whatever his rank, must be ready at all times to yield a prompt, a cheerful, and an implicit obedience to the orders of those who have a right to command him. His conduct, too, must, beyond that of all other men, be marked by vigilant self-control, and a studied avoidance of all grounds of offence in his bearings towards those with whom he mixes on a footing of equality; while towards those whom he is called upon to command, he must display mildness, never degenerating into weakness—and firmness, unalloyed by a particle of arrogance.

THE END.

THE

EAST INDIA VOYAGER.

CHAPTER I.

CHOICE OF A CABIN.

SINCE the opening of the trade to the East Indies, the facilities of making voyages to either of the three Presidencies have greatly increased; still it must be confessed that, with all the advantages which are now attainable, a visit to our Asiatic territories is a formidable undertaking. Many persons, up to the very moment in which their destination is absolutely fixed, know nothing at all of the country which is to be their future residence, and are consequently at a great loss to set about their preparations, or to obtain instructions from former travellers, who are supposed to be competent to afford them. It is not always those who have enjoyed the best means of acquiring information, who are capable of imparting it; and, generally speaking, the advice given to inexperienced people meditating a long voyage, is so vague and indefinite as to be of little real service. It is therefore scarcely necessary to offer any apology for a series of papers which are intended to supply the voyagers to the East Indies with useful hints for their guidance, and by pointing out those methods which personal acquaintance with the subject has proved the most advantageous, to save a great deal of anxiety, trouble, and expence.

Upon the choice and furniture of a cabin a large portion of the comfort of a voyage must necessarily depend. To young men who spend the greater part of their time upon deck, the situation of their sleeping-place is not important; but, however desirous to practise economy, and to accustom themselves, according to the common phrase, to rough it through life, they should endeavour to secure themselves a part at least of a cabin, a berth in the steerage being particularly disagreeable under any circumstances. To ladies, whether married or single, the upper, or poop-cabins are certainly the most desirable, the disadvantages of the noise overhead being more than counterbalanced by the enjoyment of many favourable circumstances unattainable below. In the first place, these cabins are much more light and airy: it is seldom, even in the very roughest weather, that the ports are compelled to be shut; and it is almost inconceivable to those who have never been at sea, how great a difference it makes in the comforts or discomforts of a voyage, weather a delicate person can have the enjoyment of light and air in bad weather, or be deprived of both, condemned in illness to a dark close cabin, without the possibility of diverting the mind by reading, or any other employment. There is also another great advantage above stairs, which is the comparative degree of seclusion attainable in these cabins. A few steps lead from them all to the cuddy, or general apartment: there is no necessity to go out upon deck, or to go up or down stairs to meals; thus avoiding much of the annoyance of a rolling vessel, and all the disagreeables attendant upon encountering persons engaged in the duties of the ship. It may seem fastidious to object to meeting sailors employed in getting up different stores from the hold, or to pass and repass other cabins, or the neighbourhood of the steward's pantry; nevertheless, if ladies have the opportunity of avoiding these things, they will do well to embrace it; for, however trivial they may be in a well-regulated ship, very offensive circumstances may arise from them. The two after-cabins on the lower deck are generally considered to be the best in the ship; and when, as is sometimes the case, there is a communication immediately from them to the cuddy, without the necessity of passing through the steerage, much of the inconvenience is removed. They are certainly more free from noise than any others in the vessel; but there is a greater difficulty in keeping them clean, and a much greater danger of their being infested with rats or other vermin. The upper cabins, on the other hand, may with a little care be always neat and comfortable; nor are they liable to have the sea wash into them, which may be the case in fine weather below, if by any awkwardness in the management, the ship should make a sudden dip: but they are certainly noisy. Neither during the night nor the day can the inmates of the poop-cabins expect peace: persons on duty are always stationed above their heads, and it is a favourite walk with the passengers; added to this, the hen-coops are usually placed upon the poop, and though the unfortunate denizens of these prisons may occasionally be quiescent, every movement of the ship causes the feet of the coops to strike against the deck. In bad weather, or during the working of the vessel, the noises made by trampling overhead, ropes dragging, blocks falling, &c. &c., are very sensibly augmented by the cackling, chuckling, and screaming of the poultry, while throughout the day, whether fair or foul, they are scarcely ever silent. In those ships in which the comfort and convenience of the passengers are paramount considerations, the hen-coops do not occupy a place upon the poop, and it is probable that a general doom of banishment will shortly be pronounced against them. Perhaps by making the proper representations before the cabin is finally engaged, the passenger may procure the removal of these noisy neighbours, even when another destination had not been previously contemplated. Without, however, wishing to alarm those persons whose destinies are fixed in India, it may be said that the noise on board ship should be looked upon with some indulgence, it being merely preparatory to the disturbances which must be endured on shore. So many circumstances combine to destroy the quietude of night in India, that it is only accustomed ears that can sleep during the concerts maintained by the jackalls, the incessant chirping and humming of insects, and the loud vociferations of the natives perambulating the streets and roads at all hours. It is advisable, both on board ship and on shore, to stop the ears with cotton; but good sleepers will soon become inured to the numerous sounds which in the first instance effectually prevent repose.

Ladies who study their comfort, will always, in going out to India, be provided with a couch and a cot; the latter is almost indispensable in rough weather, while the former will be found very essential during the day, since, when the ship is rolling, a recumbent attitude is exceedingly desirable: an easy chair also, lashed in some snug corner, with a box or other rest to put the feet against, will be found to add much to the enjoyment of a voyage; and as these articles of furniture will be useful in India, they should in all cases be procured, where it is possible to incur the expence; a second light chair, easily moved about, and a washing table, to shut up, will complete the list of that class of furniture. Ship-couches are always furnished with drawers, and are exceedingly convenient upon this account, as they may be made to contain the greater portion of the wearing apparel necessary for the voyage; a soft wool mattress should be provided to fit into the couch, or the cot, together with three or four blankets, a counterpane, and two or three extra pillows. Both during the voyage, and in India, an abundance of feather pillows will be found very conducive to comfort; and as they are not liable to so many accidents as the air pillows, they will prove more serviceable. The cabin floor should either be covered with a carpet or a mat, and ladies should be provided with a small rug, to put under their feet when sitting at their meals in the cuddy; an essential point to those who have never been accustomed to encounter cold boards, the change of latitudes rendering the change of temperature very sensibly felt: a small sweeping broom, and dust pan or shovel, are also essentials, as are likewise a swinging lamp, and a candlestick. The carpenter of the ship will furnish one or two swinging shelves, to be suspended from convenient places in the roof; and it will be found advantageous to have a narrow slip of board nailed up as a standing shelf, and perforated with holes of different sizes, for a wine glass or two, a tumbler, tea-cups, &c. No one to whom expence is not the first object, should be unprovided with a filtering machine. The quantity of water usually allowed to passengers on board ship is very small, and that is frequently rendered almost useless, even for the purpose of washing, by its impurities: good managers will always contrive to have a day's supply in advance, and by allowing it to pass through the filtering-machine, they will be furnished with a fair portion of wholesome water with which to perform their ablutions, instead of having every sense offended by the wretched stuff so often served out from the casks. Looking-glasses being expensive articles in India, ladies are recommended to take out a large-sized dressing-glass, which must be screwed against the cabin wall, the choice of the place depending more upon security than convenience; it can afterwards be mounted upon a stand for the toilet table.

It will be necessary to have a very large supply of cleets, hooks, staples, and nails, together with a hammer; for a neglect in providing these things, under the idea that they are always attainable on board ship, will be certainly followed by great inconvenience and annoyance. An experienced carpenter from the shore should in all cases be employed, under the direction of the passenger, or an efficient friend, to secure the furniture in their right places, to cleet all the trunks, and to lash heavy articles to staples firmly fixed in the panels. Unless these precautions should be attended to, in the first heavy sea every thing will be adrift; and as it is quite impossible for the carpenters belonging to the ship to do all the work in the cabins of the passengers, no dependence ought to be placed upon them, since the greater necessity for their services, in consequence of the state of the weather, the more difficult it will be to procure them, the performance of their own duties employing all their time and attention. Spare cleets, nails, hooks, staples, and, above all things, a hammer, will be found most useful, both in the event of any omission on the part of the passenger, and for the purpose of doing an act of kindness to those who may be in want of such things; some improvident persons being always to be found who, notwithstanding their want of thought, it may be a pleasure to oblige.

Upon certain days in the week the hold of the ship is opened for the purpose of allowing the passengers an opportunity of sending for such trunks as they may require; but if the cabin be of a tolerable size, a lady may always manage to have every thing that she can want during the voyage close at hand: the trunks or boxes can be rendered both useful and ornamental, by being furnished with cushions covered with some cheap chintz, which can afterwards be turned to good account, as sofa-covers, &c., in India. If there should be little accommodation for trunks, &c., every box should be numbered, and an inventory of its contents taken, in order that there may be no mistake or disappointment in sending for them.

The stores to be laid in for sea consumption, in addition to perfumery, soap, and wax candles, depend in a great measure upon circumstances in which the passenger alone is qualified to judge. A certain quantity of brandy will always be found useful; for, without wishing to encourage intemperance, we may be permitted to repay any little service performed by the artizans of the vessel in the manner most acceptable to them. There are many sailors who have a great aversion to the rum served out on board ship, and upon whom a glass of brandy produces a most beneficial effect, and they will gladly come into the cabin and repair any damage, or remedy any inconvenience, when they know that they will be repaid by the taste of a cordial unattainable in any other way. To landsmen, when suffering under nausea, it exercises a very reviving influence; and even a Swede, who never drank spirits himself, was always thankful for a glass of brandy, which he took away with him for a regale for some one of his companions. Tobacco is generally a drug on board ship, but bars of common soap will be found useful gifts amongst the sailors, who are seldom provided with any article of the kind for washing their clothes.

Generally speaking, Indiamen are so well supplied with every thing which can be reasonably required, that there is little or no necessity for private stores; a few bottles of essence of coffee may, however, be found useful, a tea-spoonful being sufficient for a cup, mixed with boiling water. Boiling water may be obtained from the steward at the morning watch on board most ships; but passengers occasionally carry an apparatus in their own cabins, by which it can be procured at all times: this it must be confessed is a dangerous indulgence; for, however carefully a lamp may be managed, there is always a risk of setting fire to the ship. To those who suffer from sea-sickness, a chest of soda water will be a great comfort, but this is an expensive luxury; a chest of plain water also, containing four or six dozen of bottles, will conduce greatly to the comfort of the passenger; and perhaps it may be advisable to take a case of portable soup. Some persons provide themselves with preserved milk, and cases of Le Mann's biscuits; but these last are never wanted where there is a liberal captain; and the experience of the writer limits the private supplies to water, soda water, and coffee. Cases of liqueurs, confectionary, plum cakes, &c., may be taken by those who desire to celebrate fête-days on board ship, and who, in entertaining company, either in their own cabins or at the cuddy table, wish to produce some unwonted luxury.

Ladies carrying out pianos should, unless they engage very large cabins, be content to have them packed up and deposited in the hold; they take up a very inconvenient quantity of space, are liable to be damaged in heavy seas, and are, moreover, in nine cases out of ten, dreadful nuisances to the rest of the passengers. Musical instruments on board ship form the annoyance in fine weather; half a dozen performers, instead of playing in concert, will vex the ears of all on board by executing at the same time as many different pieces of music, which altogether create the most horrid discord imaginable.

Every thing on board ship should be rendered as compact as possible; and passengers, particularly in the lower cabins, will find canvas or large carpet bags very useful: these should be suspended from the ceiling in some snug corner; their contents are not so liable to get wetted by the salt water as those in trunks upon the ground, and in the very finest weather there is no security below against shipping a sea, which will inevitably spoil every thing that it penetrates. Gentlemen taking out valuable dogs, should see themselves that they are carefully attended to: terriers are sufficiently hardy to make the voyage without risk to their health; but spaniels, pointers, and hounds will not escape sickness unless they are well brushed every day. Experience has shewn that brushing the coat of a dog on board ship is a better preventive from illness than washing, and for a trifling remuneration some person will be found to perform the office. Young dogs are frequently kept in health by a cup of tea being given to them every day—green tea has the preference—rendered palatable by sugar and milk; but any tea is advantageous. All puppies should in India, have a portion of tea every morning—a prescription recommended by Youatt, the most celebrated dog-doctor of the day, and which will be verified by those who take a strong interest in the kennel.

Young men, in going to sea for the first time, will find their account in providing themselves with odds and ends of various kinds for dresses and decorations, should they be inclined to join in private theatricals on board. As the ladies are always applied to on such occasions, they are recommended to carry with them any frippery which they would otherwise discard. It is not always that dramatic amusements take place; but as they frequently occur on board outward-bound ships, it is advantageous to be able to supply the performers with the necessary costume. There is, generally speaking, more gaiety on board outward, than homeward bound vessels; few of the former sail without taking passengers visiting India for the first time, and these, buoyant in spirit, and enjoying the freshness of youth, usually endeavour to beguile the tediousness of the voyage by getting up a play or a concert. Those who are returning to India gladly join in these amusements, which seem to be unnecessary to persons coming home, it being seldom that passengers require more than a sober game at cards, or an occasional dance, to vary the monotony of the voyage. Of course any entertainment of the kind must depend in a great measure upon the sort of encouragement given by the captain, and the temper and dispositions of the people on board. It is scarcely possible in England to have any previous acquaintance with the parties who are to sail in the same vessel, or to obtain any very accurate information respecting the character of the captain. If it can be managed, it is always an advantage for the ladies of the party to be introduced to each other before they meet on board ship; for, in consequence of some ill-timed reserve in the first instance, a coolness may take place which will last during the whole voyage. Strangers who have no India connections find it very difficult in London to make themselves acquainted with the temper and disposition of the captain, since, unless he should be very notorious for stinginess or tyranny, little or nothing can be known concerning him. In some instances he may obtain a bad name very undeservedly; for unfortunately quarrels occasionally take place between the passengers, both in outward and homeward-bound ships, which involve the captain in a great deal of trouble; and unless he happen to be a first-rate diplomatist, in very unjust condemnations. Where, however, it can be discovered that numerous instances of misconduct on the part of the captain towards his passengers have taken place, it will be very advisable to look out for another ship, since an ill-tempered, or even an injudicious person placed in command, has it in his power to render the voyage exceedingly disagreeable. There are rules and regulations established on board every ship which the captain is bound to enforce; these will come under a separate head; but there are so many ways of doing the same thing, that very improper means may be resorted to in furtherance of a justifiable object.

CHAPTER II.

LADIES' OUTFIT.

Ladies proceeding to India are earnestly recommended to purchase nothing for the voyage which will not be useful after their arrival at the place of their destination. An idea that any thing is good enough for ship-board, sometimes induces persons to throw away their money upon coarse cheap things, which would not be wearable on shore. Cotton goods being best suited to the climate of India, the linen, if it may be so called, should be made of very fine cambric muslin, the only description of calico suited to the hot season. There being, however, a period of cold weather, varying from four to five months, it will be advantageous to have at least one dozen of day, and the same of night linen, made of fine thick long-cloth. The length of the voyage may be estimated in a sailing vessel at a hundred days, and it will therefore be easy to calculate the quantity required. It is not prudent to depend upon any opportunity of getting clothes washed at the Cape, or any other port at which the vessel may touch, since there is always a chance of disappointment, and a certainty of every thing being hurriedly and badly done, besides the risk of losses, which are irremediable. French stays are the best adapted to the climate; and as there is generally some difficulty in obtaining these articles, not fewer than six pairs should be provided. Cotton stockings will be found much more agreeable for constant wear than silk, and much more easily washed. The very fine open-worked thread hose, suitable for full dress, will be advantageously substituted for silk, which, in consequence of their not absorbing the moisture on the skin, and their liability to be stained by the shoe-binding or sandal, are disagreeable wear, while it is so very difficult to get them properly washed, that they are soon entirely spoiled. Shoes may be purchased ad libitum; for those of European make, whether English or French, are very superior to the articles manufactured by China-men. The greater number should be light, fitted for the house or carriage; but half a dozen or more pairs of a stronger description—kid, or even soft Spanish leather, with thick soles—will be found useful in the cold weather, and for walking about in gardens, &c. A considerable quantity of flannel should be taken, it being absolutely essential at some periods of the year; with the exception of the portion necessary for the voyage, it will be advisable to take it in the piece—indeed piece-goods of all kinds are strongly recommended. The numbers and quality of the dresses provided for a lady's outfit must necessarily depend upon the amount of the funds placed at her disposal. One handsome full dress will at least be required; and this should be constructed of the richest and most fashionable material of the day. It is not, however, advisable to carry out many expensive satins under any circumstances; because rich goods of the kind are always purchaseable in the country, without the risk, which must in all cases be hazarded, of the colour flying in the voyage. Pinks and blues, the latter especially, can never be depended upon, and it is impossible to say what dyes or shades will stand, and what will not, out of half a dozen ribbons of the self-same tint; but in different pieces, one or two may stand, while the remainder, though taken equal care of, will be faded and gone. In England, where so great a variety of fancy goods can be obtained, ladies will find it advisable to purchase the cheaper kinds, such being the most difficult to procure in India, where large investments are sent out of particular goods, and where those lighter articles, which have only a short reign in London, seldom find their way. There are few things more annoying than the being compelled to purchase from the self-same piece of which every lady in the circle has already bought a dress; and this is the predicament to which those who are most anxious about their toilet may be reduced when the private stores fail. Cheap edgings of lace, light gauze handkerchiefs, ribbons, and fancy goods of every description, will be useful; and the money laid out in this way will go farther, and be of more real service than if spent in a rich satin dress, which may be unwearable by the time it is landed. Handsome worked muslin dresses will be found extremely serviceable, and also coloured printed muslins for morning wear, and plain book or mull muslin; any thing thicker is not fitted for the hot season; silks, satins, Mousseline de laine, or Challi, will be only endurable to a new arrival in the cold weather, with the exception, perhaps, of a satin full dress for evening parties, with short sleeves, which a lady, anxious for her first appearance, will manage to endure. After the process of acclimation has been carried on for a year or two, silk gowns may be borne during the rains at least; but the first hot season is generally very trying, and demands all the alleviation which thin garments can afford: preparations, however, must be made for the change of temperature, which occurs after the autumnal equinox. From the middle of October until the beginning of March warm clothing will be very necessary as a protection from the cold; and those who go out in the morning upon elephants, or in open carriages, will require a well-wadded cloak, or one that is lined with fur. A handsome cloak of this description will last a long time in India with common care, and as fur is not a purchaseable article, should be taken out from England. These remarks, however, only apply to the Bengal Presidency, the climate of Madras or Bombay, not permitting velvets and furs at any season. A fashionable velvet bonnet is desirable for the cold weather; velvet is not so liable to spot, or lose its colour as satin, and therefore is more economical in the end. Bonnets may be dispensed with altogether in the hot season; but a lady who is anxious about her appearance, will always be seen in some light gauzy article of the kind in the evening drive, while in cold weather a covering for the head is indispensable. Mantilles, scarves, pelerines, or any other article of the kind which happens to be the mode of the day, should be provided for the different seasons. Handsome English shawls are much admired in India, as also light fancy shawls of all descriptions, of home manufacture. A good-sized parasol, and a black and white lace veil, should be added to the items. The silk or thread mittens or gloves now so much worn, are infinitely better fitted to the Indian climate than leather, and will be found far more agreeable and useful; and if the lady have it in her power to indulge in such things, feathers, artificial flowers, guazes of all kinds, and ribbons should be purchased in large quantities. Bobbinett, both figured and plain, of the best quality, will always turn to good account, as also thread-lace. Every lady should be provided with a box containing a store of the best needles, pins, the best description of bobbin and tape, buttons, hooks and eyes, and an extra thimble or two. The papers containing the needles should be greased, to prevent them from rusting, or they may be packed in emery paper. Scissars and penknives must also be carefully packed, and carefully looked after; for nothing can be more trying to the honesty of an Indian servant than articles of the kind, which, if of native construction, are worthless, and which, if European, are expensive, and not easily procured. Whatever materials may be required for any favourite fancy-work must be purchased in England, the supply being very precarious in India, and likewise exceedingly limited—what is vulgarly termed Hobson's choice being frequently the only alternative. Nothing intended for the toilet after the arrival in India should be previously worn in England; but if kid-gloves be taken, they should all be tried on, and thus suffered to take the form of the hand, otherwise they may shrink, and not be wearable; but a silk dress will be utterly spoiled after a single evening, for it will always be tarnished by some subtle agent, which it is impossible to detect. In packing for India, every thing should be placed in a room with a fire in it for a couple of days even in summer, in order that the articles may be thoroughly dry; they must then be put into tin cases, and soldered up, the tins to be enclosed in wood. Tin boxes of every description are extremely useful in India; the strong kind, japanned, are frequently to be purchased very cheaply in England, second-hand, such as muff-boxes, &c., while the mere tin case cannot be turned to good account after the voyage. It will be advisable also to line the boxes well with thin oil-skins containing delicate articles, of which the colour is apt to fly, the oil-skin to be carefully lapped over and secured. Ladies who are going out to military relatives, or who expect to travel in the interior, should get a pair of small chests of drawers, three drawers in each, which can be slung on either side of a camel; bullock-trunks also are useful upon such occasions, and are to be had at the principal shops in London. Ladies are frequently advised to wear black during the voyage; but it is the most uncomfortable costume that can be adopted, being so disagreeable as scarcely to be borne during the hot weather. Since, with the exception of washing things, all the dresses destined for India must be new, ladies may dedicate their previous wardrobe to the ship; the different degrees of temperature in the different latitudes will require various descriptions of clothing. Those who are expert with the needle, may employ themselves during the voyage by making up a new dress occasionally from any cheap material they may have purchased. Persons who study economy may always get great bargains by buying up articles that are just going out of season, in London—for instance, summer goods in autumn, and winter goods in spring, which will be ready for the corresponding seasons in India. A vessel sailing from London in January, arrives in India about the beginning of June, consequently in the hottest period of the year; while ships sailing in June will just come in at the commencement of the cold weather in October, and for the three following months even velvet dresses will not be found too warm in Bengal. Formerly there was a strong prejudice in India against dresses trimmed or embroidered in gold or silver, as such ornaments were considered too much in the native taste to be proper for European ladies; but strangers are now permitted a wider latitude, and whatever may be the fashion in Paris or London is eligible in Calcutta at least, and may be risked at the other Presidencies. With respect to trinkets, a watch seems to be the only thing essential; all other European ornaments, with the single exception of fashion, are decidedly inferior to those which may be purchased of the natives. The native gold is worked up with little or no alloy, and the workmanship is beautiful. If a lady can draw, she will get her own patterns executed in the best manner; or she may bring out drawings of every ornament in fashion, and have them manufactured in India. Money thus spent is not a bad investment, for the cost of the workmanship is not high; whereas European jewellery is scarcely intrinsically worth a tenth part of the sum paid for it. It is not advisable to carry out any trumpery in the way of ornament; for all sorts of gilt and glass goods of the kind may be purchased in the Bazaars for almost nothing, large investments being sent out, which are frequently sold at less than the cost price. There is one advantage in wearing such things, since they can always be regilt in India at a very small expence, and thus be made to look as good as new. The finer kinds of perfumery, prettily cut-glass bottles, and all sorts of bijouterie for the toilet or drawing-room table, good plaister casts, and in fact every thing ornamental, as far as the pecuniary means can afford, should be taken. In India there is no variety of these fancy things to be had, excepting of Chinese or native manufacture; and they are, as a matter of course, less esteemed than foreign rarities. Portfolios of prints and pretty books in pretty bindings are desirable. Though oils are plentiful enough in India, hair-oil is not so nice as that prepared in England. Eau de Cologne, lavender, and rose water are cheap and plentiful; but any thing exceedingly recherché must be taken out. Violet hair-powder is a very essential article, as it forms the greatest alleviation of the prickly heat, and is somewhat of a preservative against the stings of musquitoes. If presents to natives are contemplated, single, or cases of cut-glass bottles, or those of purple and gold, or gorgeous looking china, will be found very acceptable; also small cases containing spirits of red lavender, peppermint, aniseed, or the like, which both Mohammedans and Hindus will take unscrupulously under the name of medicine. Those of course are intended for the richer class of natives, as a return for any civility received from them; and to the last, small looking-glasses may be added, many Asiatic ladies being unprovided with any mirror except that which is set in a thumb-ring. For the domestic servants pieces of leno, such as are used for window-curtains in England, will be much esteemed for veils; and if liveries be given to the men, English cloth should be taken of the required colour, while cheap shawls, of the long scarf kind, will form a great gift as a reward for good behaviour: for instance, a lady marrying a gentleman who is going back to India, and who expects his old servants to return to him again, should take out something of the kind as presents. A married lady setting up as housekeeper in India, should supply herself with china and glass of every description; these articles are much cheaper in England than in India. And there is a greater variety of patterns to choose from. Table linen is another desideratum, nothing but cotton table-cloths and napkins being procurable in India. The impossibility of getting damask mangled, has been brought forward as an objection to its employment; but the absence of a mangle is well supplied by the exceedingly heavy irons employed by the washermen. Moulds of all kinds for jellies, puddings, &c., and even the common delf fluted pudding basins are useful; as also a set of seives, a coffee-pot with percolator, or an apparatus with a lamp under it fitted up with a saucepan; and there are several descriptions of conjurers, peripurists, &c., to he had in the shops in London, by which many kinds of cookery may be carried on in the anterooms and verandas, and which are especially convenient at night, and in travelling. Bottles of essences of various herbs are often wanted in India, and are seldom procurable. Smyrna currants are dear, and their place ill supplied by kist-mists and other raisins; while English preserves, raspberry jam especially, are in great demand. The Indian products will supply substitutes for every other kind of preserve; but the raspberries of the Himilaya not yet having been brought into the market, the jam made from that fruit must still be imported from England. In pickles, walnuts are the only things which cannot at present be easily obtained, although shortly great supplies may be expected from the Himalaya; nor is mushroom catsup made in India. Mushrooms can be procured, though not, perhaps, in sufficient quantities to make catsup: the natives are always doubtful about them, and seem to think that they are eaten at a risk; thus they are never brought to market. Hermetically sealed cases of preserved lobster and salmon are great luxuries at an Indian table, more particularly in the Upper Provinces; therefore, if expence should not be an object, they ought to be added to the list of stores. Turtle-soup, if required for grand entertainments, must be preserved in England; it, with all other preserved meats, may be purchased of excellent quality of Gamble, the original patentee, Cornhill. Hams and cheeses are best packed with charcoal, which preserves them more completely during the voyage than any thing else. Very good hams, however, may be purchased in India, and the Hissar cheeses are superexcellent; but the supply of these latter is not very great. Liqueurs of all kinds may be taken out to India with advantage; as also cakes of chocolate, and every sort of bon-bon, the latter being useful as patterns, since there is nothing that an Indian confectioner cannot imitate. It should be observed that none of these things are absolutely necessary, but merely mentioned as guides to persons who, having plenty of money to spend, wish to lay it out in the best manner. In the event of a selection being made, it should be in favour of glass, china, the essences of herbs, and raspberry jam. Plate, if not procured a great bargain second-hand in England, is cheaper and perhaps better in India, where it is manufactured according to the fashion of the country. A common European milk-jug would be of scarcely any use, and would make a poor figure in comparison with the splendid vases placed upon the breakfast table in India. Knives and forks, every sort of cutlery in fact, ought to be purchased in England, and of the very best makers. A pretty looking portable grate, to fit into a fire-place, with fender and fire-irons, and front of some kind of lackered metal, as light as it can be procured consistantly with the proper strength, will prove very acceptable, both in the event of living for any period in a standing camp, or for a residence in the Upper Provinces of Bengal or any of the Hill sanitariums. The grates found in the Bungalows of India are the most miserable looking concerns imaginable; and there being scarcely any probability of getting any thing better, it is certainly worth while to take out an ornamental article of the kind. Desks, dressing-cases, and work-boxes, if made of wood, should be provided with thick woollen covers, in order to preserve them from the heat; piano-fortes, guitars, &c., must be covered up in the same manner. Performers upon any instrument should supply themselves with a large collection of music, and commission some friend at home to send out occasionally assortments of the most popular compositions. Every thing that can be put into a scrap-book is useful, and all sorts of amusing games, the toys invented for children of a larger growth, such as boxes full of landscapes, that may be put together in all manner of ways; moveable heads, panoramas, &c., which serve to beguile time, and may interest by their novelty. English dolls and English toys of every kind will be acceptable to little nephews and nieces, and the children of friends; patterns for work; all sorts of drawing materials; the best patent ink, and if quills be essential, Bramah's pens made for the purpose: when they get dry, if soaked for a few minutes in salt and water, their flexibility will be restored. Should steel pens be taken out, a patent handle will be required; it is best to make trial of the country reed-pens, which many people find excellent. Ornamental stationery of every kind, white and coloured, forms very valuable stock.

CHAPTER III.

DESULTORY REMARKS.

Amid the multitudes of children, the offspring of Anglo-Indian parents, sent home to England for their education, and who are, should no unforeseen circumstance occur to prevent it, destined to return to the land of their birth, very few, if any, are so fortunate as to receive instruction upon points which would be very serviceable for their future guidance. Young men enter the Indian army, and young ladies return to their families, without knowing any thing at all about the country which they are going to visit; and probably without the slightest acquaintance with the language which it is necessary that they should speak, in order to be able to give a single direction to their servants. Upon their arrival in England, children generally can converse very fluently in Hindostanee; and it would not be difficult to the persons to whom their education is entrusted, to keep up this knowledge by the assistance of the works of Gilchrist, published for the purpose of enabling tyros going to India, to acquire a complete knowledge of the language, without the aid of a teacher. Hindostanee, is, however, usually forgotten in the first six months; and the beau ideal respecting India, which has been so long entertained, still filling the minds of people who know nothing at all about it, a few showy accomplishments are alone considered necessary for the female part of the community. Useful knowledge seems indeed to be wholly omitted in the education of young ladies, who in most cases are left to pick it up in the best way they can; those who have the advantage of private tuition at home, enjoying better opportunities of making themselves acquainted with domestic economy than it is possible to attain under the present system of scholastic establishment, and the means of rendering themselves in some degree independent of the assistance of others. Young people who come to England merely for their education, usually spend the whole period of their sojourn at school, where they have little, if any opportunity of acquiring that homely species of knowledge, which, though not in the slightest degree incompatible with the cultivation of the mind, appears to be considered quite derogatory to gentlewomen. The indolent lives which ladies are reported to lead in India, the crowds of servants, or, as it is sometimes supposed, slaves, entertained to do their bidding, seem to render it unnecessary that they should attain any art excepting that of amusing themselves; but although the fair sex are not called upon to perform any thing akin to domestic drudgery, and may, if they please, entirely relinquish the cares of housekeeping, their own comfort, and their appearance also, will be much enhanced by active and industrious habits, and an acquaintance with useful things. Not to shock prejudice too much at the onset, we will commence with the accomplishments which are the most desirable for a residence in India. In order to render music available, an acquaintance with it should not be of a superficial nature: a slight knowledge of the art is very soon lost, while there is little chance of improvement; whereas persons who possess real musical tastes, and have cultivated their talents to advantage, can generally manage to draw a musical society around them, and thus find a delightful method of beguiling time, which otherwise would lag heavily upon hand. Drawing is perhaps the more independent and more useful accomplishment of the two. There never can be wanting subjects for the pencil in a country, and amid a people so truly picturesque; but for these also it will be necessary to study under a good master, and to understand the principles of the art; for there is little in the way of tuition to be found in India, and no paintings from which amateurs can take hints for their improvement.—Floricultural and horticultural knowledge will be found extremely useful, leading to pursuits which amuse while they elevate the mind. Persons who are condemned to a wandering life in India—and there are few comparatively who are settled at Calcutta or any large station for more than a limited period—are often compelled either to lay out new ground for gardens, or to be content with native gardeners who have had no opportunities of improvement. In such circumstances the garden which may be superintended in person before sunrise and after sunset, will be made much more productive by an acquaintance with the nature and best methods of cultivating plants. In the cold weather a very considerable portion of the day may, in the Upper Provinces of Bengal, be spent in the garden; and this being the season in which European vegetables and flowers arrive at perfection, the interest of the plantation is much heightened. Although there is some difficulty in raising English flowers in India, still it is to be overcome; and the superiority of the gardens which boast these beautiful exotics is so great, that it is worth taking pains to secure it. Fresh seeds brought out from England are necessary to keep up the stock; for all foreign productions soon dwindle in the gardens of India, if propagated from their own seeds; but when it is not possible to obtain supplies from the country where they flourish in the fullest perfection, exchanges may be made with much advantage with gardens at distant stations. Mignionette will blow very freely in India, and exhale its richest perfume both morning and evening; while balsams, which grow wild over the country, and many other flowers, both indigenous and imported, may be much improved, and rendered double, by cultivation. Generally speaking, the hollyhocks, dahlias, and other favourites of home-scenes shock our eyes by their miserable appearance, their stunted growth, and single flowers; for where the climate has done so much for vegetation, the hand of the cultivator is suffered to relax, and, with some exceptions, we find flowers, natives of Asiatic countries, arriving at fuller perfection in England than in the land of their birth. The parterres in India, though very superb, are more indebted to shrubs than to the smaller families of plants, annuals, perennials, &c., which bloom so beautifully in our flower-beds in England. There are at present no collections of dahlias in India which comprise the numerous varieties known in Europe. The ordinary kind, which is very common, is the double purple; crimson is more rare, while other sorts are very seldom seen. The dahlia is readily propagated by seed; but the preferable method is by slips planted at the end of the rains, which root freely, and produce larger flowers than those produced by seed. Floricultural and horticultural knowledge will enable the parties possessing it to make very interesting experiments in the improvement of native and foreign products; while it will prevent those attempts which are rendered abortive by the ignorance of the projector, who is compelled to trust entirely to his own fancies, and may consequently fall into errors which entirely defeat the object in view.—The care and management of birds will be found a useful branch of knowledge, and also the best method of rearing poultry. In some parts of India, Guinea fowl will thrive exceedingly well, while in others it is scarcely possible to rear the young broods: there is also great difficulty in breeding turkeys; and it is obvious, therefore, that some acquaintance with this portion of domestic economy may be turned to good account. As a general rule with regard to poultry of every kind, garlick should be given in all cases where the mortality is expected to be great: it should be put down the throats of young birds in small quantities like peppercorns; but care must be taken not to give any thing of the kind during the fattening process, or otherwise the flesh will be uneatable:—the eggs of laying hens will also tase of garlick; the fowls, therefore, must not be allowed indiscriminate access to this powerful root, for they will eat freely of it, soon becoming fond of a vegetable which diffuses warmth and strength throughout their bodies. Excellent butter may be made in India, if care be taken that the cows be well fed. Where they can get plenty of lucerne and other nourishing grasses, their milk is rich, and easily churned into the very best description of butter; but under less favourable circumstances it will never attain the proper degree of consistence. It is necessary, in order to ensure proper attention to live stock, that the master or mistress should themselves see these animals fed. The task is one which does not involve much trouble. It is only necessary to order the cattle, sheep, and goats to be driven up, just before the sun disappears, to the front of one of the verandahs of the house, where the party may be seated at their ease, while the cows eat their trusses of grass, and the sheep and goats are fed from a trough with the grain which the bunneah, or grain-dealer, will weigh out for them. This is not one of the things which it is prudent to entrust to servants in India; for though implicit confidence may be placed in many individuals, generally speaking there is a risk of carelessness, or of the appropriation of the money charged for the food by the purveyor. Good veal is a desideratum in most of the farm yards in India; yet there appears to be no good reason why the calves should not be as well fattened as those in England: little attention is paid to the subject; though young men who desire to be thought very learned in horses, might be expected to contrive to gain some acquaintance with the method of breeding cattle. There is a mixture of flour, milk, and gin made into boluses, which is given to calves in England with great advantage, and which is worthy of a trial in India; while, however trifling the knowledge that is previously obtained of domestic concerns may be, to those who pitch their tents amid the natives of a foreign country every item will be found of importance. The people of India, though a very teachable race, and easily falling into the methods proposed to them by Europeans, are proverbially deficient in every thing relating to the present system of agriculture. Englishmen are very apt to blame the ignorance and unskilfulness of those who serve them, without considering that they ought to have taken care to make themselves acquainted, while at home, with the details of arrangements which are essential to their own comfort in a foreign land. The native mode of living in India differs so widely from ours, that it is astonishing, when we consider how small a portion of the community is formed by Europeans, that we find so much already done to our hands: servants in any number, well acquainted with our ways and habits, our style of living, cookery, &c., are always attainable. The bread eaten by the natives differs very widely from our own, and the food both of Mohammedans and Hindus is prepared in a very different manner; but, taught by the parties who first established themselves in the country, the native domestics have reached a very high degree of perfection in many branches of culinary art formerly perfectly unknown. It is a generally received opinion amid people who have never been in the country, that neither bread nor butter are made in India; and though the heat of the climate might afford some reason for the latter supposition, the former has nothing better for its support than the fact of cases of Le Mann's biscuits being amongst the exports. There are many bakers in India who might compete with Le Mann himself, the variety and excellence of the fancy-bread produced at many tables not being to be surpassed;

while, if the slightest pains are taken to instruct the cooks or the confectioners in the method of preparing European novelties, the teacher will be certain to be rewarded by complete success. Every thing that requires reformation at an Anglo-Indian's table, or in any large Indian establishment, is entirely owing to the indolence or ignorance of the heads of the family. If they are content to leave the management wholly to native servants, they will of course take care to have their own way; and it certainly requires no small degree of judgment to decide on what points interference would be advantageous, and when it is best to leave the domestics to their own devices. Nothing very essential can be done on the part of the European masters without an adequate acquaintance with the language; and those who are too idle to set seriously about its attainment, must be content to relinquish all their arrangements to the will of others, and to adopt ways and measures which may be diametrically opposed to their own inclinations.

Amid the whole number of Indian servants, the ayah, or lady's maid, is the least efficient out of the bathing-room, which is her peculiar province. In nine cases out of ten she knows little or nothing of her business, and will not be at the trouble to learn, and, though a necessary appendage, contrives to render herself as useless as possible. Her acquaintance with dressing hair extends no farther than brushing and plaiting; and, generally speaking, she is very awkward at the processes of pinning, tying bows, hooking, or buttoning, and she seldom or ever knows how to fold up a gown: a lady therefore who goes out to India, ought to be as independent as possible in all these particulars, for otherwise her patience will be sorely tried. An ayah having rumpled and crumpled her mistress's gown into the most terrible figure possible, carries it off to the *Istree Wallah*, or ironer, to have it smoothed out again; and these frequent ironings prove very detrimental to silk dresses, which are, however, scarcely wearable without them. It is ten to one whether the ayah ever knows where any thing under her charge has been placed: it has consequently to be hunted for throughout the whole wardrobe, and is probably found at last in a most misused condition, while carelessness and inattention are manifested in all that she undertakes. There are, of course, some exceptions, but unfortunately few, in comparison to the idle and dissipated native women who enter an European establishment. The Portuguese who are Christians, and certainly a far better class, make very superior ayahs; but these persons are not easily attainable out of Calcutta, and as their wages are higher than those given to a Mohammedan woman, it is only ladies, who need not regard expense, who can secure their services. An European waiting maid is out of the question, excepting in the family of a Governor, Commander-in-Chief, or some functionary of nearly equal rank, and it therefore becomes necessary to make the best of what is to be had; and those ladies who know how every thing ought to be done, and can give their instructions accordingly, have the greatest chance of being well served. The cause of the general worthlessness of ayahs in India arises from the impossibility of getting a respectable Moosulmanee woman to outrage all her feelings of propriety by engaging in a service in which she will be required to mix indiscriminately with men: it is only those who have fallen into a disreputable mode of life, and have little or no character to lose, who can be induced to take service in an European family, and it is not from such persons that industrious habits can be expected. Many have not even learned to thread a needle; and the greater number seem to think of nothing but smoking and gossiping with the men-servants. The needlework of the domestic establishment in India is performed by a tailor, or *dirzee*, as he is called; and those men who are employed upon the wardrobes of ladies, are usually very expert, but they undertake nothing beyond the mere sewing, hemming, stitching, and copying departments. They will make a gown from a given pattern with tolerable accuracy; but they do not consider it to be their business to try it on; and they would refuse if required to do so, on the plea of indecorum, which it is rather curious should come from them instead of the lady. On this account some acquaintance with the method of cutting out a gown, and trying it on, will be found very important in India; for the expence of having new dresses from the Marchands de Mode of the Presidencies is too great for the majority of female residents; while, without the lady can contrive to assist in the manufacture, books and prints of fashions are totally useless. A gown made by a dirzee who is left entirely to his own skill and discretion, is usually pulled to pieces, and put together again so frequently, that it looks old before it has been worn; and in many places in the Provinces there is absolutely no remedy, no European woman being to be found throughout the whole station capable of affording the slightest assistance. The art of cutting out and fitting on, although so necessary, is very difficult of acquirement in India, where the circle may be so small as to furnish no one person able or willing to give the necessary instructions; while there is nothing to prevent a young lady in England from obtaining a sufficient acquaintance with the process, to enable her to make a fashionable appearance. The toil is not great, since the executive may always be left to the tailor, who will follow the directions given with great accuracy.

The millinery art, though not quite so essential, since a single hat or cap will suffice where many gowns are necessary, is very advantageous to those who study the graces of the toilet in India. To be able to trim, and modify, and alter, will be found most useful when at the distance of perhaps a hundred miles from any person who can perform these constantly required services. At all the large stations men may be found who undertake to make hats and bonnets after any given pattern, but who are totally unequal to the task of placing feathers, bows, or any other ornament in their proper positions, taste and elegance being quite out of the question. If the lady herself cannot supply this omission, she must be content to make a very poor figure in the circle in which she moves. It has been said that people must be born milliners, to succeed in an art which requires a very peculiar and perhaps unattainable talent; but though it may be difficult or impossible to excel, a certain degree of dexterity may be arrived at, which will turn to good account in places where nothing very much better can be found. As an Indian voyage is seldom undertaken without a few months of previous preparation, ladies, who have not the prospect of being permanently settled at one of the three Presidencies, should endeavour to render themselves acquainted with this very useful branch of feminine economy; for, however ingenious they may be, and equal to remedy all deficiencies of the kind, their natural cleverness will be much assisted by a little practical knowledge. India has been for so long a period represented as a perfect paradise for women, that it is difficult to dissipate an idea which seems to have gained possession of every mind; and certainly rich ladies, either at the Presidencies or elsewhere, may obtain every thing they can want, and nearly every thing they can wish for. The rich, however, form a very small portion of Anglo-Indian society; by far the greater number of the wives and daughters of European families being restricted within very limited means. Cheap materials, which are frequently attainable, will be of very little use to such persons, unless they have some skill in the art of making them up; and though it is esteemed little less than high treason to find fault with the toilets of Anglo-Indian ladies, truth compels me to say that there is great room for improvement, more especially in the Upper Provinces. Girls who go out to their parents, under the idea that they will find their wants supplied with the same readiness as at home, will be much disappointed; and though there are many resources which may be rendered available as substitutes, active habits, and a readiness at contrivance, are necessary to bring them into the service. There are so very few methods for the employment of the time of the softer sex in India, that a more than ordinary devotion of it to the subject of dress is not only pardonable, but praiseworthy, especially as many causes operate to induce negligence. The indulgence of the indolence which the oppressive nature of the climate is so apt to produce, is but too frequently attended by an unwillingness to give up the comfort of a loose and careless attire for the restraints of the toilet. When this habit is suffered to grow upon the parties who have given way to it, they are indisposed to receive company in a morning; and the interests of society suffer very considerably from the seclusion of the female portion of a family in their chambers. So much of the happiness of life in India depends upon the exertions of the ladies, that they should consider very deeply, before they go out, the responsibility which they incur while becoming such important members of the community: every accomplishment and every useful and amiable quality will have a wide field for its display; and there can be no doubt that the exertion of well directed female influence will always be productive of the happiest results. Where the ladies of a Station patronize public amusements, and encourage social visiting, the gentlemen seldom or ever abandon themselves to gambling, or any other destructive pursuit; and a ready concurrence with any scheme proposed for the furtherance of harmless entertainment, forms one of the best means of keeping society together, since a captious temper, caprice, or the want of inclination to oblige in one single individual may often mar the happiest arrangements which a limited society can propose. Single women—spinsters as they are universally termed in India—have not much in their power beyond the effect produced by pleasing manners; and the slightest departure from established and often arbitrary rule subjects them to so much remark, that their situation is not so agreeable as in England, where they enjoy numerous innocent privileges denied to them in the East; but when they marry, or if they go out married, the case is very different, and they may, if they choose to exert themselves, make a considerable reformation in the affairs of the household. It is a singular thing that while Anglo-Indians put themselves very frequently to considerable inconvenience by unnecessary deference to native opinion, they should have lessened the respectability of European ladies in the eyes of their Asiatic associates by customs which cannot fail to be disagreeable to English women, and to which they can only be reconciled under the idea that they are inevitable. In an Anglo-Indian establishment a certain class of men-servants, the bearers, have nearly constant access into the sleeping apartments: they make the beds, dust the furniture, take charge of the lamps, and are so frequently called upon during the day to perform one or other of these offices, that they seem to think themselves privileged to walk in and out whenever they please.

How such a custom could ever have originated it is difficult to say, since every body, in the slightest degree acquainted with the native character, must have known that nothing could be more likely to shock its prejudices than so unnecessary an invasion of female privacy. No native of India could be persuaded that the ladies in England do not suffer their footmen to enter their bedchambers; and as women servants are kept in every family, there seems no good reason why they should not be made to perform the work which, to our great scandal, now devolves upon the men. Too little attention has hitherto been paid to the opinion which the natives of India may form of our character from the conduct we pursue when settled amongst them. Considering our own customs to be very superior to those which obtain in Asia, we should be exceedingly wrong were we to take up any of their absurd notions regarding the regulation of society, or to relinquish dancing merely because they view it in a different light; but why we should actually adopt customs which are, or ought to be, equally revolting to us as to them, appears to be perfectly unaccountable. In consequence, perhaps, of the bearers proving better servants than the ayahs, they have been permitted to usurp their places; and the custom of employing them in the bedchambers of ladies, as well as of gentlemen, seems now to be almost invariably established. There appears, however, to be no absolute necessity for its continuance, a little female resolution alone being wanted to cause the abolition of a practice which involves so many indecorums. Anglo-Indian ladies are most justly celebrated for the propriety of their conduct; generally speaking, nothing can be more blameless than their manners both in public and in private: why, therefore, when they shew themselves thus anxious to uphold the dignity of the sex in the eyes of their own country people, should they be so careless of the impressions which they may make upon the surrounding natives? There are other and numerous items connected with an Anglo-Indian establishment which are susceptible of great improvement, and in which a lady may interfere with infinite advantage. Hitherto the sole management has, in most houses, been at the entire discretion of the master of the family, who has been content to leave it entirely to the servants, and who has usually deprecated every kind of innovation on the part of the wife. Fashions have grown up in this way, and become so deeply rooted, that it is seldom that a stranger can muster sufficient courage to alter or abolish them; and though many are both expensive and unnecessary, while others are exceedingly barbarous, they are still retained (on the score of custom) with unyielding tenacity. Women, however, if they choose to exert themselves, can always manage to become the mistresses of the domestic department; and that they have not already succeeded in producing a new order of things, is entirely owing to their youth and inexperience at the period of their landing in India. Knowing little or nothing concerning the domestic economy at home, they perpetuate the defects of the system pursued in their new residence, by a blind adoption of every custom, good, bad, or indifferent; while those who go out at a later period of life, are too few to effect much in the way of general improvement.

CHAPTER IV.

DOMESTIC ECONOMY, DIET, CLOTHING, ETC.

INDIA becomes either the temporary home, or the residence of the later years of life, of many persons who unexpectedly find their destiny cast in the eastern world, and who have neither time nor opportunity to obtain information of interest and importance to their future welfare: to individuals thus circumstanced the following observations are addressed.

Families going out to Calcutta may now be entirely independent of the private hospitality formerly so essential to the comfort of a stranger, but at Madras and Bombay it is still necessary to be provided with letters of introduction to residents, since no places of public entertainment have yet been established for their accommodation. In Calcutta there are several excellent hotels conducted in a manner admirably adapted to secure the comfort of those who take up their abode in them. They are divided into separate suites of apartments for the use of families, while bachelors can have single chambers with the use of a public room, and a table d'hote. All the expences are included in a certain sum, amounting to one, two, or three hundred rupees a month, according to the accommodation afforded, and for this charge an excellent table is kept, servants supplied, and every comfort provided, the expence being less in fact than housekeeping unless upon the most economical scale. The great public convenience resulting from these hotels has entirely conquered the prejudices with which, in the first instance they had to contend, even the old residents in the country, civil servants of long standing, availing themselves of the advantages which they hold out, when proceeding to the seat of Government upon business or pleasure. Individuals or families establishing themselves at one of these hotels, have time to look about them before they finally settle, and should they be destined to travel to the Upper Provinces, they cannot do better than take up their abode in them during the whole of their sojourn at the Presidency.

Though the rents of houses have fallen considerably during the last few years, they are still high in Calcutta, and indeed all over India, and when persons expect to be settled for any long period, it is advisable to purchase; the health and comfort of a family depending greatly upon improvements and conveniences which are not always to be found in a hired house, and for which a tenant-at-will does not like to incur the expence. There are many very respectable mansions in Calcutta, and indeed throughout Bengal which are only glazed on what is called the weather-side, and which are entirely destitute of fire-places, the latter though very conducive to comfort are not perhaps absolutely essential, for although the weather is frequently very cold, by shutting up the doors and windows and by having tin feet-warmers filled with hot water, an agreeable temperature may be kept up, but the glazing should never be dispensed with. During the continuance of the typhoons or squalls, (which are of common occurrence both in hot and rainy seasons,) and for some hours afterwards, until the sky has become quite settled, the house should be closely shut up, especially at night, the elemental disturbance affecting the air very considerably, and producing the most injurious results to delicate persons unaccustomed to such exposure. The large Venetian blinds though shutting apparently very closely, admit damp air loaded with miasma, and if strict enquiry were made into the causes which have brought on fevers, cholera, and other dangerous, and often fatal attacks, they would be found to proceed from inattention to circumstances most essential to the preservation of health.

The choice of the position of the bed in sleeping rooms is of great importance, especially to persons who visit India at any advanced period of life, and with whom the process of acclimating is attended with more danger than to the younger and more hardy. Bed chambers in India are usually constructed wholly with a view to secure the greatest quantity of air, and this of course is very desirable in the hot weather. During the most sultry nights, however, the means are insufficient for the end, and at other times to sleep exposed to all the winds of heaven is very dangerous. Throughout the rainy season especially, a change always takes place in the atmosphere towards morning; just as the false dawn breaks, a rush of cold air is perceptible, those who are wakeful and watchful may rise and shut one of the windows, but it is better to be out of the reach of its immediate influence. For this purpose the bed ought to be placed in some part of the room in which no wind can actually blow over it; let the circulation of air be as free as possible throughout the apartment but do not be exposed to a draught. Nearly all the sleeping apartments in India have doors or windows on every side, the former, in Bengal, and not unfrequently in the Upper Provinces, when they open into other apartments being nothing more than gigantic Venetians, or as they are called in India, jhil mils. One of these at least should be closed at night, if it is impracticable to place the bed in such a position as to secure it from a draught. It is impossible to attend too scrupulously to these precautions, since more than half the illnesses sustained by Europeans in India arise from the neglect of them. Nothing is more common than for persons desirous to avail themselves of all the air that can be obtained, to awaken with a stroke of the land-wind, which in some instances will deprive the individual so attacked, of the use of his limbs, and will at any rate be productive of severe pain.

During the hot winds in the Upper Provinces many persons sleep outside the houses with perfect impunity, the air being perfectly dry, but this indulgence can only be enjoyed in particular places, and at particular seasons of the year, the moment that any change in the state of the atmosphere may be expected, it is dangerous to the last degree. Persons impatient of heat are apt to dispense with their musquito curtains under the idea that they prevent the free circulation of the air. It is never advisable to relinquish this protection, slight as it may be, from the miasma with which the atmosphere is frequently loaded, the moisture which is often found on the outside of these curtains showing how much they tend to preserve the party sleeping within them from actual contact with baleful influences. To those who can afford it the best plan is to shut up the bedchamber entirely, and have a punkah pulled all night, but this luxury is only to be obtained at present at the expence of keeping extra servants; when machinery shall be more extensively introduced into India, the residents will be enabled to keep punkahs constantly going in every room in the house at a comparatively small expence, a blessing of most inestimable importance in such a country. Few persons sleep in the hot weather with more than a sheet over them, though a greater degree of coolness is secured by excluding the hot air by means of a thick coverlet. The contact with clothes is certainly very distressing during hot nights, and great comfort would be produced by having the sheet and counterpane extended over a framework at about a foot and a half or two feet distant from the body. The natives who are well aware of the danger of exposure to the atmosphere when sleeping as they often do, in the open air, always take care to wrap themselves up from head to foot, having acquired the method of breathing with their faces covered. The apartments of their houses are seldom open on more than one side, and can be closed at pleasure with thick curtains or purdahs as they are called.

Attention to clothing is also of very great importance to European residents in India, and in order to be secure from the ill effects of sudden changes in the atmosphere, it is advisable to wear flannel next the skin. This in the hot season may be rendered easily supportable by being lined with mull muslin, and as it absorbs the perspiration, the wearer will feel more comfortable and even some degrees cooler than those who profess not to be able to bear any thing but the lightest and thinnest apparel. Every house to be really comfortable should be furnished with two fire-places, one in the best drawing-room, and one in some inferior apartment, which in case of illness during the cold season, may be appropriated to the use of an invalid. In this apartment it will be advisable to light a fire during the rains, it will render the atmosphere throughout the whole house much more wholesome, and will materially assist in the preservation of the contents of any boxes which may be placed within it. The want of a fire is often very sensibly felt during the rains, when every thing in the house is, what is termed, wringing wet; when writing paper must be ironed before it can be used, and every article of wearing apparel feels as if it had just come out of the water. Much has been said and written about Indian luxury, but comfort is a thing still to be studied; while the carelessness and indifference manifested concerning the most obviously necessary arrangements, occasion a wanton sacrifice of health. Strangers often purchase experience (which ought to be supplied by long residents) at a very dear rate, while they cannot fail to be astonished at the utter contempt for improvement shewn by the Anglo-Indian community, who seem perfectly content to perpetuate all the errors and mistakes made by the early settlers in the country.

Considerable caution should be exercised by new arrivals, with respect to bathing, which ought to be regulated according to the constitution. The general practice is to repair to a bathing room attached to each suite of apartments, and to have from half a dozen to a dozen large jars of cold water poured over the shoulders by an attendant. This water if taken from the wells in the morning is piercingly cold, it is therefore customary for those who cannot bear the sudden shocks to permit the water to remain all night in the jars in the hot weather, and vice versâ in the cold season. Any kind of cold bathing often disagrees, and when this is the case, a large kettle full of boiling water should be distributed throughout the jars in order to render the whole tepid, which is perhaps the most refreshing, and certainly the most healthy system to pursue. As native servants are not the best judges of the degrees of heat and cold, it will be necessary to try all the jars with the hand, in order to prevent the chance of alternate scalding and freezing; this kind of bath, with the free use of soap and friction, will be found both delightful and salutary, and may be enjoyed without danger by the most delicate persons, whereas any predisposition to fever or cholera is accelerated by cold bathing. Many young men plunge unadvisedly in the heat of the day into a swimming bath, a place roofed in and at a very low temperature, and by this means sow the seeds of illness from which they never afterwards recover.

The subject of diet is one in which persons going out to India rather late in life, usually feel great anxiety and alarm, and in their determination to avoid any thing like excess, they frequently fall into the opposite extreme. Two of the Bishops who died in Calcutta were said to have sacrificed themselves to abstinence, carried to too great an extent. It is of course impossible to prescribe a regimen which will suit every constitution, and each individual must be guided by experience, and the knowledge he has attained of what is hurtful, or the reverse. Many persons are afraid to touch fruit, which nevertheless may be eaten in moderation, with advantage. A certain quantity of stimulant seems absolutely necessary, taken in the shape of wine, beer, or weak brandy and water, but every body should discourage as much as possible the habit of drinking between meals; iced water is to many persons a pleasant and a wholesome stimulant, soda water taken in moderation, is also very agreeable and salutary, and occasionally a tea spoonful of sal-volatile in a tumbler full of cold water will be found beneficial. The native servants prepare many kinds of sherbets of the most palateable description, but it is advisable to partake very sparingly of them, a wine glassful of milk punch in a tumbler of cold water, forms a refreshing drink, the small quantity of spirit contained preventing the acid from disagreeing. Beer is a good thing in moderation, but should not be drank between meals, it is difficult when thirst is excessive to refrain, but it should be borne in mind that the means employed are never adequate to the end, encouraging rather than preventing the evil, those who drink frequently soon finding their thirst unquenchable. Hot tea, and all cold weak liquids bring on attacks of prickly heat, but these the sufferer must learn to bear, since there is neither prevention nor cure. The only safe alleviation is the application of powder, or when friction can be borne, warm soap and water rubbed with a flannel on the part affected. Prickly heat is occasioned by very minute blisters suddenly rising on the skin, and filled with water at a boiling pitch, the pain it produces being sometimes so violent as only to be compared to cutting with knives.

Persons possessed of sufficient means can upon their arrival in India, in setting up housekeeping, be supplied with every thing requisite for the most magnificent display; those whose pecuniary resources are of a more limited description should be cautious in their proceedings. The furniture absolutely essential to a house in India is trifling, compared to what is necessary to ensure a respectable appearance at home. The floors must in the first place be covered with mats, and the walls supplied with glass shades to hold the lamps, for the sitting rooms in India are too large to be lighted by the methods usually employed in England; a few chairs and tables will complete the items, while the bed chambers, *pro tem*, will require little more than the cabin furniture used on board ship. There are constant sales going on at the Presidencies, and indeed in all large stations, at which the most beautiful ornamental furniture is frequently to be purchased at a very cheap rate. The master of the house may either attend himself or employ a sircar. These sircars are usually great rogues, but they may be made very useful with good looking after. By mentioning a price which you will not exceed, they will exert themselves to procure the article wanted for that sum, and though in all probability they have made a good profit, you have been saved all the trouble, while it would be impossible for a European to pick up things as cheaply as a native. There are many commodities in Calcutta and other large stations, so completely hidden up in warehouses, that their existence would not be known to a stranger without the assistance of a sircar, particularly with respect to native products, shawls, &c. These fellows will sometimes take a real interest in the welfare of the persons who employ them as agents in a small way, and though it is always desirable to keep out of their debt, yet as they charge nothing for their services, being content with the commission which they get upon all purchases, they are a useful set of people when not trusted too far. It will not do to engage servants upon the recommendation of a sircar, who in few cases will refuse to take a bribe from the least reputable characters who could not otherwise hope for employment. While sojourning at an hotel, time will be permitted to look out for fitting persons to form the establishment, and for this purpose application should be made to the head men belonging to some respectable resident family, who has lived many years in his service. Advice with regard to servants will be given so often in the course of these pages, that its introduction may appear impertinent; yet care in the choice of these necessary appendages cannot be too strongly insisted upon. If good servants are not obtained at first, it will be very difficult to get them at all, for they are not fond of engaging in places previously filled by thieves and vagabonds.

The difference in manners and customs, and the difficulty of making orders comprehended, and of understanding what is passing around, prove very severe trials to the temper of a stranger, and without the exertion of considerable self-control the greatest personal discomfort will ensue, while the lives of dependents will be made wretched. Excepting in those individuals who are blessed with a more than ordinary portion of benevolence, the natives of India have less chance of kind treatment from men who visit the country rather late in life, than from younger residents, who are brought up as it were amongst them. Persons whose habits and manners are fixed, cannot so readily adapt themselves to strange customs, they are unwilling to commence their education anew, and are impatient of contradiction. Easily disgusted with a state of things of which they entertained no previous idea, they seldom or ever become reconciled to the people, or the country. It must be confessed that however kind and hospitable in other respects old Anglo-Indian residents may be, they manifest an unwillingness to assist new arrivals with information or advice, being much more disposed to laugh at and encourage the mistakes of Griffins, as they are termed, than to put them in the right way. Many persons who would gladly have availed themselves of the experience of their associates, are left to blunder on in their errors, until they make the most mortifying discoveries, it being considered a good joke to perplex and mislead; the gaucheries of the uninitiated affording a fund of amusement. Stories are told, which if true show that the highest functionaries have been most unmercifully treated in this way upon their first arrival. In laughing at the credulity of their dupes, the quizzers do not consider the great difficulty of separating the false from the true, in a scene in which all is strange, and where such extraordinary things are perpetrated, as may well induce the spectator to believe any thing he is told. It is therefore advisable for a stranger to have all his wits about him, and the sooner he can acquire a competent knowledge of the language, the more readily will he be able to see and judge for himself.

There is perhaps no place in which every thing essential for an establishment can be obtained so easily as at Calcutta, carriages and horses are to be hired at a not unreasonable rate, palanquins by the day or half day, and servants of all descriptions of a very respectable class also by the day, these people are called ticca, and if recommended by individuals of known good character, may be trusted. A whole house may be furnished from the bazaars in the course of a few hours, with articles either of an expensive or an economical description, according to the means of the purchaser, a well filled purse answering all the purposes of Aladdin's wonderful lamp. Never was there a place in which there are greater bargains, for if sales happen to be frequent, the most costly articles, carriages, horses, &c., are to be had for a mere song.

While letters of recommendation are not necessary in Calcutta to procure houseroom upon the first arrival, those persons who do not go out in any appointment which gives them a certain rank, will do well to provide themselves with introductions to resident families, which may be useful in obtaining attentions they might not otherwise receive; for the society of Calcutta is now so extensive, that strangers may be almost as much overlooked there as in London. Formerly there were only two circles; composed of those who had the *entrée* to Government House, and those who had not. Admission to the vice regal public parties does not however ensure invitations to the saloons of the *elite*, and the higher classes of the community are divided into cliques, the bond of union being as in other large places in England, equality of rank, fortune, and style of living. Introductions to persons somewhat of the same class as the party going to settle, are therefore the most advisable, and every body should endeavour, without absurdly seeking to raise themselves far above their natural condition, to establish as good a position as they can, a great deal depending upon the first step, while some caution is necessary to avoid ineligible connexions, which however inconvenient cannot afterwards be readily shaken off.

Officers belonging to the Queen's Service who go out to India, although they may be destined to spend many years of their lives in the country in which their regiment is stationed, usually look upon it as a place of temporary sojourn, and trouble themselves very little concerning manners and habits which are very uninteresting in their eyes. The society of their brother officers renders them in a great degree independent of that of the resident community, and each is apt to underrate and disparage the other. The Company's officers have privileges which those of the Queen's Service do not possess, comparatively few staff appointments or other lucrative situations being open to them, a jealousy is thus engendered which can only be subdued by long residence, intimate acquaintance with the civil and military servants of the Company, and the individual friendships consequent upon such associations.

Queen's officers are apt to despise modes and customs of which they do not at once perceive the utility, and persons better acquainted with the causes which have led to their adoption, despise them in turn for the non-compliance which lessens their respectability. There are of course some very brilliant exceptions, but it too often happens that individuals belonging to the Queen's Service, remain for years in India without conquering a single prejudice, or without seeing more than the mere external surface of the very small portion of the country and the native community, coming beneath their notice. They do not usually set the example of forbearance and kindness towards the native inhabitants, and their own ignorance of the conduct necessary to be pursued, prevents them from being able to withhold the soldiers from many acts of tyranny and oppression, which they would not commit if better informed. The march of a Queen's regiment through the country is dreaded by the inhabitants, who with their cattle are pressed into the service without adequate payment, and are frequently subjected to ill-treatment besides. It is, however, always pleasant to be able to shew a reverse to a gloomy picture. "I cannot," says Colonel Fitzclarence, now Earl of Munster, in his interesting Journal "adduce a stronger instance of the good feeling which has at times been entertained by the European soldiers for the sepoys, than the following anecdote, which speaks highly for both parties, and I heard it from authorities which I have no reason to doubt. The 72d regiment served under Lord Lake for so long a period with the sepoys, that they had become attached to each other; and the former being aware of the prejudices of the latter, have been known, when they happened to arrive first in camp, to wait till Jack Sepoy, as they call him, had drawn the water he wanted from the tank or well; ought not this example, though set by common soldiers, to make those in a higher sphere, and more civilized countries, blush, who have not known how to respect and tolerate the prejudices of their fellow-creatures." The want of sympathy, but too frequently manifested by Europeans with the natives of India, in all cases when not proceeding from malevolence of disposition, arises from ignorance of their true character, and the claims they possess to a higher degree of consideration, and that such ignorance should exist at all is much to be lamented, especially when there are so many noble examples which shew that it must entirely originate in idleness or apathy. The list of writers belonging to the military service of the crown, who have displayed the information which they have obtained concerning India, in works highly interesting and instructive, is particularly brilliant, and comparatively speaking, may be called extensive. The journal of Colonel Fitzclarence, already quoted, possesses an extraordinary degree of merit, the extent and quantity of the information contained upon almost innumerable subjects connected with the country and the people, are wonderful, considering the rapid nature of the author's travels, and the difficulties which he had to contend against, it shows, however, how much may be accomplished by an active enquiring mind, while the interest manifested by Colonel Fitzclarence in every thing connected with the country, and his kind and gracious manners have given him a reputation in India of which he may well be proud, his name is never mentioned without praises from the lips of men, who though they may not have known him personally, are well acquainted with his character and conduct.

Major Skinner of Her Majesty's 31st regiment, has contributed another most valuable and interesting work on the subject of India, while his overland journey shews the intimate acquaintance with Asiatic manners obtained during his abode in a country, in which many possessed of the same means of acquiring knowledge, will reside for years without knowing a word of the language. To Major Sherer, Major

Archer, and Captain Mundy, the reading public are indebted for some very entertaining volumes illustrative of Indian manners and Indian scenery, and the drawings of Major Luard, of Lieut. White, Capt. Jump, and others, are justly esteemed as highly valuable additions to the portfolios of the lovers of art. With the exception of Bishop Heber and one or two others, who were also temporary residents in India, all the lighter and more popular works illustrative of the country have been the contributions of officers in the service of the crown, a circumstance which ought to encourage persons who are capable of turning their observations to good account, to add their quota of information to the list. Though the importance of those profound volumes emanating from men who have studied their subject long and deeply cannot be disputed, yet they have nevertheless failed in attracting public attention to the country, and it was only when the reading world at home began to be amused, as well as informed, that any thing like general interest has been directed towards India. These observations are made for the purpose of shewing, that a great deal of good may be effected by individuals destitute of many of the advantages supposed to be requisite to constitute a traveller or an historian, and of inducing all intelligent persons who go to India to make themselves acquainted with circumstances and things which are imperfectly understood at home. By interesting themselves in the history and improvement of the people with whom they are domesticated, they will add to their own enjoyment, and become more reconciled to the land of their exile.

CHAPTER V.

THE CIVIL SERVICE.

In offering the following pages to those persons who have obtained an appointment in the Honourable East India Company's Civil Service, or who contemplate this advantage for their sons, I am able to recommend them to their serious consideration, in consequence of the valuable nature of the source whence they have been derived. Aware of the great importance of the subject, and conscious of my own inability to do it justice, I applied to a gentleman, who having served during a period of fourteen years with the highest credit to himself, as a judge and magistrate, was fully competent to give the necessary information. My portion, therefore of the chapters devoted to advice to Civilians going out to the Bengal Presidency, consists merely of the queries which will be found at the head of the respective paragraphs furnishing the replies to each. These replies will be found full, complete, and satisfactory, while the copious information conveyed in this and a succeeding chapter, regarding a branch of public service so important to the best interests of India and of England, and so imperfectly known in this country, cannot fail to prove acceptable to all classes of readers.

1. What would you advise a young man in the Civil Service going to India to take with him in the way of outfit?

Some persons set about considering this question by referring to the possibility of the ship, on which the person is embarked, touching at any intermediate port between England and India, where clothes may be washed. There is but one place where ships touch in their voyages for a sufficient time to permit of washing to be executed, and also so intermediately situated as to make this point worthy of consideration—and that is the Cape of Good Hope. I would advise that all outfits be provided without reference to the vessel going to any port in Southern Africa, and I believe this to be the truest economy. The price charged for washing at the Cape (badly done as it is at all times) is enormous. The people at the Cape calculate on all comers by ship, who stay but for a short period, as being lawful prey; and they use them accordingly. The expences incurred on account of washing extensively at the Cape of Good Hope, would, if properly disbursed, provide the articles necessary to furnish a person from the Cape to India without the necessity of employing Cape laundresses, and after all leave the master owner of a property at the end of a voyage which would otherwise be at the bottom of the almost bottomless and insatiable pockets of Mrs. Krraywaygen, or Brodsternberg. Young men, fresh from the scenes of gaiety and fashion, will not take the advice of those whom years have sobered, and they will therefore be hardly persuaded to believe that dress on board of ship (I of course use the term in the conventional sense) is not only unnecessary, but unusual. Of course I do not advocate that a youth should be slovenly in his apparel, or ungentlemanly either; but a person on ship-board, spruced out for a promenade in the Parks or the Opera would be an object of ridicule; and when he, in common with his fellow passengers, comes to feel the intense oppression of the change from cold to tropical climates, he will be most glad to divest himself of his plumes and avail himself of the privilege of tolerance and relaxation. This fact and one other, viz., that the climate of India, even in the North-Western Provinces, does not permit the use of cloth clothes for more than five months of the year, and sometimes, not for that, will shew that a large stock of cloth clothes is not only not necessary to an outfit, but that it may turn out to be nearly useless. Independent of this, it must be recollected, that the major part of youths who leave this country have not ceased growing, and that, in consequence, a large stock of cloth clothes may become worthless before they are worn. To such I would advise that they should take with them a small quantity of fine cloth, which can be made up tolerably well in Calcutta, where workmen are good, but dear in their charges. To all, however, whose height and size are supposed to be fixed when leaving England, and to all whose cases may become similar in India, I would seriously recommend the establishment of a connection with some respectable house in London, who would send out to them at specified periods what might be required, and what might be estimated without difficulty, thus avoiding the heavy charges which the European tradesmen in India are in a measure obliged to exact. For this reason I have advocated the appointment on the part of those proceeding to India, of home connections; and with this, I may give a just estimate of what may be required in No. 1. This point having been settled, I come to light clothes. In a voyage out, though the weather may be sometimes cold, especially in rounding the Cape in the winter months, it is in general warm and oftentimes oppressively so; it is then necessary to wear light clothes. These, if made of white material, must dirty soon: some of white jean are required for days of unusual smartness, or for going on shore.—No. 2. Hats are but little used on board of ship, but are indispensable as part of dress in India, where, like all other things of English manufacture, they are dear and often bad. A good beaver hat in a strong box is very useful; caps are necessary on ship-board, from the liability of hats to be blown over-board in fresh winds, and from the inconvenience of wearing them between decks, in consequence of the lowness.—No. 4. Shoes are much more cool and convenient than boots; good light shoes and boots for Indian wear are made cheap in India. Strong shoes, and good hunting boots, if required, should be taken out, as they can only be procured in India from European shopkeepers, who execute your orders when it pleases *them*, instead of their customers, and then at the usual penalty of high charges. Silk stockings, French or English, are dear in India, and a good supply from England is convenient.—No. 6. Saddlery. Those who are fond of hunting should take with them their own saddles. None that are good are made in India. Harness of all sorts is procurable at a moderate rate, but not saddles. The same may be said of guns, &c., all of which are imported from England, and are sold in India at extravagant prices.

What will be his necessary expences upon landing, and how much money should he have to provide himself with them?

I hold it a matter of the very utmost importance that a youth in any service, (and the importance is almost equal to the individuals of either service,) civil or military, should be launched forth into the world free from all encumbrance. A young man going to India in the Civil Service has a certain position to maintain, that of respectability, something in relation to what he may expect hereafter to be. This, without any extravagance, will cost him money, which the allowances which he will receive during the period of his residence "in College," as it is termed, i. e. before he passes his examination and becomes qualified for the public service, and also for perhaps two or three years subsequently, will not allow him to purchase. To obtain these things, therefore, he must either purchase them on credit, or borrow the money to pay for them. Either of these courses is at once destructive of independence of character, and is but too often the forerunner of irretrievable ruin. A young man should have no excuse for incurring debt of any sort, for when it is incurred once only, for what is necessary, it soon becomes a difficult task to restrain oneself within the rather indefinite bounds of that term. And as the judge of such bounds is the party himself, self gratification generally inclines the balance towards the indulgence rather than the restraint. When once this barrier is overpast, farewell to success in life. A young man in the Civil Service will only receive 400 rupees per month for the first year and a half, so that, in reference to the expences of living, of the number of servants which it is compulsory to keep, and to house rent, he can scarcely be expected to save anything. On setting up housekeeping in Calcutta, or in the provinces, he must provide himself with bed, tables, chairs, cooking utensils, china, plate, table linen, a buggy, and buggy horse, and a riding-horse. It is perhaps useless to observe in explanation of these items, that walking in India in the day time is out of the question. Any one therefore who goes about much in the day time, must do so either in a buggy or a palanquin. The latter is a slow and expensive mode of conveyance—two years' keep of which would nearly pay the price of a buggy. The buggy being kept then principally for business, visits, and day trips, the riding-horse is requisite for morning and evening exercise. Purchasing a buggy second-hand—which may be done—I believe to be but poor economy. The article may turn out useless, and will at best but last for a short while—even if it prove serviceable, the equipage will be changed at loss when the owner's prospects rise. On the contrary, a good sound buggy from a person well known, will, when brought to sale, always bring a fair price from the lower orders of the community. New buggies of the first makers may be had from 1,000 to 1,200 rupees. Good riding and driving horses may be had from 400 to 600 rupees each. Arabs generally run higher. Plate and furniture cannot well cost less than 1,500 rupees. Thus the sum allowed to a youth on arriving in India should not be less than £400. This, however, is full and ample, and if granted, should be considered as precluding all excuse for further demands, or for incurring debts. It is seldom, if ever, that young men go to India without some introductions to people in Calcutta, and indeed hospitality is so generally practised there, that procuring introductions is comparatively easy. A writer arriving in Calcutta should immediately proceed with his papers and certificates to the Secretary to the Government, and report his arrival. The Secretary will inform him of the steps he must take, and put him in the line of his duty. Supposing, however, that the visit to the Secretary may seem hard of accomplishment to a stranger first putting his foot in Calcutta, I should advise, that he should get some experienced friend on board of ship, who had been in India and was returning thereto, to direct him how to find the persons to whom he has letters of introduction. Some one of these will not fail to bring an invitation to stay and occupy a room, until the new comer can make arrangements for himself. Should the stranger be so singularly unfortunate as not to have any such introduction, he must even seek a friend similar to that which he has often found at home—even "Mine Inn." Of these there have of late been many established, some of which are of the first respectability, and are patronised by the elite of the society of upper India, who, having no homes in Calcutta, sometimes pay it a visit. Of these, Benton's hotel, and Spence's, are the best. The latter I specially recommend from personal knowledge, and from having there experienced civility, attention, and accommodation. In either of the cases, whether the newly-arrived stranger be living at an hotel or at a friend's, he will find those who will put him in the way of doing all that is necessary as to official matters. Supposing him possessed of a sum of money necessary to set himself up, I would advise a youth to consult his friends and acquaintances before he purchases the requisite articles. There are rogues in Calcutta as elsewhere ; and if the unwary have not some one to guide them they will have to purchase their experience very dear. Above all, young men, on landing, or, indeed, until they know something of the country, will do well to have no connection with any of the Bengally Sircars, with whom they will be surrounded, and by whom they will be harassed with solicitations. The cunning of these men is proverbial, and their art in carving out for themselves a decent per centage on every rupee that passes through their hands is astonishing. If these men must be employed, (and the saving of trouble through their quiet yet active intermediate agency often tempts people to call in their services,) it is advisable to employ some one well recommended, i. e. by respectable people resident in Calcutta, whose favour they may fear to lose, and the apprehension of which may induce them to act somewhat more fairly than those over whom there is no control. The reason, too, why I have added "resident in Calcutta" to the above piece of advice is, that all written recommendations are valueless, unless their authenticity is capable of verification. Many persons in England refuse to receive servants with written characters, and the precaution may wisely be adhered to in India. The reason why the contrary practice obtains in India, is that individuals are generally well known; and that it is next to impossible to counterfeit their hand-writing. Nevertheless, instances of gross knavery in these respects are not unfrequently brought to light; and the practice of buying and selling certificates of service is common. All these observations apply with greater force to personal and menial servants, whose papers are dubious in the extreme. The names of servants in India are so common to many individuals, there are so many Buxoos and Hossains, alias John Smith and

Tom Jones,—that a great facility exists to the practice of fraud of this description. Above all things, however convenient the accommodation may be, I seriously recommend no young man to take into his service any servant who speaks English, and this for two reasons. First, such persons are scarcely ever respectable, they have learnt what they have picked up for the purpose of serving with those whose ignorance of the language puts them at the mercy of their dependants, persons whom they may plunder without scruple or measure. They have generally served much in cantonments of European troops, which are bad schools for servants. Secondly, a young man, about to enter a service where an intimate knowledge of the languages is absolutely requisite to enable him to fulfil his duty with any credit or comfort to himself, and with any satisfaction to the governed, (and whose satisfaction is an officer's best reward,) should take every opportunity of practising speaking the Indian tongues, and nothing tends more to facilitate the acquisition of a knowledge of the language than conversation, be it upon the most trivial subject of household management. A youth, not as yet intimately acquainted with the idiom of the language may feel hesitation in speaking it in public, or before others; but in his own house, he may cautiously feel his way, and try his strength. He may observe how his orders are executed, and that will be a test of the intelligibility of his jargon, for although your servant will, be your language ever so far short of the comprehensible, pretend to understand you, yet the result of his efforts will soon shew you whether he has done so or not. To this may be tacked as a carollary, which should be strongly impressed on the mind of every one, when a native servant fails to do what he has been told, consider whether his fault may not have arisen from *your* improper mode of giving the order, rather than *his* stupidity. How often would this consideration, if brought to mind at the moment, have prevented an abusive rebuke which can contaminate the utterer only, and not the hearer, however irritable it may be to his feelings. And here, albeit a digression, I cannot avoid making a dissuasive remark on this too common and degrading practice in India. Its origin is to me a mystery. How is it that a gentleman, respectable and well educated, who would think it beneath him to swear, or use profane expressions, will use words oftentimes positively indecent? Is it that the natives of rank do so to their servants, or that these servants are beings of an inferior kind, who require such treatment? Surely neither of these is a sufficient reason. To the first, I would reply, that we should not follow a bad example, but that we should shew a better. As to the second, even were not its truth altogether disputable, their feelings at least are as sensitive as our own, and a principle of consideration should prevent our unnecessarily wounding them. Let me assure all young men that this practice gains them neither good will nor credit in a place like India, where every man's character is as well known as his office under Government. The reputation of an abusive habit will deter many a respectable domestic from offering his services, and many of the higher classes of natives, though some of them say with the poet—

> " Video meliora proboque
> Sed deteriora sequor,"

are perfect gentlemen, and acute judges of good manners. Those who have ever heard a native speak feelingly on the subject can alone judge of what consequence they deem it. To return from this digression, however, I would recommend, that servants should be taken from, and on the recommendation of, some steady man, actually in employment, and who has served his master faithfully for years. A young man in the civil service, will never want a choice of domestics;

they will soon enough find out his residence when he wants his establishment completed; caution, however, as above stated, should always be taken, or you may entertain one who will abuse your confidence and abscond with all the valuables you may possess. This, however, can rarely happen, if you have respectable references from the servant by whom the man has been recommended, and who knows both his home and his relatives; should he prove unworthy of trust, the information thus easily attainable, would render the delinquent liable to speedy detection. Besides this, to obtain a good service in a respectable family is not held lightly, the more especially as it affords an opportunity of getting others of a servant's family into the same house, and thus a community of interests is established between servants and master. I had a servant in India who gradually introduced his relations, brothers or nephews, into the house; he himself had seven rupees per month, and the rest four rupees each, making a monthly total of thirty-one rupees. This is a very large sum for a family in India, and the receipt of this for many years, eventually made them all rich and respectable in their own village. Again, if one of these wished to go home, or was ill, he sent for some other of his relations and left him with me as a substitute. Now these men would hardly lose such advantages, if they could help it, by misconduct; and had they stolen property to the value of two or three hundred rupees, the risk of gain would hardly have recompensed them for the loss of so valuable a place. To these circumstances, and to general kind treatment of the natives, I attribute the fact, that during a residence of fourteen years in all parts of the country, I have never lost an article of any consequence; and that my plate, which was valuable, was sold in 1836 for what I had given for it in 1822.

Until the last few years, all young men who arrived in India as writers, went into College in the Writers' Buildings, and there remained until they were emancipated by being declared qualified for the public service. Some got out in three months, and others remained three years. This state of things could not well last, and various rules were made to alleviate these evils, until Lord W. Bentinck knocked it on the head altogether in reality, though the name still remains. The College was identified with the Writers' Buildings; and when they were thrown up, its glory was gone. It may emphatically be said, "Troja fuit." Peace to thy manes, oh, Buildings! now no longer inhabited by writers. Thou hast seen sad doings in thy day, and perhaps, though we look back with fond regret to many reminiscenses, yet it is better for the rising generation that thou art not. But as thou art not, I am reminded that I have now to show that generation, what still exists to recall the traces of thy ancient discipline, since the ordeal of examination must be passed. The period fixed within which all writers must pass the examination prescribed before they can be duly qualified for the public service, is one year. The examination consists of reading and translating Persian and Hindee—not Hindostanee; and translating English into those languages, all without assistance. A dictionary even is not allowed to be opened. It may therefore be imagined that the trial must be severe, and that though easily passed by those who really possess a sound knowledge of the grammar of those tongues, and a tolerably familiar acquaintance with its general literature, it must prove a stumbling block to those who are only slightly or superficially proficient. Nor is it to be wondered at that no trivial test is required, since after having passed this, the young man is sent to join some office to commence active duty to the people and the Government. To enable him to perform this duty a knowledge of the language is absolutely necessary, and results of a calamitous nature might accrue from any ignorance. When also such results may proceed, it is not a matter of surprise, that the examiners are something strict in performing a duty of so onerous though unpleasant a nature. If this examination be not successfully passed within the period of one year from the date of the student's arrival, he is directed to proceed back again to England, and is considered to have forfeited his appointment. This enactment is one of the many for which the Indian service stands indebted to the kind feelings of Lord W. Bentinck. It is very rigorous, and has been acted on in several instances. But the Court of Directors, who are ever ready, if possible, to afford a lenient consideration to every case, have permitted the banished to return, excepting in two or three cases, wherein gross and repeated negligence and misconduct in the individuals, shewed them to be unfit subjects for mercy. Nevertheless, young men will do well to weigh these things, and to set themselves on their arrival (if not before) to conquer the difficulties of their path; since, though the extreme penalty is not in these cases exacted, yet the punishment of being compelled to return home is sufficiently severe. It superinduces the expence of a voyage home and out, besides the loss of full three years' rank; the first of these losses is a drop in the ocean in comparison to the second, which throws him back all his life time, and can never be recovered. It is no less than suffering fifteen or twenty contemporaries, and many of a lower rank, to take the precedence, and to have a general right to good appointments in preference to himself. If these are not incentives to hard study, I do not know what are.

While young men are what is termed—in college, they may either reside in Calcutta or may proceed up the country and study there. In the first case, they are examined by the college-council; in the other, by a committee of members at the station where they may be. Of these two courses there can be no doubt that it is by far the best to proceed into the interior. Calcutta is, in all seasons, the seat of many entertainments public and private; and during the cold weather it is very gay. Young men are tempted in various ways to leave their studies, whereas in the interior of the country they are not. Morning visits, evening calls, dinners, balls, &c. are, doubtless, pleasant and seductive, but they ill-accord with serious study. Shops there are in plenty; they are magnificent, and the prices are according. A youth may walk in, order or take what he likes, and, far from any questions being asked, articles will be pressed on his attention. He will have formed acquaintances with young men who were, perhaps, ship-mates, and visits to Dum-Dum and Barrackpore, large stations, the one about eight the other fourteen miles from Calcutta, where the artillery and native infantry are respectively stationed, will occupy time which should be devoted to more profitable purposes. On the other hand, a station in the interior presents none of these seductions to idleness and expence. The members of the society will generally be a judge, a magistrate, a medical officer, and perhaps two or three assistants. All these have their various duties to attend to, and cannot trifle away their time if they would; the collegian is therefore obliged to work or do nothing. I question also (that is, if a youth have a proper feeling in respect to the situation he is about to hold, and contemplates the career before him as an honorable field for exertion, where he may do more good than any other individual in the whole world, save those similarly situated), if seeing men, and especially young men of nearly his own age, actively employed in the discharge of their duties, does not stimulate him to exertion that he may join in the work, and commence a course where he too may get a name. If all these nobler feelings, which I believe find a preponderating influence in the hearts of the majority of young men, do not exist, and if the novice look on his Indian course as merely a means of present subsistence and future luxury, even then, ignoble as such feelings are, there is yet something to spur him on to exertion in the thought, that the sooner he is emancipated from college, the sooner he will have a claim to increase of salary. I should therefore very seriously advise all young men to proceed into the interior to study. There are less temptations there than at Calcutta, and the student is brought more immediately into contact with those whose language he is learning; all of which cannot fail to facilitate his task and give him an Oriental turn of mind.

I cannot conclude these observations without adverting to one point of the utmost importance. I allude to the great advantage which those young men experience who possess such connexions and introductions in India, as may secure them something in the shape of a paternal regard from some respectable person long resident there. One main cause of errors which youths in India commit, is the want of some wholesome advice, which it is the office of the parent to give; while young men, having lost their advisers, are but too apt to think that they have no need of counsel or counsellor. It is needless to point out how many things apparently trivial but in reality of great weight in their eventual consequences, appear different to the experienced and the inexperienced, nor how the acute eye of the wary perceives a tendency to deviate from the course of propriety, while the deviator scarcely knows that he is erring, so slight is the falling off. A word in such a case, or a gentle expostulation, if given in time, may often save a man from committing that which, little as he then thinks of it, may hereafter cause him the bitterest anguish. I need not dilate on this subject, for it is an evil case, common to all mankind, old and young. Life is spent in purchasing experience at a dear rate; it is despised by nearly all but by the possessor; it is almost invariably spurned when offered in the way of advice, and when the possessor has acquired sufficient to guard himself on all points, he has no occasion for it, and he is called away ere he has been able to make use of it to any good purpose. There are yet some youths who will receive in good part what is said to them, and for such the procuring of a sound and judicious adviser is of more weight than untold gold. Few youths go to India without some letters to friends; and if, among those friends, there should be any one on whom they have a claim sufficiently strong to produce an invitation to spend a short period under the same roof after their arrival, it would be most advantageous.

What books should he possess, and what will be his best course of study?

Those which are used as class books at Haileybury, especially the Prem Saugor and the Anvari-Soheily. Richardson's Dictionary is indispensable, as containing all the more recondite meanings of the Persian and Arabic words. For all ordinary purposes, however, there is no work like Shakespear's Hindostanee Dictionary, respecting which it has always seemed a miracle to me, how it contains all the information which is there to be found; though it professes to be merely a Hindostanee Dictionary, there is scarcely a Persian word in ordinary use which may not there be found, and the explanation of each word in its usual, ordinary, and useful meaning. Richardson, on the contrary, gives fifty meanings to each word, leaving the learner to choose amidst the mass of confusion whichever may suit his pleasure, thus infinitely confusing and perplexing him. As to the course of study to be pursued, regular reading the books above alluded to gives a facility in translating. It is an advantageous custom to note down in a book the words met with in the course of the day's reading, which may be new, and to commit them to memory. As the acquiring of the idioms of these languages is absolutely necessary to a scholar. I know of no better way than this. Let the learner translate a portion of Persian, verbatim, as it stands; and then translate the same portion into free English; after that let him compare, and carefully note, how the form of the sentence and expression differ from his own tongue. Translating from English into Persian and Hindostanee, is a very good way of acquiring a knowledge; though it must be confessed that unless there be somebody to superintend the process and correct all faults, bad habits may be acquired. Still in every ship going to India, there will be some resident returning to his Eastern home, who will be able to assist the student should he be induced to labour during the voyage. If the kindly passenger be no scholar, yet in hearing the exercise read to him, he will soon be able to say whether it be intelligible or otherwise. Of course in India this objection does not exist, as regular native teachers, called moonshees, are appointed to assist the student.

CHAPTER VI.

THE CIVIL SERVICE.

Is the young man who has obtained a writership, allowed a choice in the different departments of the service, and what are the advantages and disadvantages of each?

There are only three distinctions as to the line of service. The political, the judicial and revenue, and the commercial, as I shall hereafter explain. The political department is that in which all the transactions between the British Government and Foreign Courts are carried on; as well as between the Government and Native Princes, independent or otherwise. The appointments in this department are not at first well paid, but they lead to high and splendid appointments hereafter, if the aspirant to honor succeed in his career. This line requires a perfect and entire knowledge of the native languages, as well as an intimacy with the customs, manners, and habits of the various people of India, together with their modes of thinking and acting, their prejudices and their religion. To this should be added a good acquaintance with not only the general History of British India, but of its particular states. All these requisites demand a long apprenticeship, before an officer in the political line can well aspire to the higher grade of appointments. As in these, he will oftentimes have to act in the greatest emergencies, where the credit of the

British Government, whose authorised agent he is, is at stake, and in cases where an error in judgment might produce incalculable and irremediable mischief, he cannot well hope to be trusted with such duties until Government have sufficient reason to suppose that it will suffer no detriment by confiding to him such a trust. This line leaves the successful aspirant to nearly the only offices where fame and fortune are to be obtained on any scale, such as agent to the Governor-General, and residentships. Noble as the prospect is, and eager as many of my young readers may be to throw caution and prudence to Jericho, and despite of all the difficulties to scan this hill of fame with greedy and ambitious eyes, I am sorry that I must more than partially blight their hopes. Time was when all these splendid prizes were held almost exclusively by the Company's Civil Service. Now if you look over the list you will scarcely find one civil servant holding such offices. They have been transferred to the military service. You will ask the reason why? Because it pleased that short-sighted politician Lord William Bentinck to do so, on the alleged score of economy, but whose undisguised partiality for the members of his own profession, afforded but too much reason for the belief that he might be induced to take advantage of the circumstance of that peculiar line being open to every branch of the service, in order to provide for his military friends. There was possibly another motive, and one which shews that the despotism almost inseparable from the military professional character, renders it unadvisable that men accustomed to have their mandates implicitly obeyed, should be entrusted with the government of such a country as India. A military Governor-General, unless a man of very enlarged mind, is impatient under every dissent from his sovereign will and pleasure, and the necessary subordination to which officers belonging to the army are reduced, renders them more willing instruments in the hands of authority, than men who are accustomed to have a voice in affairs of consequence, and who are allowed some degree of discretionary power. The result of this system has been manifested by disorders in Oude, a war in the Cole country protracted from 1832 to the present period, and the murder of poor Blake at Jeypoor, in 1835. These matters, however, are somewhat foreign to our present discussion, and I shall therefore only say, that the occurrence of the calamities above noticed, are not imputed to the officers in charge of the political relations of the districts in which they happened, but to the measures which they were directed to execute. The fact, however remains, that it has been found convenient by succeeding governors, to continue a practice which extends the bounds of their patronage, and so this custom still holds, and will do so, unless the Court of Directors interfere. A young man, therefore, has not the option of joining the political line. Splendid talent, far above the ordinary run, may command anything; but as a youth, even should he possess these transcendent abilities, has not had the opportunity of putting them forth, and therefore, until then, a military officer will be preferred to him should the Government want an assistant in the political department. Interest, however, if it be overwhelming, will in this, as in other things, carry all before it, provided the individual possessing it, is capable of doing the duties of his office. No interest can push on one totally incompetent, or very much so. The next line which I shall consider, is that which I have denominated the Commercial, and respecting which I must make some explanatory remarks, as the appellation is one of my own affixing, and is rather arbitrary. In former days, when the East India Company was a trading corporation, there were many very rich and valuable appointments called Commercial Agencies, the officers holding which, superintended the advances made to the cultivators of cotton, and persons employed in the production of silk, &c., and in due season received the produce and remitted it to Calcutta. The Government cultivators too were protected by especial enactments from many annoyances to which ordinary persons were subject. So that the inducement, in a country where the name of Government protection assures respect, to become the protegés of the Company were many. This subject and that of the Company's trade would form a subject for a separate paper—but it is here irrelevant. The magnitude of the Government interests, entrusted to these commercial agents, and the sums of money which they had at their disposal, rendered, I presume, these offices of high trust, for they used to be highest in remuneration in the whole service. Yet it seems singular why they should have been so, as the work was most easy, and the labour little. The agent had a fine mansion allowed him, he had little trouble in going about to visit his district, and his business was confined to looking over accounts, signing papers, and adjusting petty differences between the cultivators; while the real details of the office were conducted by his head officer or dewan. But thus it ever will be in the world where every thing like kissing goes by favour; and consequently these offices, with much pay and little work, were prizes given to individuals who had good interest, and in this line were made many of those large and princely fortunes which used to astonish the people of England. Let it, however, be recollected, that I am not now alluding to another species of commercial agency unconnected with the Government, which certainly astonished all England, and subsequently all the people of India too, by the production of immense fortunes to the persons whose names were gradually removed from the houses, and the origin of which fortunes was never accurately known until the year 1829, when all the then existing houses fell simultaneously with one crash, and left their constituents who had placed trusts and money in their hands with dividends varying from five to one-sixteenth per cent. of the original. Where the cash went to, people still wonder, unless it be, (as some say, in England still,) in the shape of fine houses, glittering plate, splendid parties, and costly viands, which may perhaps be justly considered as too good for the starving widows and orphans, from whose pittance they were derived. No, the Indian Government has been in times of old sufficiently illustrated by deeds which shun the light, or if brought to light shame the open day, to require that *this* should be laid at its door. I therefore introduce this casual remark that the reader may know that *these* "agencies" were established by certain traders within the Mahratta ditch in Calcutta, yet rejoicing in the magnificent appellation of the "Merchant-Princes of the City of Palaces." Having explained this matter, I proceed to my subject, which is the Government commercial agencies, wherein as I have said, salaries were large, and fortunes made. Alas! for the word "were," we weep because they are not. The first attack made upon these fat kine was by the Clipping Dutchman, as some wag christened his horse at one of the races in honour of the then Governor-General Lord W. Bentinck, who wisely made friends to himself of the Mammon of Leadenhall Street, by cutting down all salaries save his own enormous stipend. Still they were snug berths, but then afterwards came the new charter by which trading in all its branches was abolished save in salt and opium; with that system fell the agencies generally, and now two or three alone remain. They are well paid and lucrative appointments, but they are no sinecures, and are usually held by persons high up in the service. In former days also there were what were called inland customs, but what were, if properly denominated, the curse of India. The collection of these customs was the business of an officer, and one was stationed in each of fifteen of the largest towns in India. This system afforded such pretext to the executive native officers (generally a corrupt set who purchase their situations with a view to extortion) to oppress every one who came within their official clutches, that it almost put a stop to the internal trade of the country. Blessed be heaven this system of inland customs is now abolished, and people may carry their merchandise from one end of India to the other without being pillaged at each step by custom-house officers. Though great credit is due to the Government of India, which submitted to a present loss of revenue (though with an almost sure prospect of eventual increase) for the purpose of relieving the community of an almost intolerable evil, the greatest share of praise is due to Mr. Charles Trevelyan of the Civil Service. That gentleman published a small book on the subject, which, though containing nothing particularly new as to facts, which were indeed pretty well felt and known, yet placed those facts in such a strong light, and proved the evils to be so overwhelming that Government could no longer uphold the system without obtaining a most unenviable reputation for encouraging and supporting oppression. With this system went the custom collectors as a body, and now there are but two offices connected with customs of any description, the import and export customs at Calcutta, and one in Upper India for frontier duties. Besides these there are offices of audit and account both in the Upper and Lower Provinces; and an office of the post-master general. I have classed, therefore, all these under the head of commercial, because they have all more or less reference to commerce and accounts in general, and they are exceptions to the ordinary offices. In almost all of these, if a young man be admitted as an assistant, he must not look for speedy increase of pay and promotion. He must wait for gradation rank, and can scarcely hope to be moved over the heads of his equals or superiors, or even to hasten on his promotion by his own exertions. When chance, promotion, death, or retirement, open the road, he can in return have little fear of an interloper being put above him; and then, though perhaps later than his contemporaries, he gets into a largely salaried office, yielding greater emoluments than theirs. All these offices too, or the majority of them, are situated in the capitals of the Presidencies, and the holders of them remain stationary, while they generally have the advantage of the best society, and every comfort which can be desired—a lot which does not fall to all who take the line of the service. N. B. These comforts are not to be had without expence, however, and consequently large fortunes are seldom made in them. The remaining path to be chosen, is what I call the line, because it is the largest and ordinary branch of the service to which the Company's civil employes are attached.

I confess myself, that though I should hesitate a little on the score of fame, which may be obtained in the political department, this is the branch of the service which I prefer. It is an honest and fair course, where luck or favour can do little, though they may partially assist on occasions, where a youth soon becomes known for assiduity or otherwise, where his contest with his contemporaries is only who can be the most efficient in business, and where he has it in his power by his activity, forbearance and justice, to make the people under his charge happy. I do not specify integrity as one of the qualities wherein he may shine, as it is one so essentially necessary to every officer, as to be scarcely deemed a virtue, and its deficiency is now so rare, as hardly to form an exception to the general rule. In this line, a youth, after getting out of college, will first be made assistant in the office of magistrate and collector. He will at first be required to do many slight duties under the close inspection of his superior, and as he evinces capacity and industry, heavier and more responsible duties will be committed to his charge, until he gets a perfect insight into his duty. So sudden are the changes in office, either from exchange of officers, leave of absence, or sickness, that two years will scarce elapse before some chance will, in all probability, throw the office on his hands for a short time; or should not this happen, he will be sent into the interior of the district on deputation to perform some specific duty which could not be so well executed at the head station. In these situations his diligence and judgment, or contrariwise, will soon become manifest. From this office he will in four or five years become a joint magistrate, then a magistrate and collector, and thereafter as circumstances may turn out.

From all these statements the reader may judge which of the branches of the service he deems most to be preferred. Situations in the commercial line are not always procurable. Still less in the political, and the revenue and judicial branch is the only one fairly open. I prefer it to the commercial: it is more laborious, perhaps less paid also, but it is more intellectual, more gratifying, and brings a man into contact with the natives of India, and to an observer and those who dive deeper into things than the superficies, offers an inexhaustible subject of study and amusement

One further point remains for discussion, that is, whether a young man should pursue his fortunes in Bengal proper, or the North Western Provinces, and the pros and cons of the case are briefly resolved into climate, and the chances of promotion. In reference to climate opinions vary, and those who have lived in Bengal, aver that it is far superior to the Upper Provinces. Those from the North-West, are loud in praise of their own abode. The climate of Bengal is free from the great alterations of heat and cold to which the Upper Provinces are subject. In Bengal the climate is moist and humid. There are no hot winds, and during the cold weather no inconvenience is suffered. In Upper India the climate is dry. During three months of the year the hot winds blow like hurricanes, and in the cold weather a good box coat for a morning ride, and a couple of stout blankets on the bed, are far from unpleasant. The Bengalees say that the even nature of the temperature favours health, the North-Western replies, that the hottest wind in India is preferable to the stifling stagnant hot house atmosphere of Bengal. In fact a hot house is a perfect representation of Bengal. The hot winds of Upper India are tempered in the house by artificial means, while five months of good cold healthy weather strengthen the body against the relaxation of the rest of the year. I give the preference to Upper India, and having served in both I am tolerably well able to offer an opinion. Many a man who has passed a long period in Bengal, if sent to the Upper Provinces, becomes attached to them, but the converse is not the case. I never knew one sent in his early days to Upper India, who liked the climate or state of things in Bengal. Again, the appearance of men, women and especially children in Upper India, their healthy hue, plainly proves the superiority of that climate to the luxurious, yet relaxing air of Bengal. On the subject of promotion it is generally considered that people in Bengal are more speedily promoted than those in Upper India, and I believe it to be the case. I do not think the advantage so great as might be supposed. It is indubitable that Upper India affords the finest field for talent to display itself, which, and the superiority of the climate, are the causes of most people prefering to go there rather than to stay in Bengal, and which are in consequence indirectly productive of delay in promotion.

The wishes of young men on their first appointment to assistantships are consulted by the Government, as far as the public interests permit. A list of places where assistants are required, is usually offered to their notice, and from that they may choose where they will go. Should any special reason be offered why a youth should wish to go to a particular station, such as his having any friend or relation there, it will be in general attended to, unless there be some good reason to the contrary.

What are the principal dangers which an inexperienced person will have to encounter :—what are the best means of avoiding them?

Omitting the mention of drinking and gambling as too obvious to require reprobation, I shall specify three things which require to be guarded against, two of which have reference to a youth personally, and the third to him as an officer of Government. The first I shall touch on, is, getting into debt of any kind. This is a subject which has often been treated of, and the mention of it here might be considered superfluous. But exhortation passes away while temptation remains, and an additional word can do no harm and may do good. The worst part of getting into debt is, that when the boundary is once overpast, there is no knowing to what extent it will go. If it be necessary to obtain a loan for matters indispensable, there are many respectable sources from which it can be procured. But young men seldom want a credit at all beyond what they usually take with them to supply their necessities. If unprincipled debt be incurred, I mean if a young man borrow to gratify his taste for any particular passion, the sum required for the indulgence is far beyond what he can obtain from any respectable source. The same want of principle will induce him to get money from any source respectable or otherwise, rather than restrain his unruly appetites. For such the opulent natives are on the look out. They care little for what sum may be required, or what security is offered, or if in fact there be any at all. Their sole object is to secure their victim in such a manner that he can never free himself from the meshes of the net which encloses him. They know that the youth in process of time will arrive at office, and then will come their harvest, then will come the long-expected feast with which they will glut themselves in the face of their victim, and in spite of his virtuous but helpless indignation. When thus situated at the head of a reputable office, he will find himself compelled by demands of payment and threats of arrest and exposure, to appoint to offices, or to recommend for appointments, the kindred and servants of his creditor. The same means compel him to shut his eyes to their enormities, until matters come to such a pass that the attention of authority is attracted to the scenes of iniquity which have been committed, and then ensues disgrace almost irretrievable. Yet all this while the unfortunate victim may be mainly conscious of the evils which are committed in his name, and may vainly writhe to free himself from trammels not to be shaken off! Can any case be more shocking than this, and yet such things have been. With such a prospect before his eyes will not every youth gifted with good sense or right feeling shun the idea even of debt.

I write feelingly on this subject, because I once narrowly escaped the snare myself; for though long experience may have given me the power to advise, I do not profess myself to have been, or to be better than my neighbours. If this exposure of myself save one unthinking youth from a similar course, I shall rejoice thereat. Shortly after my arrival at Calcutta, where I then was in the Writers' Buildings, I had expended a sum of money which was given me as an outfit, and which was considerably less than was necessary. A friend, with whom I was at that time living, had formed an acquaintance with several rich natives of Calcutta, who used to come to our house. It happened that one day in the course of conversation I mentioned that I was short of money, when one of these native gentlemen who was present, politely offered me any immediate assistance which I might want, the offer was accepted, the favour was duly appreciated, and the accommodation duly used. One day my convenient friend, whom we will call Rada Mohun, paid me a visit and in the course of conversation casually asked the question, who was my sircar or house steward. When I told him the name, he remonstrated with me in having so improper a person near me, and offered to procure for me one more efficient. I thought nothing of this speech, and less of the motive by which it was dictated, and I passed the matter off by replying that the man suited me well enough, and that I did not intend to change him. Time passed and I had taken advantage of my friend's accommodating disposition to use his cash box further. In another visit Rada Mohun again more earnestly pressed on me the necessity of having another house steward, and offered to send me a relation of his own in the place of the person I employed. I was astonished at his pertinacity, and also at the nature of the demand. Rada Mohun used to come in his carriage and was a man of fortune. "How could I ask," said I naturally, "a brother of yours to go and get me half a cheese, or a dozen of beer." The remonstrance had no effect. Rada Mohun said that his brother would be but too happy to serve me. My eventual reply was that we had a custom in England, of not turning away a servant except for a fault; that my house steward had committed none, and that I should not displace him. My friend departed not in the best possible humour. Time again passed; in this interval, however, my eyes had been opened to what was going on. A book had been put into my hand called "Tytler's Considerations on India," and therein I found a detail of the condition to which men in office were reduced who were in the hands and at the mercy of their native creditors. I saw the brink of the precipice on which I stood, and felt my danger. My first thought was how to procure money from some respectable European house, wherewith to release myself from this thrall. Friends I had none, I had a slight acquaintance with one of those gentlemen who belonged to the agency houses in Calcutta, and whose misfortune it was to incur the odium and disgrace of a failure, and to bear in their own persons the consequences of the acts of others. This individual, (Mr. James Cullen,) on whom I had no claim whatever, kindly promised to do what he could with his partners on my behalf, but was at that time unable to bring them to consent to lend me the necessary amount. It was after all no very great sum, but I believe that commercial difficulties were then beginning to be felt. In deep disappointment I took leave only to meet a worse torment at home, in a visit from my friend Rada Mohun. He deemed that by this time he had fully entrapped me, and that he had only to pull in his net and pull out his fish. He was mistaken nevertheless. On this visit he assumed a more peremptory tone. He no longer expostulated and advised, but commanded; he told me I must displace my servant, and receive his relation in his place. The result of the interview was that I as decidedly refused what he most imperiously demanded; and he left me in high dudgeon. I knew the consequences, and was at my wits end to meet them. The next day brought Rada Mohun's clerk to my door with my account, the amount of which had I sold all I possessed, and myself into the bargain, I could not have paid. It was worth an effort, for submission was my only alternative. I got into my conveyance and went once more to my friend the agent. I told him the whole story and besought him to save me from ruin, which, had he refused, appeared to me inevitable. He had once more recourse to his partners and his influence prevailed. I received liberty to draw for the sum I wanted. I need not say how rejoiced I was at this event, I went home, drew a bill on the agents, and sent my house-steward with it to Rada Mohun's, and was a free man once more. It amused me to hear my servant describe the rage into which my quondam creditor fell, at finding his prey escaped; but here ends the tale.

It is instructive, and will serve to warn youth against insidious friends and the necessity of calling for their assistance. The evil originates in the man, and, like all evil in, the world, it superinduces a further and a greater evil.

I have personally known another case which ended tragically; but as parties are still alive who might recognise the allusion, I can only touch on it very generally. The gentleman in question had been unjustly hospitable and liberal in his youth, I say unjustly, because it was not with his own that he was so. He was nevertheless much beloved for his kindness, and generally esteemed; all of which facts only shew, how debt can blacken even the fairest prospects of the fairest characters. He at length in the course of service reached high office, and was, as I have before shewn to be the case, compelled to nominate his creditor's servants to places. The gentleman did his duty, and as he thought, prevented by his own uprightness all existence of evil. It was at length brought to his notice that matters were going wrong, and that the delinquent was his creditor's nephew, who held place under him. The charge having on investigation proved to be true, the gentleman hesitated not to brave all consequences, and dismissed the offender. The creditor finding all efforts to obtain his nephew's restoration from this high-minded gentlemen to be ineffectual, took out a writ against him at a time when he (the creditor) knew that his debtor must be unable to resist or to evade. The process was issued, and the attempt to execute it, so agitated the gentleman, that it brought on apoplexy and immediate death. His loss was deeply regretted, and all said, "what might he not have been had he not incurred this fatal debt."—Verbum non amplius addum.

The next point on which I shall caution youth, is a bodily evil, and one at which they will perhaps laugh—but which is nevertheless not to be lightly heeded. I mean against exposure to the sun. Young men who leave home in the flower and bloom of health, think that no climate and no exposure can hurt them. Fond of field sports, they imagine they can with impunity do in India as they have done in England, and go heedlessly in the sun for hours, and at the hottest time of the day. Nothing can be more dangerous or deceptive than this practice. It is dangerous, because the numerous instances of speedy death produced by such exposure, prove the fact. It is deceptive, because those who for some time brave the exposure, think that they have escaped scot free, and they will not suffer for their indiscretions. Here they are mistaken; after years shew it in a marked manner.

The third point refers particularly to young men entering on office. The caution I wish to impress on them is, to take heed and not shew too great partiality or favour to any one individual native. The favour of any English gentlemen in office is so valuable to a native, that there is scarcely any degree of obsequiousness and servility which they will not practise to obtain his favour. Professions of personal esteem, offers of unbounded service and devotion, in fact every thing that can create a favourable impression are employed by them, and if they once acquire a personal influence over the head of the establishment, their gain is great, and evil ensues. But what is as bad, should they have no real influence, but are permitted to wear the semblance of possessing it, they will turn it to the same account. Wherefore let no man in office have, or seem to have, particular favourites, or lend an ear to one person more than another. Equal favour, equal justice is every man's right, and any thing which disturbs the equilibrium, makes right wrong.

What are his prospects in the present state of Indian affairs, and what is the best policy to pursue, and how conduct himself until he has gained acquaintance in the country which will enable him to see his own way?

Much relative to this question has been before answered. His prospects as to promotion I have set forth. His prospects as to pecuniary matters are peculiarly bright. From the second or third year of his arrival he may commence laying by money, which should always be invested in Company's paper, unless he has any persons in whom he can really trust, who will manage his affairs for him. At the end of ten years he will be entitled to a furlough, or leave of absence of three years from the date of his quitting India, to the date of his return, and during which period he will receive an allowance of £500 per annum. After twenty-five years service, including the three years furlough, (which may be taken at any period after the lapse of ten years) he becomes entitled to a pension of £1000, for which, however, be it recollected, four per cent. is deducted from all pay and allowances. It is not unreasonable to suppose that a civilian who goes steadily through his course may accumulate from £20,000 to £30,000 of his own, independent of his pension. A discussion has arisen as to the benefit arising from a man taking his furlough. Some consider it best to stay out the whole time at once, and then to come home for good; others prefer taking their furlough as soon as they can. It is not an easy matter to decide a question which depends so much on individual feeling and circumstances. A visit home on furlough renews health, invigorates the mind, enables a man to renew his youthful connexions, see his friends, and to form in mature age a correct notion of those things which youth has erroneously coloured. A person continuing twenty-two years in India is to a certain extent cut off from his country and family, and finds it more difficult to reconnect the links of a chain so long dissevered. As also the Company will not pension a servant for twenty-two years continuous service, but will then compel him to take his furlough for three years, or to serve them out, a man may as well have his furlough when he is young, as afterwards, especially as the salaries which he will have in his older days are more likely to be higher than those more recently attained.

Until a young man can see his own way tolerably he will not have much to do in the way of business, respecting which he will not have some superior near, ready to correct him, should he go wrong. A few maxims I will note for his guidance, but they must be brief.

1. Remember old Fuller's maxim: that natives of India are images of God's creation, though they are carved in ebony instead of ivory.

2. Make yourself a perfect master of the language and idioms of your district, and with the manners and customs. To effect which—

3. Mix much with people of all classes; to bring about which—

4. Be civil, courteous, and easy of access; still preserving your respectability by preventing any undue assumption of personal familiarity when in office.

5. Official reproofs are the lot of all men, even when they think they least deserve it. Receive such, however, with good temper, and occasionally hesitate to think yourself in the right, when your reprover may have so much more experience than yourself. If the occasion be one where you and your superior may differ legitimately, acquiesce, for he has the right to obedience. If you think yourself in the right, pocket the affront and do not remonstrate. In fifty cases out of fifty-one, remonstrance is useless, as the Government almost always on principle uphold a superior against an inferior, unless the case be *clearer* than the sun at noon-day. Remonstrance seldom does any good, and procures the applicant the character of a troublesome fellow, and is a rod in pickle to be used when occasion offers. As for contumely or disobedience on the part of an inferior to a

superior, it is held as rank as high-treason and is severely handled.

6. In giving an order or decision, weigh it well beforehand and do not decide hastily, so that there need be no necessity for altering or revising it. The man who upsets his own order without new and sufficient grounds, stultifies himself, and givés all around him small ideas of his wisdom, and also—double trouble.

7. In dealing with people of India remember that though you are a servant of the Government, whose authority is paramount, you are the people's protector as well as the officer of the Company.

8. When respectable natives come to pay visits, do not converse with them on matters connected with your cases decided or to be tried. They will give you, however, on interrogation, good information as to the state of your district and of the conduct of your inferior officers.

9. Use contumelious expressions to no man—much less strike any one.

10. Remember the Queen of England's sayings and doings are not more a matter of talk and observation in the palace and out of it, than are the acts of an European officer in his district in India. Every act or saying is marked, reported and commented on, from the rising of the sun to the going down thereof. A man might almost as soon (with reverence be it spoken) hide any part of his conduct from his creator, as his household servants. No people are better judges of their rulers than the people of India, and they always estimate them at their true value, whether evil for evil, or good for good.

Having concluded the replies to the several queries addressed to me, allow me to add a few words. I most earnestly advise every civilian going to India to take with him, and to peruse attentively, Mr. Shore's Notes on Indian

Affairs, for I know no book which can for one moment be compared to it as regards information on the real state of India. Until this book appeared, the world may be said to have read of nothing but the external appearance of things; here they have the subject dissected to the back bone. There is much in the book which will astonish the youthful reader; he will be perhaps amazed to hear that what he has been taught to believe as gospel, that the British system is all perfection—is a perfection of fallacy only. He will be surprised to find that the English are detested as rulers, and that were the opportunity to offer, the people of Upper India would rise against us to a man—the Indian army excepted. These, and many other things, will cause no little wonderment; but the reader may rely on the truth of every line of this book, which treats of facts, and of the accuracy of the deductions, provided a slight, and a very slight allowance be made for the zeal of a mind full of the subject, and ardently glowing with the hope of remedying the evil so forcibly depicted. The most important effect which this book is likely to produce on a young man going to India, is the establishment of some sympathy between him and those over whom his future career must exercise, for good or for evil, such influence. It will teach him (facts I fear too lightly impressed on the minds of many) that the various descriptions of people of India have virtues to be cherished, as well as vices to be repressed; and that had they no other title to our admiration, we cannot but wonder at the exemplary patience which they have manifested under evils, as great almost as it ever fell to the lot of men to endure. I neither had the pleasure of knowing the individual who has thus established an honourable name for himself for ever by the fearless manner in which he has stood forth to hold up to the public the evils sustained in India, nor do I know the Publisher of the book, and I can therefore have no interest in penning these lines:

but I do so, for the purpose of paying a just tribute to Mr. Shore's accuracy, which a long and not inactive career in India enables me to corroborate, and with an earnest and sincere hope, nay a prayer even, that the people of India may derive a lasting benefit from the influence which this book may obtain over the minds of the rising generation of rulers.

CHAPTER VII.

CADETS.

In order to give weight and value to the advice now offered to young military men, the best authorities have been consulted; and the contents of this chapter being the result of instructions kindly communicated by several officers of long experience in the Indian army, may be received as well worthy of attention.

To a cadet, his uniform must be an object of the first importance, and therefore claims precedence. It is advisable to take out the greater portion of the materials, but not to have them made up before he leaves England, since they may be useless on arrival, not only in consequence of the prospect of outgrowing his clothes during his passage, in which an indolent, easy life, together with good living, may effect a material increase in size, but because the regimental coat may not be made agreeably to the regulations, and as it is impossible for the young officer to guess even at the particular corps to which he may be finally appointed, they will of necessity have, however correct in other respects, to undergo certain alterations relative to the facings, and individual regimental badges of distinction. The clothes in which the cadet embarks, if well and fashionably made, will be quite sufficient guides to the tailors of India, who are very good workmen and expert imitators, and young men are strongly recommended to employ a respectable *native*

Maitree tailor to make up their jackets, &c., instead of going to the European artistes, who are notoriously exorbitant in their charges, and who can only procure the same class of operatives employed by the Maitree Durzee, and therefore cannot by any possibility render their manufacture superior, in proportion to the excess of their bills. As a general rule, young and inexperienced persons going to India, should be instructed never to purchase anything of a European dealer which he can procure from a native, the actual maker of the article being in all cases the same, that is, (if constructed in India,) natives; and the difference consisting only in the price.

The officer, Colonel Smythe, to whom I am indebted for the foregoing recommendation concerning tailors, belongs himself to the Madras army, but the greater number of my authorities from Bengal are equally conclusive. The cadet being strictly enjoined to employ a native tailor, a saving of seventy-five per cent. will be thus effected, while the article will turn out of equal excellence. European tailors at the Indian Presidencies of course flourish greatly concerning their fashion, experience, &c., but it is seldom that they have emigrated from the best houses in London, or that their assumptions are in the slightest degree borne out by their proficiency.

A relative returning from Bengal, though equipped in the best suit that Calcutta could afford, sent, as a matter of course, to a first-rate artiste to take his measure for new clothes, and I can never forget the glance of mingled pity and contempt which he cast upon the garment before him. My kinsman observed, "the person who made this coat *said* that he came from London." "Very likely," replied the Grosvenor-street tailor, "I do not doubt it, there are plenty of bunglers in this metropolis." Without going the length of a Brummell or a D'Orsay, it must be admitted that in London the perfection of the craft is confined to a comparatively small number of workshops, and when these are not attainable, there is quite as good a chance of finding a clever artiste among native Indians as amid their European rivals. I am instructed by my above mentioned correspondent to state, "that young men belonging to the Madras cavalry should carry out French grey cloth for two jackets, reckoning for the ordinary size, one yard to each; sky-blue ditto for two pair of trowsers, and blue cloth for a morning frock coat. Those for the infantry, scarlet cloth for a cloak, and two shell jackets, the facing cloth of either may be procured in India. The cavalry should take silver braid and twist for a dress jacket; buttons had better be purchased in India. The infantry, a quantity of lace, and a pair of *subaltern's* epaulettes for the dress coat; a regulation sword, according to the army to which the party may belong; a hunting saddle* and bridle for both. The cavalry cadets, in addition, a military saddle and bridle, according to the pattern now in use in Madras, which differs *in toto* from those employed in the Queen's Regiments. Hawkes, in Piccadilly, will supply the cadet with a proper Madras cavalry helmet; he may take his girdles from Lambert and Brown, of Regent-street, who have them all right; but not his dress belts, *sabretache* and *cartouche box*, for they vary much in different regiments, and therefore those purchased in England might be wholly useless, while the allowance made for them by any dealer furnishing the correct article, would be so trifling that it is much better to reserve the selection until it can be done with a certainty of being correct. A cavalry cadet *should* by all means carry out a brace of pistols; an infantry officer *may* do so. They should be quite plain, bronzed barrels, carbine bore, with percussion locks, and with a spring to fix them in the waist-belt if required.

* Very good saddles are made at Cawnpore, at exceedingly reasonable prices, nevertheless as European saddles have the preference, the Bengal cadet may bring them out.

Thus much for absolutely necessary articles of equipment; the rest must be regulated according to the habits, tastes, and means of the party; where the latter are abundant, directions may be deemed superfluous; these hints being chiefly intended for persons who desire, or who are obliged to make small sums go as far as they can. On its arrival at Madras the ship will be visited by a serjeant from the officer in charge of gentlemen cadets, Lieutenant Alexander, 8th Cavalry, now holds that appointment. The serjeant will afford facilities for landing, and escort them to the building allotted by Government for their reception, services which will secure them from the impositions and annoyances of Black Town Dobashees, and harpies of a similar description, who are always on the look out to prey upon the unwary. From the Cadet Institution they may despatch their letters, if they have any, to residents at the Presidency, and their removal from the quarters with which they have been provided, will of course, depend upon the invitations they may receive. If their letters, and it is the fate of many, should not be productive of the expected hospitality, they will remain at the Institution until sent to join some corps. During their residence at this place they will be messed by the superintendent, who, on being consulted, will provide them with proper servants, and aid them with information and advice. The first named point is one of the highest importance, many young men losing more by the dishonesty of servants hastily engaged in the first instance, than by any thing else, the risk of getting improper characters about them, which is run by inexperienced persons, being very great indeed. Very speedily after a certain number of cadets are assembled, an order is issued for their departure from Madras, in order to do duty with some regiment stationed in the interior, until the arrival from home of the whole list of cadets of the season, which, by shewing their relative standing, occasions their being permanently posted to the particular regiments, to which they will ultimately belong, and which will in all probability form their home for life; and it is not until this posting takes place that they ought to attempt to make up their uniform, or procure their expensive equipments.

Up to this period a scarlet jacket, and a plain blue morning frock, which is the same throughout every corps both of infantry, and cavalry, will be quite sufficient. Having once joined their corps, they must trust to their own docility, observation, and aptitude for acquiring useful knowledge, for their future guidance. The adjutant will take them in hand, and soon render them learned in every point respecting dress and equipment, their proper appearance on parade, &c.; while on other occasions they will follow the example afforded by their companions, who from their longer residence in the country are better versed in its system of etiquette. The first thing that a young officer will require to purchase is a horse, and great care is necessary in this undertaking, for in India, as elsewhere, men, and gentlemen even, who would scorn a mean or shabby action, allow themselves great latitude in horse dealing. A cavalry cadet had better wait until he joins his regiment, before he attempts to supply himself with the two chargers he will be obliged to keep up at musters. He will be permitted, on application, to select them from the remount list of the season, and they will be paid for by fourteen stoppages from his monthly pay, of fifty rupees each, but as this stoppage will cut so deeply into his pay as to cause very serious inconvenience, his friends should arrange this; they, or at least one of them, should be paid for at once, and by thus enabling the young officer to join with undiminished resources, he may have it in his power to meet those expences which necessarily occur, such as mess and band entrance money, public rooms, racket court, library, or other subscriptions of the kind: "I look upon it," continues the high authority from which these instructions are derived, " as very important that every young officer should belong to such public institutions, and attend their social meetings; for I have generally found that the men by whom they are avoided, perhaps on the first instance from necessity, acquire low habits, become habitual smokers and drinkers, until ashamed of themselves they are ashamed to join any decent society, particularly when ladies are expected to be present. An infantry cadet had better content himself with a stout pony, a Pegue will be found the most desirable, it will cost him from 250 to 350 rupees, that is from twenty-five to thirty-five pounds; if he ask an experienced friend to aid him with advice, he will generally be sure of getting his money's worth. Cavalry cadets will not, in many instances, be content to remain altogether dismounted until they can get their remount chargers; they, with the advice of some judicious friend, would do well to purchase a smart Arab, above fourteen hands, which will probably prevent the necessity of their taking more than one remount horse; but, in general the cavalry lads keep one horse, in addition to their charger, for hunting, as they are never permitted, on any account, to hunt their first charger. The next article they will require is a tent; this can be procured, on application, from the arsenal, and may be paid for by monthly stoppages, divided in about six portions, the price being about 180 rupees. Young officers who are ordered to join corps at a distance, are generally marched off under an experienced commandant, who will explain the proper method of procedure, and who generally arranges for their mess-table *en route*. Each person will be expected to bring his own wine and beer, and also a camp kit, consisting of chairs, plates, knife and fork, spoons, silver fork, glasses, &c.; these are usually fitted up in a case, so that the chair boy carries the whole, and at the end of each day's march takes them to the mess tent, where breakfast is provided. Cadets who may be appointed to do duty with regiments at

Madras or Palaveram, are spared these arrangements until their final posting; and have time and opportunity to acquire personal experience in their new mode of life; and those who are directed to do duty at Vellore, or Arcot, which are only a night's run, generally post it in a palanquin, which can be hired by the trip; but in longer distances the usual method is by marching at the rate of about twelve miles a day."

In commencing a new paragraph from the instructions of my kind and able correspondent, Colonel Smythe, I wish to draw particular attention to the following valuable observations: "Generally speaking, a young infantry officer, on his arrival at Madras, will have to supply himself with a horse, say 300 rupees; a tent, 175; a camp cot, with canopy and curtains, 35 or 40; spoons and silver forks, two of each kind, large and small: these latter he may take out with him, knives and forks, large and small, of each two; plates, soup, dessert, and hot water; two tumblers; ditto wine glasses: I recommend one each to be of silver, breakages in camp occurring frequently; a chair, a camp stool, and a writing table. His Europe trunks he may exchange for teak wood camp trunks. I am supposing he carries out a hunting saddle and bridle, he will get a leather case for one set of his smaller traps, of plates, &c. to be carried with his chair as before directed. His horsekeeper will carry the tumbler and wine glass in a case, suspended over one shoulder, and over the other a choggal or skin containing water; and thus equipped, with his chair boy and chair on one side, and his horsekeeper on the other, the youth commences his first march. The carriage required to transport his baggage and tent will be hired and paid for out of his monthly pay, and therefore cannot be included in our scheme of necessary outfit and outlay, the officer commanding the party arranging all these things. I cannot too strongly impress upon the friends of young men, particularly those who can afford it, the advantage attending their despatching their ward or relative, to join the regiment to which he may be first appointed, free from debt, and with the means of paying for his equipments at once, so that he may not be embarrassed by stoppages from his pay, which of necessity oblige him to get into debt. There are shroffs in every bazaar who are willing to lend, but who charge enormous interest; these men, generally speaking, are not very pressing for payment, so long as the regiment continues at the station, but when the order is issued for its march, woe be to the unfortunate wight indebted to these cormorants, if he be without the means of satisfying their demands. Complaints, courts of inquiry, courts of requests, and similar annoyances, follow in rapid succession, if indeed nothing worse should ensue. A cornet receives, if on full batta, 350, if on half ditto, 280 rupees a month. I assume this in round numbers as being near the mark, for I do not know the exact amount. If he be without the means of supplying himself, he must purchase his horses from the company, paying by instalments; for his horses, 100 rupees a month are deducted during the period of fourteen months, for his tent 30 during six months, therefore 350 or 280, with these drawbacks, leaves 220 or 150 only for the first six months; his mess, and band entrance, occasion another stoppage during the same period, at least 25 rupees more. Of the remainder the butler usually gets 30, in some corps the amount is higher, in very few below this rate: his mess fund monthly subscriptions for keeping up the mess articles adds something more, but I cannot state the sum exactly, it is now I believe, usually rated at a small per centage on allowances: his other mess expenses of wine, beer, friends, public nights, and especial occasions, cannot be estimated under 50 rupees; his subscriptions to places of public resort and amusement will be 25 more; his moonshee will cost him 15 at least, even if he joins with another in this necessary expenditure. Then he has the keep of three horses, a horsekeeper to each, at 6 rupees a month, a grass cutter ditto at 5, and shoeing the horses, which usually comes to 7 more. He has also all his own servants to pay, a dressing boy 5, a matee 9, (he is a sort of head servant at this wage,) a chair boy at 5, a lasseen 7, in the field, or at distant cantonments they all get more. Three or four other lower unclean drudges, amounting to 6 or 7 at the least, an amount to which young men seldom confine themselves. If they are sportsmen they must have dogs, which require separate attendants at an additional expence. In this calculation I have made no mention of the debt he must necessarily incur in supplying himself (without private resources,) with his expensive equipments, and which he intends and is expected to pay for out of the balance left from his pay, after the more immediate stoppages detailed above, have been made: besides having to supply and keep up his wardrobe, and provide for the wear and tear of his equipments, and the not unfrequent occurrences of the death of a charger, which must be replaced out of his own resources. With all these necessary outlays, can we wonder that young Indian officers get almost invariably deeply in debt, and that this misfortune is more especially the fate of the apparently better paid cavalry officer. But while I would strenuously advise the friends of young men, particularly, as I have before said, those who can afford it, to start them up to the regiments to which they are first appointed, free of incumbrances, I would as strongly advise them not to place any large sums of money *at their own disposal, not even for that purpose.* Give them, say £50 on embarking, for incidental expences on the voyage, and credit for as much more upon landing in India. This should maintain them until they receive their first pay, after which, if it should not be broken in upon by instalments, this pay ought to keep them handsomely. To effect the object in view, an arrangement should be made with some house of agency to honor such bills for equipments, horses, mess, &c., as may be *requisite on joining*, provided they are countersigned, in token of their being actually and *bona fide* for this purpose, by the commanding officer. I should say that for the cavalry, £350 would be certainly required to meet their demands; for the infantry, £120 might suffice, taking the difference of the price of cattle into account, which are essential to the former, and the comparatively less expensive equipments which are necessary in the latter service."

When paying their respects to the Adjutant-General, to whom cadets are expected to make their bow, they are sometimes asked whether there is any particular regiment to which they would like to be posted. A good authority in such matters recommends the youth to leave the selection entirely to this functionary, but this of course must depend upon circumstances. The cadet must on no account neglect to report himself at the office of the Town Major immediately upon landing, there being a positive order to this effect. There is in Bengal of course, a superintendent of cadets as well as at the other Presidencies, whose office is close to that of the Town Major, and where arrangements will be at once made for his reception should the cadet land at the customary place, Chandpaul Ghent, he will find himself more than a mile distant from the fort, and should therefore engage one of the numerous palanquins in constant attendance, and not upon any account attempt to walk to the place of destination. Neglect of this precaution may be attended by fatal consequences; these are too often risked by thoughtless young men, who upon first touching the shore commence a series of imprudences, which may end in violent illness, or death. Should the cadet have no invitations to private houses, he will take up his quarters in Fort William, one side of the principal quadrangle being set apart for the accommodation of assistant surgeons, and cadets. It is called from its position the South Barracks, and as a matter of course is much less comfortable and convenient than the quarters allotted to more permanent residents, or officers of a higher grade. The range consists of two stories, the ground floor being employed as warehouses under the name of Godowns. A broad staircase communicates with either end of the building, and upon reaching the landing place, a passage about twenty feet wide with Venetian doors right and left, and regularly numbered, leads to the different apartments, each consisting of a single room. Should there be a greater number of cadets than vacant apartments, they are what is termed in military phraseology, " doubled up," but assistant surgeons have always a room to themselves, and should they happen to be married, on application, they are usually permitted to occupy quarters in the royal, or rampart forrests. The business of the superintendent is to see that the young officer is duly provided with every requisite, and prevented from falling into the hands of the sircars or " land sharks, as they have been aptly termed by a great oriental authority. These men are always on the look out, and by the plausibility of their address, and their great obsequiousness, insinuate themselves into the confidence of unsuspecting youth. They manifest the utmost readiness to supply the cadet with goods of every description, but the bill is never forthcoming until he is about to take his departure, when the sum total seldom fails to create astonishment and alarm.

A jacket of scarlet cloth or camblet is the first thing which a cadet will require, since he is expected to appear in his uniform at the mess table, and here too the contents of the canteen will be put into requisition. Until the close of the year 1827, a complete mess service was kept up for the use of cadets, but since this period each member has been directed to bring his own plates, knives, forks, glasses, &c. with him, this being what is called camp fashion, a custom almost invariably adopted in the Upper Provinces. The period of residence in Fort William varies, partly depending upon the season of the year in which the cadets land, and partly on the number that have arrived, it is generally however from two to three months. The cadet is not required to keep up any establishment while residing in the garrison, being provided with breakfast at 8 A. M., tiffin, 2 P. M., and dinner at 7 P. M. at the mess. The breakfast consists, like most Indian repasts of the kind, of fish and rice, curries, and cold meat with tea and coffee. The tiffen is spread with fruit and the cold meat left from the previous night's dinner, and the dinner of good joints with the dishes most in season. The quantity of wine allowed to each member is limited, and confined to Madeira and sherry, beer is also placed upon the table, but the above mentioned comprise the whole of the liquors admitted at the board. Neither occupation nor amusements are provided for the cadets, who must carve out their own employments in the best way they can. The days therefore seem intolerably long to those who are not blessed with many personal resources. When the barracks are pretty full there is generally something going forward in the shape of mischief. The studiously disposed are frequently exposed to an annoyance of which in all probability they have had a foretaste on board ship. "Our ears," observes a correspondent in Fort William, "are continually assailed by the doleful sound of a flute, the luckless performer ensconced in his solitary apartment, giving vent to his anguish by playing out of tune, and out of time. Just as we have reconciled ourselves to this infliction, a more vigorous youth, ambitious of excellence on the violin, favours us with a grand crash, and perhaps in self-defence our next door neighbour will complete the discord by doing his best upon the key bugle. When our measure of affliction may be said to be full." It is usual for cadets to proceed to the military stations in the interior of

Bengal by water, and when the order for departure arrives, an experienced officer about to join his corps is placed in charge of the fleet, a medical officer being also appointed. It is the duty of the superintendent to provide the boats, and to take care that they are sea, or rather river-worthy. In order to meet the several demands consequent upon their entrance into the service, Government has for several years past allowed the cadet to draw the sum of 200 rupees in excess of his pay, to be refunded by instalments after he has been six months doing duty with his corps; a regulation which by prudent management may be made very advantageous. By a recent order of Lord W. Bentinck, the infantry cadet is only permitted to draw boat allowance to Benares, and the cavalry cadet to Cawnpore. Should a young officer wish to do duty with a corps cantoned beyond these stations, he must proceed thither at his own expence. The conduct of the cadets while upon the river of course materially depends upon the influence which the commanding officer possesses over them, and the discipline which he keeps up. It is a charge of great responsibility, and is sometimes attended by very unpleasant circumstances, chiefly resulting from wanton aggressions upon the natives. The fatal results which in many instances ensue, occur sufficiently often to render it necessary to warn the cadet against the rashness with which some are apt to point their guns against the defenceless creatures who may chance to offend them. A slight wound, a trifling blow, will in many cases produce death amongst the ill-fed and ill-lodged classes of India, who are subdued by privations to a degree of feebleness which is not suspected until they die from some apparently inadequate cause. Accidents, if they may be so called, of this kind are occasionally hushed up, the demand for justice from the surviving relatives, being satisfied by a few rupees; but they are liable to be brought before a public tribunal. Even if escaping this penalty, the individual who has, however, unpremeditatedly taken the life of a fellow-creature, must, if he possess any feeling, always be haunted by a painful remembrance. Without the slightest desire to make any sweeping imputation against the conduct of the Company's servants on their first arrival in India, it must be said that instances of cruelty and oppression towards the lower orders of natives are too numerous. Much of what is reprehensible arises from thoughtlessness, while ignorance of the manners, habits, and customs of the people, lead also to many indiscretions. The period passed at the Presidency will be well spent in gathering knowledge concerning the duties which a young man will have to perform in his new career, and the dangers he must avoid: and he should lose no opportunity of gaining instruction upon these subjects, either from books, or conversation with intelligent persons. The advice of a judicious friend, some old and experienced officer, who will give a youth the benefits of the information which he has himself acquired during his own residence in the country, forms one of the greatest advantages which a cadet can possibly enjoy upon landing. Letters of recommendation, generally speaking, are of very little use when addressed to the residents of Calcutta, who receive so many, that they do not think themselves bound to take notice of more than one out of twenty, while the most beneficial result which can now be expected from these epistles, is an invitation to dinner. However agreeable the society of families settled in Calcutta may be, the cadet will gain little or no information which may prove useful for his own particular guidance at the table of these residents. With the exception of officials of high rank, who are usually content to leave young men to find their own path through life, the Calcutta palaces are not tenanted by military men. Others know little of the service, and care still less, but there are always numerous officers to be found either on duty or upon leave of absence at the seat of Government, to whom the cadet will require no introduction from home, and whose character, (for in India every person's character is known,) will be a sufficient guarantee for the excellence and importance of the instruction he may afford. To such a person the cadet should apply when desirous to engage the servants which he will require to attend him in his progress up the country. It is scarcely possible to repeat too often the caution which should be observed in this particular. In Calcutta, there are multitudes of servants anxious and eager to engage, and though the sircar attached to the establishment of the superintendent of cadets, may probably take care that no person of notoriously bad character shall be admitted to the service of the officers placed under his charge, this functionary will scarcely have the best description of domestics at his disposal, while he himself cannot always be trusted. The Bengal sircars, as it has been before stated, are proverbial for their knavery, and however carefully selected, the one who has secured the appointment in the superintendent's office, would be *a rara avis* indeed if he did not pocket large sums in addition to his pay and allowances, from the proceeds of unwarranted taxes levied on the cadets.

This man probably receives a heavy per centage upon the pay of the person he recommends, who if he be honest may do well enough for a temporary attendant, and therefore it is advisable for the cadet to take what are called ticca servants, while in Calcutta, that is, men who will engage by the day. In going up the country, and comparatively few young men are stationed at or near the Presidency, natives belonging to the Upper Provinces, who are a finer and better class of men, are much more desirable than Bengallies, and there are always a sufficient number, who have attended gentlemen going home, in Calcutta, to supply the wants of new arrivals. An officer who has retained his own servants during a series of years, and this is the test of respectability both of master and man, can procure any number of people of the best character whenever he may require them for himself or his friend. He has only to employ his khansamah, or his sirdar bearer, as the case may be, who will collect the whole suite immediately. In order however to induce these men to remain, or even to engage with him, the cadet must be cautious in his own conduct. If he have by his violence or ill-temper acquired a bad character in the fort, he must be content to be served by rogues and vagabonds, who not being admissible into any respectable establishment, will submit to maltreatment for the sake of a living, and indemnify themselves by neglecting his interests if they do not plunder their master. In proceeding by water from Calcutta to join a regiment, very few servants are necessary, a khidmutghar, a bearer, a sweeper, and a dhobee, or washerman will suffice, if going up in a fleet under the charge of an officer, who will establish a mess. In a steamer still fewer will be required, and if proceeding in a budgerow alone, a massalchee need only be added, for the khidmutghar will undertake the cooking department.

In river travelling a horse proves an embarrassing companion, it may be despatched by land under the care of the syce, or groom, but in most cases it is advisable to delay the purchase until arriving at the first place of destination.

In the list of articles supplied by an experienced officer belonging to the Bengal army, appended to the present work, the prices of uniform coats and jackets for the infantry purchased in Calcutta, are given. Authorities differ, and this Bengal correspondent seems to approve of their being obtained from an European tailor; it will however be optional for the cadet to take out the cloth, and get his regimentals made up by some worthy, domiciled in the old China bazaar, Surroop Chunder Bhur, 315, should he be alive, being especially recommended. The cadet on embarkation should by no means cast aside the refuse of his wardrobe, provided there is a chance that the articles may continue to fit him; he will find them useful should there be any such thing as theatrical amusements on board. Officers in the Indian army are always expected to appear in uniform, whether they are with their regiments, or absent upon leave in any part of the Presidency; plain clothes, therefore, can only be worn upon particular occasions, such as at a race course, upon the stage, or other permitted places; but a young man wishing to enter into the fun of the thing, will find it an advantage to be able to supply his masquerade suits from his own stores. If he belong to the sporting world, a scarlet coat, well lined jockey cap, and other essentials will prove useful, also fancy waistcoats, such as are affected by the grooms, Sam Wellers, and other queer characters at home. A driving coat with many capes, a knowing hat, a dreadnought, or any other unshapeable garment which gives to a gentleman the appearance of a white or a brown bear, will come into employment, while too much cannot be said in favour of a Macintosh of the most uncouth description imaginable. The first youth who could make his *debut* upon an Indian race course in such a costume must have been a very enviable personage. It is impossible to over-rate the merits of top-boots and leather gaiters, and the youth should study the appearance of smart English farmers at a fair at home, for the style of their coloured handkerchiefs, high-lows, &c. No mention has yet been made of a gun, that much prized acquisition of masculine youth; there are always plenty of excellent quality to be purchased in Calcutta, but as, notwithstanding the most prudential resolves, there will be many unexpected and imperative demands upon the purse of the new arrival, it would be just as well to take one out.

A young man quitting his friends and relatives at home

for a foreign country, and for an indefinite period, may expect to receive a few presents as keepsakes from those who can afford to lavish upon him some token of their kindness. We will suppose that he is possessed of a watch, and a writing desk of a strong description, mounted in brass, with a Bramah lock; a telescope which will be found very useful; a moderately sized dressing case, fitted up with razors manufactured by Weiss, Mechi, or some equally celebrated person, will be an acceptable gift; ditto a gun, and all patent appurtenances thereunto belonging, and a brace of pistols; a collection of whips and canes, or walking sticks, fancy articles of the latter being expensive, and not always procurable in remote places; a case of perfumery, and a small assortment of pins, needles, black sewing silk, thread, buttons, and shoe ribbons. These latter should all be packed in a small case, and so arranged as to be ready for the most inexpert and unaccustomed hands. Books will also prove very desirable presents, both as an amusement on board ship and as valuable guides and references for the information and instruction of the young soldier. In a succeeding chapter, a catalogue will be given of the works which will be found most useful in the library of a cadet; at present it need only be remarked, that none of an unobjectional tendency will come amiss, for though it may not be advisable to increase the baggage to any great extent, the quantity taken on board ship is immaterial, and should the books be lost, destroyed, or given away before landing in India, their perusal will have, in all probability been very advantageous both to the owner and many of his companions. Should the youth be fond of fishing, the proper tackle, &c., may be added to the items of friendly gifts. Dogs of a pure and valuable breed are always desirable in India, and few captains of vessels will object to receive them, they will add a little to the expence of the voyage, but prove agreeable companions. Terriers are the strongest description, and the least troublesome on board ship, while they will be found very useful in every part of the Peninsula. Bird fanciers should take out canaries, which are hardy and much prized in India, while English cages are in particular request.

CHAPTER VIII.

CADETS.

AMID the popular delusions regarding India, which time and more extensive information relative to the country have scarcely yet dissipated, few were more prevalent than the idea that a young military officer on landing, stepped at once into large pay and allowances, and might perchance have a considerable sum of money at his disposal, by way of arrears. The relatives of the supposed fortunate youth, were apt to indulge in expectations of rich presents by the earliest opportunity, and never for a moment contemplated the possibility of exposure to hardships and privations, and the suffering produced by the oppressive weight of a heavy debt incurred for absolute necessaries.* It has been shewn that this latter circumstance must be the inevitable result, when the cadet is left to his own resources; and if it should continue to perplex and distress him through life, must depend entirely upon the chances of procuring a staff appointment, and the exertions which he makes to qualify himself for the purpose. An officer is not eligible for the general staff until after he has served four years with his

* In the Appendix will be found the report of a special committee formed to ascertain the average of monthly expence of 1st and 2nd Lieutenants of Artillery, which will shew how difficult it is for subaltern officers to keep clear from debt.

regiment; but there are the adjutancy, and the interpretership of the corps which may be obtained at an earlier period, either of which will place a subaltern in comfortable circumstances. At the risk of appearing impertinent by the repetition of musty truisms, the advantage, indeed the necessity of considering the importance of the opening years of a young man's career must still be strongly urged. The unprofitable waste of this precious period of existence is but too frequently irremediable, and the whole future welfare in many cases is sacrificed in consequence of errors and indiscretions committed at the outset of life in India. The first thing to which a cadet should apply himself is the study of the language in common use. He must engage a moonshee for this purpose, since without a competent knowledge of Hindostanee he can never hope to succeed in any public department, or to emerge from a state of Griffinhood, as it is called; for however quick and clever he may be in other respects, he will never understand the true state of the country, or be qualified to take a leading part in the administration of its affairs. An acquaintance with the character, disposition, habits, and peculiar turn of mind of the natives is exceedingly essential, not only with regard to the conduct which it is expedient to pursue towards them, but in order to ensure their respect. It has been too much the custom for Europeans resident in India to despise native opinions, and to treat every class of persons with whom they may come into contact, with rude indifference, or with studied contumely. In many instances the contempt, imbibed without just cause, and cherished in consequence of ignorance, has degenerated into hatred, and without having any justifiable excuse for their enmity, a considerable portion of Anglo-Indians entertain the strongest aversion to the people whom they have alienated by their haughty and imperious manners. A black fellow, the invidious epithet with which they designate every native, however high in the scale of intellectuality, is, according to their opinion, scarcely superior to the brute creation, and may be treated accordingly, an idea which must always be unjust and absurd, and is now more than ever impolitic. There cannot be a better proof of the shrewdness and capacity for forming an accurate judgment of the character and conduct of the stranger resident amongst them, exhibited by the natives, than the fact that every European is estimated according to his deserts. They are ever ready to do justice to the virtues of the good and amiable portion of the community, while they are equally clear-sighted to the faults and vices of the weak and the wicked. In India, popularity is not an unstable and a fleeting thing, dependent upon the fickleness and caprice of the multitude; it must in the first place be gained by desert, and when once obtained, is never endangered excepting by the personal misconduct of the party: while, on the other hand, there is scarcely any such thing as getting over a bad name when it has been fully established. It is quite as important to the ensign as to the colonel, that he shall have the good will of the natives, for in nine cases out of ten the character first attained will cling to him through life, and in looking over the great names connected with India, few, if any, will be found amid men who have not secured the attachment of the natives, and who have not on every occasion been willing to afford their testimony in favour of the native character. In fact, in order to rise to eminence in the country, the confidence and esteem of the people must be obtained; while in private life there can be no sort of comfort without it. Ignorance of the language leads to so many sources of irritability, that it is scarcely possible for the best tempered person to avoid being ruffled, when he finds commands that have been misunderstood, disobeyed; and instructions inaccurately conveyed, producing nothing but confusion and disorder. Seldom it is that the annoyed parties are sufficiently just to admit that they themselves have occasioned the inconveniences of which they complain; they get angry, visiting their own mistakes upon the shoulders of their dependents, finding it more easy to beat their domestics than to conquer the difficulties of their form of speech. The British Government has endeavoured by every means in its power to protect the natives from this kind of aggression; and military men are liable to very severe punishment if the offence can be proved against them; nevertheless the practice exists to a very considerable extent, and the feelings of the humane portion of the community are frequently outraged, by witnessing the maltreatment which the servants of their friends and associates are compelled to endure. The tone and temper of many of the Indian periodicals shew that a strong prejudice exists against the native community; from these manifestations of popular opinion, it appears but too evident that a very large proportion of Anglo-Indians entertain an idea that a native will never undertake any service unless stimulated either by self-interest or by fear, a pecuniary reward or corporal punishment. These persons have probably found it so, because in the first instance, acting upon this supposition, they have never been able to engage the services of high-minded and respectable men, whom they could attach by kindness, and upon whose gratitude they might depend with the fullest reliance.

It is of all things essential that a young man should enter India with a desire to think well of the natives, he will necessarily be thrown a great deal amongst them, and must be in a great measure dependent upon them for his comforts and enjoyments. Let him proceed cautiously at first, not placing a blind confidence in the people whom he may have about him, but studying them closely, and showing by his willingness to do justice to all, that he will neither impose upon others nor be imposed upon himself. How often is it that Anglo-Indians forfeit all the confidence of the natives by the shabbiness and the meanness of their conduct towards them, by engaging their services, and taking their products, and paying them inadequately, or not at all; allowing their people to commit any act of rapacity and injustice by which they themselves may profit, or, if not parties in the aggression, laughing at the distress it occasions, instead of immediately redressing the wrong. A traveller who follows upon the footsteps of a person of this description, will find the greatest difficulty in getting supplies, the peasants fly at his approach, hiding commodities which they would be glad to sell if they could hope to obtain a fair price for them. Parties upon shooting expeditions will be disappointed of their expected sport if they have been preceded by men who have neglected to fulfil their engagements with the natives. This neglect having obliged the contributors of the Bengal Sporting Magazine to insist strenuously upon the necessity of paying the market price for the hire of scouts and beaters, and the products of the bazaars. A man who in England should go into the country to shoot, and having quartered himself, his horses and dogs, upon the peasants, should evade the payment of their just demands, would be looked upon in the light of a swindler, and be liable to be treated accordingly. Sometimes the injury is inflicted unintentionally, in consequence of the party being unacquainted with the customs of the country, and the established rates, but this can only happen when ignorance of the language prevents a direct communication with the villagers. Those Europeans who are well versed in Hindostanee, and who have made themselves familiar with the habits, feelings, and prejudices of the people, will, unless utterly unprincipled, deal with them in a manner which will preclude all just grounds for complaint, while they, in return, will meet with the greatest respect and attention. No native whether high or low, gentle or simple, presumes to take liberties where he knows that the attempt will be discovered, but a thousand impositions are practised on the unwary, who becomes the dupe of the very persons whom he holds in the greatest contempt. Mussalman and Hindoo servants will often pretend that they are prevented from performing offices upon the score of their religion, when in reality they have no excuse of the kind, and would not dare to urge the objection were they not secure in the ignorance of their employers. Unknown to himself they load him with indignities, thus revenging their own wrongs by degrading him in the eyes of the community. In higher life it is the same; those who know how to treat native gentlemen and are well aware of what is expected on their part, and the degree of respect which they themselves ought to receive, will seldom or ever have any cause of complaint; but the ill-bred person who offends against all the laws of native etiquette, will on the contrary, be liable to meet with incivility, or at any rate unconsciously receive insults, which, though they may be incomprehensible to him, are well understood by the surrounding spectators. In England, rudeness and ungracious conduct pursued towards any class of persons would render the individual guilty of those indecorums liable to the imputation of being exceedingly ill-bred, but unfortunately in India, courtesy towards the native is not considered as a test of good manners, and persons offending in every material point are not the less regarded by their countrymen.

Were a haughty imperious demeanour and tyrannical oppression, and even fraudulent conduct towards the dark population, confined only to unprincipled and evil-minded persons, we should have to record comparatively few instances worthy of censure; but unfortunately there are but too many, who, while conducting themselves with strict propriety in every point connected with their European relations, are guilty of very reprehensible practices with regard to the natives. An apathetic indifference concerning the welfare of a class of people whom they have taught themselves to look upon as an inferior race of beings, utterly depraved, and wholly irreclaimable, is sometimes the cause of a contemptuous disregard, which frequently deepens into a stronger feeling; while in other cases, dislike to the country, and the mode of life pursued in it, extends itself to the native inhabitants, and the repining exile, who cannot reconcile himself to a sojourn in a foreign land, imbibes a strong aversion to every thing belonging to it.

A young man embarking in any profession, and more especially should he choose a military life, ought to devote his whole mind to the service which he has embraced. In order to make a good soldier, he must be satisfied with the prospect of passing the greater portion of his life in a distant country, and looking only to the highest rank in the army, should seek zealously and toil patiently to attain it. Those officers whose entire thoughts centre in home, and in the hope of retiring early from the Indian army, seldom prove valuable members of it, belonging generally to that class which comes under the denomination of the Company's hard bargains. A discontented and a murmuring spirit which teaches itself to look upon all duty as a hardship, which sinks under privation and disappointment, and which is more eagerly desirous of easily obtained emoluments, than for the high reputation resulting from good conduct and activity, is very unfitted for a profession subject to so many chances and vicissitudes, and in which the consciousness of desert is so frequently the sole reward. It is very difficult for persons whose lot is cast in India to preserve the happy medium, to cherish love for home, and yet experience contentment abroad; but much may be done, in the first instance, by endeavouring to conquer prejudices, and by a steady contemplation of the course which it is most expedient to pursue. India should be looked upon as the scene of a protracted residence, and of the principal events of a busy and active life. Though many sources of wealth may be dried up, and there are now fewer prizes to be obtained in either service than of yore, still sufficient remains to stimulate those who are blessed with a laudable ambition; and every individual who enters the country should be guided by a determination to make the best of the lot to which his destiny has called him, recollecting, at the same time, that in every transaction of life, however trifling, he is bound to uphold the British character and the Christian religion, in the eyes of the native multitude around him.

It is impossible to write about Anglo-Indian society without falling into nearly the same anomalies, which present themselves when describing the state of native feeling. It may be said with the greatest justice, that a more high-minded, honourable and intellectual class of persons than the Civil and Military Servants of the India Company does not exist. A young man going out to India, in either capacity, has much less risk of being corrupted by evil example than in any other situation of life whatsoever; strictly speaking, there is little dissipation or profligacy to be found at the Presidencies, and in the upcountry-stations it is still more rare; should there be a black sheep in any regiment, he finds few to support him in his evil courses, and he generally gets into some scrape which obliges him to quit the service. Neither drinking nor gaming are common vices in India, and those who are engaged upon the turf have rendered racing a comparatively harmless amusement, since it has never led to the disgraceful practices common in England; in fact, a regular *leg* is a character perfectly unknown. It must further be admitted, that many bright examples of excellence are to be found in every European community throughout the country, men who apply their talents to the noblest purposes, and whose scientific attainments, and philosophical research, prove in the highest degree beneficial to themselves and to others. The general decorum of society, though it may be equalled, cannot be surpassed; the instances of female misconduct are very few, and, generally speaking, much less flagrant then at home; while no person can offend against established usages with impunity. Notwithstanding all this, there are still great defects which all who possess discernment must perceive, and those who wish well to India must deplore. We have made little or no attempt to render our virtues attractive in the eyes of others, or to render our religious creed respected. The task, however, of calling attention to the faults and errors of our countrymen abroad, is an invidious one; and as the subject has been ably handled by another pen, it will only be necessary to direct the attention of persons going out to our Eastern colonies to the Hon. Frederic Shore's work, entitled "Notes on Indian Affairs." The picture which he has drawn can scarcely be said to be too highly colored, while it presents so accurate a view of the country and the people, and is so just in its estimate of the latter, that every intelligent person should avail himself of the fruits of an experience not always easily attainable. It is quite certain that no philanthropic mind will rise from the perusal of this book without a determination to avoid the evils which are pointed out. Although provoking considerable hostility at the time in which it appeared in a series of letters, printed in one of the Calcutta newspapers, it has remained unanswered and unrefuted. The letters have been collected and printed in two volumes, in London, and no well-educated individual who sails for India should be without it.

The opening of the political department in the relations of Government with native powers to young military officers has been very advantageous to the service, and forms a strong inducement to the study of those works necessary to qualify a subaltern for such appointments. In the first instance, however, military men should study their own profession, and endeavour to become good soldiers. Many who enter the Indian army have not had the doubtful advantage, for such it is considered, of probationary residence at the college at Addiscombe, but go on board ship in perfect ignorance of the nature of the duties which they will be called upon to perform. In consequence of the establishment of Regimental Book Clubs which have been formed in nearly every corps throughout the service, a young man on being posted to a regiment will have ready access to every work of importance: many months, however, must elapse between the period of his getting a cadetship, and the time in which he can join his corps. This interval will be well employed in the perusal of works which it is essential that he should ultimately study, and the following list has been especially recommended by experienced military men, as part of the collection to be taken on board ship. Torrens' Drill Instructions, and Military Movements (last edition). Hough's Practice of Courts-Martial, and all other Military Courts of Inquest, Request, &c. A cavalry cadet should secure for himself the latest edition of cavalry exercise books, and a work of Jomini's upon military strategy will be found very useful to both services. These works, in fact, are essential to all military officers as books of reference, to which they must necessarily have occasion to resort when upon detachment, or in other circumstances, when the club collection is not at hand. The cadet should also possess himself of a good map of India, fitting into a case, the one of six sheets on cloth is the best which is extant at the present period, and he will do well to peruse the following works relative to India, at the earliest opportunity. Memoirs of the Moghul Emperor Timur, translated by Major Stewart. Memoirs of the Emperor Baber, written by himself, which has been translated into English. Memoirs of the Moghul Emperor Akber. Memoirs of the Emperor Jehanguire, translated by Major Price. History of the Mohammedan Power in India during the last century, translated by Colonel

Briggs; Stewart's History of Bengal to the Invasion of the British; Orme's History of British Military Transactions in India; Mill's History of India, the new edition of which, now preparing for publication, edited by Professor Horace Hayman Wilson, will be indispensable. If these works should be procurable on board ship, their perusal will certainly be advantageous to a young man who, on going out to India, should endeavour to obtain all the information in his power respecting the history and manners of the country which he is about to visit. He will, if previously acquainted with the subject, find many objects of interest which he would overlook unless he had obtained preliminary information concerning them. The Quanoôn-Islam, Manners and Customs of the Mussulmans of India, translated by Dr. Herklots, and Mrs. Meer Hassans able work on the same subject, will be found both useful and entertaining. Illustrations of the History and Practice of Thugs is a very curious work; the Journal of Bishop Heber should be in every body's hands; and feeling this, it would be only false delicacy which would occasion the omission of the Scenes and Characteristics of Hindostan, written for the purpose of affording accurate information concerning India, by the author of the present paper: I do not hesitate to recommend it to persons who wish to make themselves acquainted with the features of the country and the manners of its society. Shipp's Adventures is an entertaining, and also a very useful book, containing excellent advice resulting from the writer's own experience. There is a difference of opinion respecting the expedience of studying the Oriental languages previous to departure from England, some persons feeling assured that it can never be attended with any advantage. These authorities consider the best method of acquirement to consist, in sitting down seriously to work immediately after their arrival in India, under the superintendence of a Moonshee, and in all circumstances it is necessary to have recourse to a tutor of this description, as persons who have learned Hindostanee in England, know little or nothing about the proper pronunciation. To land in India, however, without being acquainted with a word of the language, is very distressing, and as the smallest quantity, which may be picked up during the voyage, can be turned into immediate use, it is certainly advisable to employ the numerous hours of leisure permitted on board ship to the attainment of this very necessary branch of knowledge. The books recommended for the purpose are the "Hindostanee Grammar;" "Hindostanee Dictionary, Hindostanee and English, and English and Hindostanee;" "Gilchrist's Hindostanee Dialogues;" "Ukhlaki Hindee;" "Bagh o Buhar," translated from the Persian; "Prem Sagur" and "Luta ifi Hindee." Persian is not so essential since the late regulations concerning it, but if studied, the following works should be taken. "Dictionary, Persian and English, English and Persian;" "Gladwin's Persian Moonshee;" "Gulistan of Shaikh Sadee;" "Anwari Sohyly."*

It is a very fortunate circumstance for young men when they find fellow passengers, in more experienced persons, well acquainted with the languages spoken in India, and ready to assist others in attaining some degree of proficiency in them. Hitherto there have been many Bengal officers shamefully ignorant of the native dialects, and a still greater number have only been able to converse in the commonest jargon. Nothing can be more reprehensible than the idleness which prevents a gentleman from expressing himself in suitable language to persons of any rank with whom he may be compelled to converse. No observations can be more just than those of Mr. Shore, when he assures us that "no native servant can ever believe a foreigner, whom he knows to have resided several years in the country, to be a gentleman, nor will he really respect him, unless he speak

* The whole of the books named in this chapter can be obtained of the Publishers of this work.

Hindostanee as one of their own native gentry would do." The opinion of the natives, and especially of native servants, unfortunately, has not yet been considered of sufficient importance to be worth attention. This has always been a great mistake, and in our present position in India, and with the prospects before us, unless rectified in time may become fatal. It is necessary to understand the jargon spoken by the lower classes, since without this knowledge it is scarcely possible to carry on the domestic concerns, or to comprehend the information given by villagers, witnesses at Courts-martial, &c.; but to adopt such phraseology must necessarily bring the party, thus identifying himself with the most ignorant portion of the community, into contempt. An accurate acquaintance with the language, and correctness in speaking it, are necessary to endear an officer to the sepoys. Every military man who takes any pride in his profession will desire to be an object of esteem and regard to the soldiers under his command, and there is no set of persons more easily conciliated, more faithful, and more strongly attached, than the sepoys of the Indian army. The officers of the Company's service have this advantage over those belonging to Queen's regiments, that familiarity with the privates of the corps does not occasion any inconvenience, or tend to destroy the respect entertained for them. The habits, manners, and customs of Europeans and natives differ so essentially, that an intercourse maintained by superiors on the one hand and inferiors on the other will not break down any one of the barriers which it is so essential to maintain. So far from the respect of the sepoys for their officers being diminished by those officers making themselves acquainted with the condition, prospects in life, feelings and hopes of the soldiery, the greater interest which they take in their concerns, the more strongly will the bonds of attachment be rivetted. A young man loses a vast fund of useful information by being unable to converse with the sepoys, and in the event of any disturbance, outbreak, or difficulty, when confidence is established between the two parties, half the obstacles and inconveniences which others less happily situated must encounter, will vanish. Nothing can be more laudable in a military man than to aim at popularity by every legitimate means; but though the instances upon record are rare, it may be necessary to say, that some young enthusiasts have become so enamoured of the amiable qualities which they have found in their dependents, as to become converts to their least justifiable prejudices, and to adopt several of their habits and religious opinions. Many officers abstain from eating pork on account of its being considered an impure and unclean food by the natives, and because its appearance at their tables might lessen the respect entertained for them by their inferiors; but others refuse to partake of the forbidden food in consequence of having imbibed the opinions of the followers of the prophet upon the subject. Again we find men who will neither kill nor eat beef, because they will not shock the Hindoos, who look upon the slaughter of the sacred animal as a crime, and who relinquish their own John Bull propensity from an unwillingness to give offence to any religious creed. Such conduct is in many instances both politic and praiseworthy, but to go farther is to shew too great a respect for idolatry, while a mistaken compliance with the superstitious notions of a people whose religious belief has assumed the lowest and most degraded forms, may lead to the worst consequences.

CHAPTER IX.

CADETS.

There are numerous persons who, if living in any part of Europe, would manage to find occupation for their time, who are in India utterly unable to discover a method of employing many hours of leisure, and therefore become a prey to ennui: military men have frequently a considerable quantity of spare time upon their hands, and should they accustom themselves to bestow it wholly upon the billiard room, they will suffer proportionately when that resource fails them, as it often must, since there are numerous stations in the country unprovided with such a refuge for the destitute. It is therefore of infinate importance to the youth who has obtained a cadetship, that he should cultivate and encourage some useful pursuit, and so great now is the spread of intelligence, and the facilities of acquiring knowledge are so many, that few need go out to India wholly dependent upon society for the means of beguiling time. Those who have a taste for drawing will find in it an inexhaustible source of amusement, and should lose no opportunity whatever in obtaining proficiency in sketching from nature. The study of architecture will likewise be found exceedingly useful, buildings being continually required in India; officers, in many places, having to construct their own bungalows, stables, or outhouses of various kinds. A competent knowledge of the art of surveying and making maps will frequently advance a young officer, who can make himself useful to Government when taking possession of new territory, and civil as well as military engineering may be studied with great advantage by officers not belonging to that particular branch of the service. Instances frequently occur when it is of consequence that some person should be found upon the spot adequate to the undertaking of works of importance, which otherwise must be postponed until the arrival of an officer of Engineers. The principles of road making should always be understood, together with the construction of temporary bridges, rafts, and, in fact, an acquaintance with mechanics of every kind may be turned to good account in India; where Europeans are continually thrown amongst expert workmen, who are perfectly ignorant of science, and who, though following with great precision the instructions which they receive, can originate nothing. Many officers in India superintend the building of their own carriages, turning out very handsome equipages in remote stations where a vehicle of the kind had never been seen before; others make up articles of furniture in the same way in their own houses, for labour being cheap, and the greater part of the materials required at hand, there is no difficulty whatsoever in procuring anything after a given pattern. The armourer of a native regiment made some excellent Italian irons from a model cut in paper, while a common carpenter constructed very beautiful bird cages, though he had never seen any thing of the kind before, from a pattern cut in pasteboard, and strung with cotton threads.

The advantage afforded by an acquaintance with horticultural science has been already mentioned, but it is of such great importance, that no apology need be made for recurring to it again. A piece of garden ground is usually attached to every European residence in India, and excepting in large stations, where experienced gardeners are attainable, its productiveness, particularly with respect to European vegetables, must in a very great measure depend upon the owner of the mansion. The Mallees, or gardeners, are in India, generally stationary, an appendage to the garden, and coming into the service of the new tenant, instead of following the fortunes of the late resident. These men, if left to themselves, will fill the ground with tobacco plants and other things convertible to their own use, either for family consumption, or for sale. It will be necessary to supply them with the seeds for exotics of every kind, and slips of pot herbs, which may easily be conveyed from station to station, in mould. To an early riser the care and culture of a garden affords delightful occupation, it will also give employment to the hour which marks the sun's decline, and, likewise, during many days in the rainy season, as well as the cold weather, the period in which it is most interesting, European vegetables being planted immediately after the rains have ceased. Some persons refuse to take any pains in the cultivation of their gardens upon the plea that they may often sow that which they cannot reap. By the regulations of the service, regiments are removed at the end of every three years, and numerous contingencies occur to shorten this period to many individuals of the corps, but to neglect any improvement in their gardens merely because they may be spending their time for the benefit of others, is a very selfish and a very shortsighted consideration, since they, in turn, may experience all the advantages of the labours of their predecessors, while, if their own principles were generally acted upon, they must depend solely upon themselves. A philanthropic mind will take pleasure in spreading useful knowledge amongst the natives, whom he is serving very essentially in introducing any new production or improved method of cultivation, and every individual belonging to the Anglo-Indian community, must, at some time or other, be indebted to those persons who have interested themselves in horticultural experiments, since, excepting in very remote places, European vegetables may now be purchased in the native bazaars. Indian gardeners have found their account in cultivating potatoes, peas, cauliflowers, lettuces, &c.; and in travelling particularly, it is of great importance to be able to procure such useful and agreeable additions to the table. A knowledge of agriculture will enable the owner of cattle to supply his animals with excellent fodder, there being several grasses neglected in India, which will grow in almost the worst situations, while waste ground, generally speaking, is abundant, and green food so scarce, that the grass cutters are frequently compelled to seek the roots of dried-up grass at the distance of several miles from the place of residence. There are many noble examples in India of the perseverance with which British gentlemen have devoted themselves to the improvement of native cultivation; amid numerous meritorious instances, the exertions of Major Sleeman, in the introduction of a superior sugar cane, will doubtless prove a stimulant to all who entertain a desire to render themselves useful to the community at large. Dr. Spry, of the Bengal army, has given a very interesting account of the methods pursued by Major Sleeman, in the furtherance of his philanthropic views, in his valuable work, entitled "Modern India,"* which those who wish to study the resources and capabilities of the country, will do well to peruse. To his, Dr. Spry's exertions, the station of Saugor in central India was indebted for the pine apple, which, previously to his attempts, could only be made to grow in particular situations, and his account of the method he employed, will shew the great public benefit to be derived from those who turn their acquaintance with science to useful purposes. "At Jubbulpore, which is about 136 miles distant from Saugor, pine-apple plants thrive in the greatest luxuriance, but they never could be made to grow in Saugor.

* Two Vols., Whittaker and Co.

All the plants which came over from the former place became in a few months sickly. As they had hitherto been planted in the ordinary garden soil, which is a rich black mould, it struck me that the introduction of a third part of silicious earth would have the effect of keeping the soil loose, by allowing the roots to shoot more easily through it: I desired the gardener, therefore, to make a mixture of one third garden earth, one third manure, and one third red sand-stone earth, and having mixed them well together, to transplant the three plants then in the garden to this new soil. The benefit was immediate. The plants which had only been existing during three preceding years, for vegetation is too strong an expression, soon began to recover from their sickly condition. The leaves, instead of being tipped with the marks of decay, became green throughout, and clearly indicated the restoration of the plant to vigorous vegetation. The plan was adopted about the same time by another gentleman, whose garden lay contiguous to mine, and whose plants were in a more forward state; and the following season, 1833, he had the gratification of cutting a large pine apple of most exquisite flavour, which was the first that had been produced at Saugor." Ill health obliged Dr. Spry to leave Saugor before he could enjoy the luxury which he had taken so much pains to procure; but it was a source of great satisfaction to him that he had put other persons in the way of bringing to perfection a delicious fruit which is rarely seen in the Upper Provinces of India. The transplantation and successful culture of the Lichi, a Chinese fruit which flourishes in great luxuriance in Bengal, would be highly beneficial in the Upper Provinces of India, where at present it is not known, while there are many native vegetables which would be improved into great delicacies, were persons to take pains in suiting the soil and method of rearing to their peculiar tendencies.

A love of natural history opens endless fields of pleasurable research to those who have encouraged a taste for it; but at the same time, it must be said, that the enthusiastic pursuit of any one of its branches may prove fatal to the party thus ardently engaged in it. India, unfortunately, can show a list of victims who have lost their lives from exposure to the climate in their unwearied desire to extend their acquaintance with the wild tribes of the jungle, and to enrich their collections of specimens. Geology cannot always be followed up without peril, since it too often leads men who are devoted to this interesting branch of science, to remain out under a burning sun much longer than is consistent with safety; pursued with moderation, and a due regard to health, however, it forms a delightful resource, every day revealing new and valuable products in a country, of which hitherto, comparatively speaking, little or nothing has been known. In a volume of the Asiatic Annual Register for 1808, there is a very useful paper entitled "Memoranda, by Dr. Walker, Professor of Natural History, Edinburgh, to a young gentleman going out to India," and the directions given are so applicable to the present time, that it is deemed advisable to republish the greater number for the benefit of those who may not be able to consult the work in which they originally appeared. "To be provided with a good Fahrenheit's thermometer, enclosed in a glass tube, that can be laid in water, for taking the heat of the sea in different latitudes, and especially for taking the heat of springs in India, whenever you may meet with them. To be careful to pick up at sea, all sea-weeds and marine animals that come within reach of the ship, and to dry and preserve them in paper or otherwise. To be attentive to all birds that are seen from the ship, to mark the English or other names, by which they are known among the sailors, and the latitudes when they first appear and disappear. To keep a regular journal from day to day, including the above, and all other observations in natural history that may occur, particularly any remarkable appearances in the weather, respecting the winds, rains, thunder and lightning, calms, tornadoes, whirlwinds, or waterspouts. To notice the alterations in the colour of the sea, and, if possible, the causes from whence they proceed; especially the colours proceeding from minute animals, with a description of these animals. On approaching the Cape of Good Hope, the Cape pigeons or Pinto birds are numerous: it would be worth while, if opportunity offers, to preserve one or two of them by stuffing their skins, and to mark what distance from the Cape they are first seen, and when they first disappear. The head, jaws, or teeth of the different species of sharks,* that may be caught upon the voyage, to be preserved. Also the different flying fishes. It is much to be wished that one of the small fishes which always accompany the blue shark, called the pilot fish, might be caught and preserved. Whereever the cable or sounding line is used, it should be carefully examined, when hove into the ship, as there are frequently found curious animals adhering to both. Between the Cape and Madagascar, and other parts of the India voyage, various sea animals can be easily taken on board, such as what the sailors call Portuguese men-of-war, and others, to be preserved, if possible, in paper or in spirits. If the ship touches either at Madagascar or the island of Johanne, there are many curious plants, fossils, and animals which may be preserved. At Bombay, many interesting articles may be obtained, which are there articles of commerce from Surat and the Gulf of Persia. Drugs, the different gums and resins, the largest pearl oysters, or mother-of-pearl and tortoise-shells, the sandalum album or white sandal wood

* In one species of shark there is usually found a small fish which burrows in the body of the larger animal, either sucking its blood or feeding on its substance, and which must prove an endless source of torment to the ferocious monster thus assailed. This creature might be easily preserved, and would form an interesting addition to the museum.

and ebony: the fine red Persian ochre, called at Bombay, Indian red. The skins of the zebra, Persian lambskins, jackall, leopard, panthers, and other Asiatic quadrupeds; also the horns, and if possible, the heads of the different antelopes and gazelles. At Bombay, Madras, and Calcutta, to collect specimens of every fossil, even of the most common that come within reach. To visit often the shops of the lapidaries, where all the finest lethidia, chalcedony, cornelia, onyx, sardonyx, agate, mocho, are cut in great quantities, and sold very cheap. To enquire at Madras concerning the cochineal discovered by Dr. Anderson, and to preserve and send home the species of grass on which it feeds. At Calcutta, to preserve good specimens with the flower of all the important plants of the country, and as much of their history as possible. To be attentive, especially to all the productions of China which may be brought there whether fossil, vegetable, or animal. To collect at Calcutta, shells, corals, corallines, sponges and other fine marine productions, which are brought there from all parts of India. To collect all the fine insects wherever they occur, some collections are to be purchased at an easy rate. I should particularly recommend preserving them in paper books, in preference to preserving them loose or upon pins. The fresh insects may be placed in folds of paper and pressed for a day or two, with a sufficient weight, when they will be dry and sufficiently prepared, even those which have been preserved on pins, when put for two minutes in spirits, may then be pressed and dried in the same manner. To pick up as often as you can find them, skins of all quadrupeds, especially those noted for any peculiar quality; being very careful to mark down as many particulars respecting their natural history as you can learn, and the uses that are made of them in the economy of arts. These skins, if dried and laid back to back with some ground pepper between them, and a few small grains of camphor, may be easily brought safe to Europe. To enquire particularly at Calcutta concerning the great quadrupeds called by the English a buffalo, but by the natives the Arnee. It does not come down lower upon the Ganges than about the plain of Plassey. It is said to be about fourteen hands high, and is a superb animal, whose history is yet unknown in Europe. As also every particular that can be learned respecting the Chittagong cows, (the Yak) whose tails are used as fly-flaps in India."

Since the period mentioned by Dr. Walker, 1808, the zoology of India has been much studied, and the history of many interesting animals previously little known, rendered familiar to every reader. There is still, however, a wide field for research. By the accounts offered by intelligent writers to that very useful and entertaining miscellany the "Bengal Sporting Magazine," we learn that there are very considerable variations found in the shape of the horns of the buffalo, in different districts, and therefore it is expedient that every person having the opportunity of visiting remote places, should note down the peculiarities falling under his observation. To sportsmen, the scientific world owe many useful discoveries; the existence of one or two varieties of wild dog, has been ascertained by these means. They were the first to prove the lion to be a denizen of Asia, and to the exertions of Capt. Smee, of the Bombay army, we are indebted for the settlement of a long disputed question regarding the maneless lion. The examination of the skin and skeleton of this animal killed by him in Guzerat, has established the claims of England to the nobler beast as a supporter to the arms, a gratifying circumstance not only to antiquaries, but to all who glory in the British lion, and who felt indignant at the attempt to degrade it into a leopard. There is a comparatively lately discovered animal in India, constituting a new type of the bovida, and an intermediate form between the bos and the bison. The construction, natural history, and habits of the Gauri Gau, or Gaour, have been stated at great length in the Journal of the Asiatic Society of Bengal; and previously to the publication of Mr. B. H. Hodgson's scientific paper, it had been mentioned by other writers; Dr. Spry in particular attracting the attention of the English reader, by an account which he has published in his work, "Modern India." The domestication of this superb creature is now a desideratum, and it is noticed here for the purpose of stimulating the youth who go out to the country where it is to be found, to exert themselves in the accomplishment of this object. Much may be done by those who are in the habit of petting animals, and of attending to the minute points so necessary to preserve them when removed from the parent during the early stages of existence.

Beautiful and interesting collections of birds may be made in India at a small cost of trouble or expense, their skins, as well as those of other animals may be kept unstuffed till after their arrival in England, with very little disadvantage to their capability of being set up in all their pristine beauty. It is advisable not to remove the skull bone, as that materially assists in preserving the shape of the head. The following receipt for a solution which has been found very effectual, is given for the purpose of enabling the traveller either at sea or on shore, to enrich his collection with whatever interesting animal may fall in his way. Take of common soap, or shavings, four drachms; gum Arabic in powder, two ditto; white oxide of arsenic in powder, six grains; boil these ingredients in four ounces of water, for about twenty minutes, taking care to stir it well during the time, and label the bottle which contains it, with the word "Poison." This solution is to be laid on sparingly on the inside of the skin with a brush or feather, two or three applications will in general suffice for the purpose. A deal box lined with lead foil, similar to that which guards the interior of a tea chest, is recommended as the best depository for a traveller's museum, and when the skins are perfectly dried, they may be placed between layers of cotton, well peppered, or impregnated with camphor. In all the bazaars of India a seed is sold which is very effectual in keeping off the attacks of insects, and will always be supplied by native servants for the purpose. The presence of a naturalist as a passenger on board ship is exceedingly desirable, since nothing can contribute more agreeably to the amusements and the employments of a voyage, than scientific researches directed towards objects of general interest. A taste is hereby diffused among persons who never troubled themselves before about natural philosophy, and those who may have found the study to be dry and unproductive, perceive its great utility, and find their enjoyments materially increased in looking at common objects with a view to ascertain their peculiar properties, the manner of their formation, and the uses to which they may be applied. Although it may be desirable to attain the very highest degree of science in every department undertaken by the student, slight observations upon anything new or striking which meets the eye of a traveller, are of importance in directing the attention of more experienced persons to the subject. The periodicals of India afford great facilities to those who desire to make the fruits of their researches known. Vast quantities of the most useful information are to be found in these valuable productions, as yet almost wholly supported by amateur contributors, who neither writing for money, nor ambitious of shining by their style, communicate the results of their experience in an easy unaffected manner, very much to the purpose. While colonial politics, parties, and factions, are, with the exception of very few interesting instances, looked upon in England as complete travesties of the grand game of life, the mighty warfare which decides the destinies of the world; the great value of the services performed by those who employ their pens in the developement of the natural resources of the country, are universally acknowledged.

Sporting in India opens so many avenues for amusement, that although not unaccompanied by danger of various kinds, it is scarcely possible to withhold encouragement to a pursuit which is at once so exciting and so absorbing in its nature. Notwithstanding the deleterious description of the atmosphere to which the pursuers of the savage game of an Indian jungle are frequently exposed, the malaria, which sometimes renders the air so thick and so strongly impregnated with disagreeable odours, as to be scarcely respirable, the excitement often suffices to preserve the party thus situated from any injurious effect. Many persons of course break down, and retire from the field with the seeds of a fatal disease, or a constitution which never can recover the shock; but others escape, and it need hardly be said, that after undergoing so severe a process of acclimization, the worst dangers of the climate may be braved with impunity. Fishing is a far more perilous amusement than hunting, it must be carried on at seasons of the year when frequent changes of temperature occur, to which the exposure is very injurious. Long intervals may elapse without producing the pleasing agitation of the mind which renders the body insensible to external sensations, and it is almost impossible to avoid the contact of wet clothing, since it is necessary to wade through pools, and to stand perhaps knee deep in the water. The rod has not so many votaries in India as the rifle, still the angler pursues his sport in many of the streams; delighting more particularly in the capture of the Mahasseer, a splendid fish which is said to afford as much excitement as the capture of salmon in the rivers of Scotland or Ireland. As nothing in India can be so detrimental as idleness, and as an amusing pursuit is not always incompatible with the highest scientific attainments, those who have any talent for the stage will do well to cultivate it. There is no record in India to shew that the slightest disadvantage has ever resulted to those gentlemen who have taken up the sock or the buskin. In fact, some of the most distinguished names in the country might be adduced to prove that success upon the boards has not been prejudicial to the morals, or injurious to the prospects of the votaries of Thalia, or her more sombre sister. A clever actor is a personage of infinite importance all over India; and one Governor-General was said to have given an appointment in Calcutta, for the purpose of retaining the Keeley of the Chowringhee Theatre, at the Presidency. It was well bestowed in other respects, and no individual has had reason to regret the motive should it in reality have been the one assigned. In the Upper Provinces it is sometimes found to be impossible to get up a play without the assistance of some neighbouring star, who travels perhaps seventy or a hundred miles without fee or reward, save that which is conferred by the applause bestowed upon him for the purpose of exhibiting for a single night. The female characters in India, being with the exception of Calcutta, where two or three actresses are engaged, personated by the most ladylike looking youths of the station, nearly all the objections urged against amateur acting are removed. It brings the parties engaging in it into female society, which is always desirable in India, for youths who feel, or fancy that they have few qualities to recommend them to the companionship of the ladies, are apt to indulge their shyness, until it degenerates into rusticity. They begin to be afraid of encountering the respectable portion of the sex, and gradually acquire pernicious habits, or enter into connexions which prove destructive to them through life. Some young men there are who never mix with European ladies at all, others may be seen in clusters in remote corners of ballrooms, anxious, but not daring, to approach them; these shy youths should always be encouraged, since in no part of the world can female influence be more beneficially exercised.

While advocating rational employment of every kind to the cadet, he should not in other pursuits forget those strictly belonging to his profession. The study of military jurisprudence is one especially to be recommended; a high degree of attainment will qualify the party for the office of judge advocate, while no individual liable to be called upon to sit upon a court-martial, should be ignorant of its leading principles, an ignorance which in many instances has led to the most flagrant acts of injustice.

CHAPTER X.

CADETS.

AMID the different kinds of duty which devolve upon military men, that of sitting upon courts-martial is one unfortunately of frequent occurrence. It is astonishing, considering the education given to youths who have the prospect of obtaining a commission in the army, how very few are properly qualified to fill the important office of member of a tribunal, which is strictly one of equity, and which ought to be of the purest and most honourable nature. Many young men are summoned to attend a court-martial, who have never given a single thought to the subject, have never made themselves acquainted with its forms, and have only vague notions concerning its object. This ignorance may be excusable in the junior members of the court, who will probably in acquiring experience take a stronger degree of interest in a subject most deeply interesting to their brother officers, and which at one period or other may seriously affect themselves. It is however not exclusively confined to the young, the idle, or the less highly gifted portion of the military community; many men not destitute of talents, and tolerably well informed upon other subjects, having grown grey in the service without advancing in a species of knowledge so intimately connected with the welfare of the army; while it is much more difficult to find an officer qualified for the appointment of deputy judge advocate, than for that of any other staff employment at the disposal of Government.

The study of military jurisprudence has been discouraged in consequence of a very erroneous supposition that it would tend to foster a litigious spirit, which, according to general opinion, has already been too strongly manifested in the army of the India Company. In all probability it is the want of the requisite knowledge which has led to the obstinacy and contention that have called forth some just reproofs upon the subject, and while so much injustice, always the accompaniment of ignorance, prevails, no set of men can be found tamely to submit to practices which are inimical to the service, and prejudicial to themselves. As it is at present constituted in India, there need be no hesitation in saying, that not the slightest reliance can be placed upon the conduct of a court-martial, its arriving at a true and just judgment, depending wholly upon accidental circumstances; the temper and disposition of the President, the talents and learning of the deputy judge advocate, and the number of persons present who happen to know what they are about. The proceedings it is true go to head quarters, and are subjected to the investigation of the judge advocate general, and the commander-in-chief, and when these authorities chance to be efficient, able, and unprejudiced men, the occasional severity of their remarks shews how greatly they have differed from the opinions on which the conclusions arrived at by a court-martial, have been founded. Unfortunately, however, there is no security that these high functionaries can, or will exercise a calm, dispassionate and wise judgment; that they will remedy injustice by the exercise of the prerogative vested in the hands of the supreme power, and visit flagrant instances of criminal indulgence towards favoured parties with severity of censure.

A court-martial ought always to be able to arrive at the truth, or at least to form a correct judgment upon the evidence placed before it, and to elicit that evidence according to the forms prescribed by law, neither suffering any illegal practice to vitiate its proceedings, nor endeavouring to suppress the truth. When exercising a judgment founded upon just notions of right and wrong, and supported by sound knowledge of the law of the case, the members of a court-martial thus guided, and pursuing a straightforward course, may defy the efforts of the president, deputy judge advocate, judge advocate general, and commander-in-chief, even should the whole be arrayed against them. They may be commanded to revise their proceedings, but if strong in the assurance of their integrity, and the authority upon which they have acted, they will come to the same conclusion, and if that conclusion be upon the side of mercy, it must be respected.* If courts-martial were always conducted according to the principles upon which they are supposed to be constituted, they would be much fewer in number. In India one appears to grow out of another in a most marvellous manner, until they threaten to have no end; and the evil becomes so intolerable that it redresses itself.

In no part of the world is it necessary to exercise a more rigid adherence to the rules and regulations laid down upon the subject of military law, than in the Company's territories, where the case which is to be brought before a court-martial, becomes the topic of conversation in every circle; and opinions are given respecting its merits without the slightest hesitation. The court is one of honour, and in regarding it in so noble a light, the errors and evil feelings

* The Crown, and the Court of Directors have the privilege of summarily displacing an officer belonging to their respective armies, with, or without a court-martial, but it is exercised only upon rare occasions, and under very peculiar circumstances: and in all instances the commander-in-chief can remit a sentence which he considers to be too severe, or suspend an officer, that is, prevent him from doing duty, without prejudice to rank or pay, until the pleasure of the authorities at home can be known.

to which human nature is prone, are put out of the question. To evince the slightest doubt concerning the honour of an officer, who may be summoned as a member of this most virtuous tribunal, would not only be to make him an enemy, but to draw down the indignation of the whole body; while to challenge a man who has perhaps openly expressed the strongest sentiments upon the subject in dispute, would create a hostile spirit throughout the army. Shielded therefore by a reputation which no one can be daring enough to attack, the members of a court-martial shew the utmost degree of affection and favour towards the accuser, or the accused, as the case may be, with perfect impunity. Corrupt motives probably in the strictest sense of the word may not be applicable to them, but the consequences are the same; and are not only very frequently highly detrimental to the prospects of those who are victims of party spirit, but exceedingly injurious to the service. The prosecutor has in some instances been actually received as an inmate of the house of a member of a court, sitting to decide a case which involved the life and honour of the accused party, and no one appeared to think that there would be any impropriety in thus permitting constant and intimate intercourse; both gentlemen having the credit of never speaking to each other upon the subject before the court.

In India and indeed in all small communities composed of the same classes, a hostile feeling is very easily excited against the unfortunate individual committing an act of imprudence which is magnified into a crime. Accusation is too frequently taken for proof, and without being aware of the true cause which has induced them to espouse a particular side, the gratification of a novel excitement prompts many persons to uphold or condemn with the utmost violence, and without a proper consideration of the merits of the question placed before them. Should the majority of the residents of a large European station in India, unfortunately arrive at a wrong conclusion, they have little chance of being set right until it is too late for the luckless object of persecution to benefit by a change of opinions, the society is composed of persons whose habits, feelings, prejudices and views are all in common, and have grown out of the circumstances in which they are placed. There is not, as in the smallest country town in England, other influential bodies, of a higher or a lower order, who may be inclined to take a different, and more enlarged view of the case, neither can the party who has been made the subject of general reprehension, insist upon being tried in a distant part of the country, where the whole affair in which he has been engaged has not been canvassed, and sentence passed by general consent beforehand. Courts-martial assembled under such circumstances have been guilty of the greatest injustice, disregarding the few warning voices which pointed out the errors of their proceedings, they have persisted in them, determined perchance in the sheer spirit of opposition, to carry their point, without reference to law or equity. Unfortunately it has happened that the commander-in-chief, either suffering himself to be biassed by the opinions of persons about him, hostile to the individual who espoused the cause of the oppressed, or from physical infirmities incapable of arriving at the truth, has confirmed sentences flagrantly unjust; refusing to do the injured party justice, when it has been shewn that they were obtained under false pretences, and against every established rule. More than one officer will have to regret to the day of his death, the departure of Lord Combermere from India, that gallant, straightforward and true hearted soldier, who united in his person a rare union of the various qualities requisite to those who have not only to lead an army into the field, but to regulate its internal discipline, and decide upon every question relative to its honour and well being. Sooner or later of course, wherever injustice has prevailed, a re-action will take place, and matters too hastily and too peremptorily decided, will be reconsidered with very different results. But this in many instances avails nothing, the arbitrary proceedings consequent upon prejudicial views, cannot be reversed; and too seldom does the conviction of error, act as a warning; though most fortunately it requires a series of extraordinary circumstances such as followed upon the departure of Lord Combermere, to produce the disastrous consequences occurring during the command of his successor.

If, as it has been before remarked, the members of a court-martial possess sufficient legal knowledge to prevent their being led away by the dicta of an ignorant and prejudiced president, or judge advocate, or will exercise a certain degree of common sense, they will always be independent of the opinions and wishes at head quarters; and they owe it as a duty not less to their brother officers than to themselves, to afford a security against every species of tyranny and oppression, by resolutely upholding the truth in despite of those who may employ their authority in the cause of despotism.

In some instances a court-martial has come to a very erroneous conclusion in consequence of not understanding the precise meaning of the words in the indictment, and being too proud to attend to the explanation offered by more learned persons. Generally speaking, nothing can be in worse taste than the style of the charges brought against an officer, who is said to have transgressed some military regulation, or to have misconducted himself in private life. Not content with a clear and simple statement of the nature of his alleged offence, he is loaded with opprobrious epithets; the words scandalous and disgraceful, being set forth in addition to unofficer like, and ungentlemanly, which would certainly be quite sufficient in all ordinary cases; and while these and other offensive words are employed upon nearly every occasion, the terms fully and honourably acquitted, when allegations of the kind, have been successfully rebutted, are frequently omitted, even when they are most strongly called for. The ends of justice cannot be answered by gross and unnecessary exaggerations, which are calculated to prejudice the minds of persons not blessed with very keen discernment, against a party, who upon some trifling occasion has a long list of charges brought against him, count heaped upon count, and all characterized by the most outrageous language. It is seldom that the manner in which these charges have been couched, meets with the notice and reprehension of a court-martial, which ought, when violent accusations fail of proof, to comment very severely upon an attempt to brand the party brought before it, with shameful epithets which have no just foundation. The court may sit during a long period, and a still longer may elapse before the judgment it has pronounced, is promulgated, and all this time the officer who has been tried, labours under the disadvantage of imputations, which should they do no injury to his character, must be very galling to his feelings. The nature and wording of the charges ought therefore to be subjects of serious consideration to a court-martial, since, unless it has been preceded by a court of enquiry, the accused has not had the advantage of any previous examination into the merits of the case, no grand jury to pass, or ignore the bill, and though in reality the charges may be frivolous and vexatious, they may be made to assume a very serious appearance, and be so involved, and so ingeniously contrived to force the prisoner to prove a negative, as to menace the most fatal consequences, unless they should undergo a strict scrutiny. Some cases are of so straightforward a nature that no doubt can be entertained upon the subject, but there are others arising out of perhaps trifling circumstances, which become so difficult and complicated, as to be very puzzling and perplexing to men who are not prepared by a previous acquaintance with the practice of courts-martial to unravel them. A rash, imprudent, and it may be, not over-gifted person, gets into some scrape, and probably commits himself still more by an incautious attempt at extrication, or by not sufficiently considering the predicament in which he is placed. He becomes amenable to a court-martial, and the same deficiency of talent, and the same hastiness of temper which have been the original causes of his misfortune, prevent him from defending himself in the most judicious manner, either in the examination of his own, or his opponent's witnesses, or by setting the affair in its true light. However willing, there perhaps may not be a single individual even at a large military station, able to assist him; his brother officers have not turned their attention to the subject, and he is at the mercy of all the mistakes, blunders, and ignorance of a court, which if the prosecutor be clever, generally sides with him—or the court may possibly be composed of men quite equal to the duty, but should the case not be properly placed before it, and the questions so framed as to elicit the most material points in the evidence, it is compelled to come to a conclusion which would have been very different had the case been differently conducted.

Few military men can afford to send for counsel from the seat of Government, and if they could, the distrust which such a step would evince, would raise an outcry very prejudicial to their interests. The Deputy Judge Advocate is sometimes the prosecutor, and sometimes draws up the charges, but this is not always the case, though the prosecutor, if choosing to come forward in his own person, is bound to consult with him; the prisoner is also allowed to have the benefit of his advice, and much of course depends upon the acuteness, temper, feelings, knowledge of the law, and acquaintance with his duties of this officer. No interest ought to obtain such an appointment, unless the party seeking it can shew that he is perfectly qualified in every respect for so responsible an office. Nor is a certain degree of information upon the subject of military jurisprudence, less necessary on the part of the members of a court-martial, who if incapable of detecting an error committed by the law officer, may be deceived by specious representations, and induced to sanction injustice. Every military man is liable to be placed in a situation in which he may be called upon to take the part of Judge Advocate, and therefore it is incumbent on him to study the subject, not, as it has been before observed, with a view to make himself a lawyer in the offensive sense of the word, but for the purpose of getting at the truth, and of preventing men in authority from using their power tyranically. It is most especially necessary where the accused person is totally helpless and unable to vindicate himself, or clear away the obstacles opposed to his attempt: or where a private soldier or non-commissioned officer has no friend to consult, and may be the victim of unmerited oppression. Each member of the court, subject to the opinion of the whole, if differing from that of the law officer, has a right to question the witnesses, and it is of the greatest consequence that these questions should be so framed as to bring out the whole truth. Many persons in giving evidence, who could have substantiated points of the highest importance, have been disappointed and distressed by not being called upon to afford the necessary information, and by this kind of mismanagement much unmerited suffering has been occasioned, which never could have taken place had the members of the court been expert at cross examination.

Instances have been known in which two officers have been tried for the same offence, under precisely the same circumstances, the first has been found guilty and dismissed the service, the second acquitted; the court-martial in either case deciding upon the evidence brought before it. The charge was that of calumniating the commanding officer. In the first case, the prisoner perhaps too confident in the consciousness of his innocence, and unaware of the necessity of proving it technically, did not make the truth of his observations upon the conduct of the prosecutor, manifest; in the second, the officer having the advantage of the assistance of an experienced friend, proved successfully that truth is not calumny, and that he was justified in the remarks which he had made, and which were repeated upon his authority. Strange to say, the sentence in the first instance was not reversed by the commander-in-chief of the time being, notwithstanding the memorials forwarded upon the subject, which clearly pointed out the hardship of the case; nor was it until the whole was re-heard before the Court of Directors at home, and every circumstance relating to it fully stated, that any redress could be obtained. Restoration to the service was then too late, for it could not have been granted without some injustice, and much inconvenience to others. Upon no subject perhaps connected with the local Government, have the Court of Directors been more perplexed than that relating to the decisions of court's-martial improperly conducted. In forwarding the case, either by accident or design, some of the most material points have been omitted, or the party in strengthening his cause by legal opinions at the Presidency, has lost time; and before he could arrive in England the question has been mooted before the court, and decided, not according to its true merits, but according to the statements placed before it. A re-consideration has been given, and a pension granted as some recompense for undeserved suffering, whereas if the whole had been known at first, restoration to the service would have followed. Occasionally, though the instances are too rare to produce much effect, an officer unjustly dismissed, has returned to take his place in his corps, like one arising from the dead, dispossessing his heirs and successors of his estates.

In addition to the grievance caused by an attempt to vilify the character of the accused, by multiplying charges, eleven men in buckram suits often growing out of two, and making them out to be of the most heinous nature, persons tried by courts-martial have other disadvantages to contend against. Should the members be raw, inexperienced, and dogmatic, the latter being often a natural consequence of the two former, they are apt to get into an ill-temper at what they are pleased to term the litigious spirit of the prisoner, who may not be disposed to permit his adversaries to have every thing their own way. They will perhaps allow all kinds of irrelevant matter to be brought forward, and object to its refutation. The glorious uncertainty of the law, ought not to apply to trials by a court-martial, which should be strictly a court of honour and of equity, where truth is the object of all concerned, but abuses will creep into the best intentioned institutions, and law having been laid down upon the subject of the proceedings, it should be generally understood, and scrupulously followed.

The prosecutor has been permitted to open his case with a flourishing speech, in the style of the Court of Queen's Bench, or the Old Bailey, in which the strongest language has been used, and accusations advanced calculated to prejudice the minds of the members of the court, which subsequently there has been no attempt to make good, or which have utterly broken down. All this must be endured with the most exemplary patience on the part of the prisoner, or the court takes offence, and after indulging in a mockery of justice, if the errors of its conduct are pointed out, and commented upon, it may get furious. Nothing is more difficult than to frame a defence which shall answer all the purposes for which it is intended, even when the prisoner is wholly innocent of the charges preferred against him. Should there have been any vexatious proceedings on the part of the court, which it is absolutely necessary to notice, the perplexities increase. To impute the slightest blame, to shew that the members have suffered themselves to be misled throughout, is to provoke the majority to increased hostility; few have the magnanimity to admit that they have been in the wrong, and accidental errors are too frequently followed up by determined perseverance. When the Mark Anthony style, which is rather the favourite, is adopted, it may not produce the intended effect upon the court, while it will seriously impede the prospect of success before another tribunal. All sorts of compliments are expected by officers sitting at a court-martial, they are to be called honourable men, to be exonerated from all improper feelings and intentions, let them conduct themselves as they will. Even when pains have been taken to prevent all just cause of offence, a court which has tolerated the most indecorous language, or the most bare-faced chicanery on the one hand, has objected to the tone and temper of the defence, and, not satisfied with passing an iniquitous sentence, affecting the life of the prisoner, thus exacting the severest penalty of the law, has added insult to injury, by tacking on a censure on the mode in which he presumed to rebut the charges preferred against him. In the endeavour to obtain redress in England by instituting civil actions against the President and members of this court-martial, the counsel consulted, expressed an opinion that it could not be maintained, because in this very defence which had occasioned so much clamour, he had not imputed malicious motives, having addressed his judges as men of honour, who though misled, desired to be impartial. Great allowances ought to be made for the indignation expressed by a party suffering under injurious treatment, and who has not received the protection from the court which it is bound to afford; while it is absolutely necessary to point out its failures for the information of the commander-in-chief.

The measure of punishment also to be awarded upon conviction, ought to be the subject of very serious consideration on the part of a member of a court-martial, and especially in the suspension of rank and pay, which involves many nice distinctions, and may occasion a greater excess of rigour than was contemplated at the time. An accurate knowledge of the law and all its bearings will be found extremely useful when points of this nature are discussed, and will prevent many of those haphazard random decisions which are often productive of incalculable mischief. Again, it is exceedingly essential to know exactly what does, and what does not constitute a military misdemeanour, and to be assured that the court has a right to take cognizance of offences brought before it. Transactions of a strictly private, and domestic nature, with which neither a court of law or of honour have anything to do, have been often mixed up with, or attempted to be passed off, as breaches of discipline, or actions unbecoming the character of an officer and a gentleman. Upon more than one occasion the contraction of debt has been attempted to be set up as a military crime, although unconnected with any attempt to defraud, or to evade payment by unjustifiable means. It is certainly essential to the character of an officer, and to the honour of the army, that all pecuniary affairs shall be carried on with the strictest integrity, but the mere circumstance of being unable to discharge a demand for money, though it may arise from a reprehensible degree of extravagance, forms no legitimate ground for a court-martial. Officers should scrupulously unite in guarding against the interference in affairs of private life, which it has been the object of some persons in authority to establish, although it cannot be justified by the most strained interpretations of military law, or the most rigid system of military discipline.

In numerous cases the appeal to a court-martial might be avoided by a timely reference to some person well instructed upon all points connected with military affairs, and who is acquainted with the exact nature of the duty which officers owe to others and to themselves. Such an authority will recommend an apology where it can be made with propriety, and thus the consequences of one false step, so frequently leading to others of the most fatal nature, will be avoided. He can also point out the necessity of submission to acts which, however arbitrary, may be enforced by authority, and will prevent rash and intemperate proceedings which tend to increase the hazard already incurred. However desirous an officer may be to afford this kind of assistance to his friends and companions, it can only be efficiently supplied by those who have given a great portion of their attention to the subject, and it is astonishing how very few amid a large and highly intelligent body, are qualified to perform a service of such great importance, and one which is so constantly required.

It is not without considerable reluctance that the foregoing remarks are hazarded, since feminine animadversion upon military jurisprudence may be considered presumptuous, impertinent, and out of place. In attempting however to direct young officers, destined to follow their profession in a distant land, to those pursuits which promise to insure their personal advantage, and to promote the best interests of society, it seemed imperative to notice at some length the neglect of a study which is so intimately connected with the welfare of the army. The observations thus offered have been elicited by a most conscientious desire to render a residence in India, not idly spent, useful to the community at large; and in the hope that more able pens may take up the subject. An abode of eight months in a house in which a court-martial was constantly sitting, afforded opportunities of becoming acquainted with the numerous evils resulting from a culpable degree of ignorance and indifference upon the part of persons who ought to have taken a deep and lively interest in the proceedings. Unwilling to give offence, personal allusions have been as much as possible carefully avoided, or many cases in point might have been adduced in support of the view now given of the manner in which courts-martial are too frequently conducted throughout British India.

CHAPTER XI.

THE MEDICAL SERVICE.

As the medical officers who receive appointments from the East India Company have usually passed the period of extreme youth, and therefore may be supposed to have entered the service of their own free choice, and after duly weighing its advantages and disadvantages, the present chapter may be deemed a work of supererogation. Nevertheless, it frequently happens that professional men of very respectable standing in the world, go out to the Presidency, to which they may be attached, almost as ignorant of the nature of their prospects, as the young cadet, who has only just left school. This ignorance is certainly not occasioned by indifference upon their part to a subject so important to their future interests, but from the difficulty of prócuring accurate information.

It is with some diffidence that the following observations are offered to those gentlemen who look to India as a field for the pursuit of their professional career, not because the subject has not been attentively considered, but on account of its extended nature, and the impossibility of doing justice to the numerous points which claim attention. Persons of great experience have shrunk from the task, and I am therefore compelled to present the remarks and opinions gathered during my residence in India, unassisted by the better judgment of gentlemen far more capable of fulfilling this duty. In the first instance I feel particularly anxious to disavow any intention in the following observations, to cast the slightest shadow upon the illustrious names which compose the body of Indian medical officers; nevertheless, without disparagement to the numbers of highly gifted individuals who belong to this branch of the service, it appears to me to be upon its present footing the most inefficient of any of the Indian departments. In the improvements which have been introduced with a view to the advantages, effectiveness, and economy of the service, the medical branch has been less fortunate than any of the others. An appendage on the civil and military establishments, and on account of its peculiar functions unconnected with political power or authority, it has met with a smaller degree of attention, than those apparently more important departments; nor are its details arranged in the manner best calculated to do justice to its own body, or to supply the wants of the service at the most economical rate to the Company. On this subject I may offer some remarks at the close of my paper, but in the first place, it is necessary to advert to its present position, and the prospects of those who enter it. The establishment in Bengal amounts, I believe, to 350, that of Madras to 230, and that of Bombay to 150 medical officers; making on the whole 730. At each Presidency there is a Medical Board composed of the three senior medical servants, which forms the highest grade in the service; the next is that of superintending surgeon, of which there are a certain number attached to each Presidency, this grade has the rank of lieutenant-colonel in the army, and the duties correspond with those of inspectors of hospitals in the British service. Then come the regimental surgeons, and assistant surgeons, corresponding in rank and pay with those of captains and lieutenants in the corps to which they are attached. The period of service, before promotion can be expected in this department, (which, as one of strict seniority, varies according to peculiar circumstances) may, generally upon an average be calculated at about fifteen years in the rank of assistant surgeon, twelve to fourteen in that of surgeon, eight in that of superintending surgeon, or in all about thirty-six or thirty-seven years in Bengal, before the medical officer can reach a seat at the Board. At Madras the period is usually shortened by four or five years, and at Bombay it is still less, the numbers to be got through in the latter named establishment, being fewer when compared to those of Bengal. This is one of the greatest grievances of which the Bengal medical officer has to complain, for as the advantages, and especially the retiring pensions attached to the Indian medical service depend entirely upon the rank attained by the individual, those in Bengal are obliged to serve much longer than in the sister Presidencies, before they can obtain the promotion, and consequent increase of pay and allowances, which follow upon shorter periods of service at Madras and Bombay. In no one single branch of the East India Company's establishment, have the advantages and emoluments been so extensively reduced and curtailed as in the medical department, and there is reason to fear that in many respects the zeal thus displayed has been of a very injudicious character. About every eight or ten years a sweeping and radical change of system appears to have taken place, introduced by, and under the sanction of the Government, each change being accompanied by important reductions to all except the highest grades of the service. Some of these alterations and regulations may have been requisite and proper, but in the opinion of those who are the most competent to form an accurate judgment upon the subject, they have exceeded the just bounds, and will be found to operate prejudicially, in consequence of the extent to which this principle of change has been carried. In pushing a theoretical principle, good perhaps in itself, to an unnecessary extent, when opposed to a practice that was found to work well, Government has overlooked some important considerations. The result of the late changes deprives the officer belonging to the medical branch of the Indian service, of all hope of deriving any pecuniary advantage from Government beyond his pay and staff allowances, and these are fixed, amounting when in the execution of his duties while in the medical charge of a regiment, to about 700 rupees a month to a surgeon, and 450 to an assistant surgeon. The cavalry regiments, and the European corps, are paid at a higher rate, since a surgeon's income who is attached to either may be estimated at about 1000 rupees per month. Under the former system, in addition to these advantages, it constantly happened that there were vacant medical charges of detachments or regiments, which fell to the care of the surgeon already in possession of the pay and allowances before mentioned, and if he were content to work double tides, that is, to perform these extra duties, he obtained large additional emoluments which often doubled and trebled his monthy income. Thus a man possessed of energy, industry, and talent, could improve both his fortune and his professional experience, whereas now, these additional duties bring with them no adequate remuneration in return, and consequently the great stimulus to exertion is taken away. Under the present system whether a regimental surgeon has much or little to do, his emoluments remain the same, and therefore, it is obviously his interest to undertake as small a portion of duty as possible. With these discouragements to contend against, the professional character of the department can scarcely improve, and it is no fault of the Government if it does not deteriorate.

Private professional practice is handsomely remunerated at Calcutta only, the other Presidencies, and a few of the large stations in the interior. Military surgeons in India are rarely offered fees, and those attached to civil stations, depend almost solely upon their public allowances. With respect to remunerating practice amongst the native population, according to the best information I could gain upon the subject, it is my belief that it is never regarded in a promising light. Instances of natives of rank applying to European physicians occasionally occur beyond the Presidencies, but these instances are so rare, that they form the exception, not the rule. The natives themselves possess a certain degree of medical information amongst their Hakeems, derived chiefly from the Arabian schools; and in some of the principal cities, as at Benares, Agra, and Delhi, natives of high repute practise medicine, and are often sent for from great distances to attend chieftains of rank. Their profits, however, are small, the fee of a native physician seldom exceeding one rupee. His prescription is taken to the Utter or native druggist, with whom he has often an arrangement for a share in the profits of the sale of the medicines prescribed, this latter source forming the chief portion of his emoluments. The greater number of a native doctor's patients, especially those who go to his residence to consult him, receive their prescriptions gratis, being too poor to pay a fee for the advice thus obtained. A few of the most eminent of the Hakeems at Lucknow, Benares, Delhi, and Agra, may acquire by the pursuit of their profession an income of from one to three hundred rupees per month, while some of them support this dignity on ten and twenty. Surgery is also practised amongst the natives, but in a rude and barbarous manner by the Gunas, or barber surgeons, who possessing no acquaintance with anatomy, often commit grievous mistakes, yet it is surprising that they should succeed at all. Ophthalmic diseases prevail much in India, probably in consequence of the heat and glare of the sun, and the sand and dust which fill the air, and cataracts or opacity in the lens of the eye is a common complaint. In the warm weather these Gunas may occasionally be seen in the streets of Agra or Delhi, seated in the morning with their rude instruments for extracting the cataract, consisting of a lancet and a steel probe. With the former the operator makes an incision in the eye, into which he introduces the blunt end of the probe, and by gentle friction on the diseased lens, he gradually detaches it from the affected part. Binding up the eye, the patient is sent home with injunctions to keep quiet, and to live low, and considering the rude method in which the operation is performed, and the nature of the instruments employed, it is wonderful that success should so frequently attend the experiment. The native population of India appear to place great confidence in their native practitioners, both physicians and surgeons, which is yet wanting to the more scientific attainments of European skill; and beyond the precincts of Calcutta, where knowledge is now advanced, it does not seem to me that the native feeling is sufficiently favorable to warrant any expectation of a profitable employment of professional talent to European practitioners in India.

At Calcutta and the sister Presidencies, medical practice forms a source of large emoluments, both European and native families paying handsomely, and generally by the year, for medical attendance. The usual fee amounts, I believe, to from 600 to 1000 sicca rupees per annum, and is often higher, so that a medical officer in good private practice makes his £5000 or £6000 a year; but, as it has been before stated, beyond the Presidencies private practice is not depended upon as a source of emolument, medical fees being seldom to be taken into calculation by that part of the profession resident at a distance from the seat of Government, or the large civil stations. The great object, therefore, of a medical officer in the Company's service is to obtain an appointment, however trifling, at the Presidencies, since though the allowances may be small, it will enable him to engage in private practice. Otherwise there is nothing to look forward to excepting the rise by seniority in the service, and a small number of lucrative appointments; and as the system of the Government seems with few and rare exceptions, bent upon the exclusion of its medical servants from every situation not belonging to their own particular department, their prospects are limited indeed. They cannot expect to share in the hopes of those who may look forward to the diplomatic and political line, to which both civil and military officers may aspire. Formerly, to those disposed to engage in commercial enterprize, advantageous openings were made by appointments to civil stations, where mercantile speculations could be successfully pursued. Even, however, in those halcyon times, for one fortunate person who obtained wealth, many were ruined; and now that India is open to every adventurer, the slight advantages formerly held out by the exclusive nature of the trade, being removed, such prospects are justly considered extremely hazardous, and are seldom made available by the service. From this statement it would appear that the medical department of the Indian establishment is certainly at present the one affording the lowest prospects to those who enter it, holding out nothing more than a moderate competency to the survivors after lengthened periods of service. There is also one great disadvantage which this department labours under, and which indicates very decidedly the inferior interest taken in its prospects by the higher authorities. The medical service is excluded from that very important boon lately granted to all other Indian military officers, the grant of pensions according to length of Indian service, as well as according to rank. The justice of their claim to participation in this boon is too clear and evident to be long withheld, but its postponement marks very strongly the feeling which their position in the service creates with the controuling powers at home, as compared with that manifested towards other military officers. The career of a medical officer in India may generally be described by the following routine. Upon his first arrival he is sent to the European Government hospital at the Presidency to act under the surgeon, quarters being found him, and his general allowance being about 230 rupees per month. He will, in all probability, be speedily removed to some regimental European hospital, to act under the regimental surgeon, until he shall have time to acquire some knowledge of the native language, and should he find his own quarters, his allowances will be about 260 rupees per month. After a time he may expect to be removed and posted to the charge of a native infantry battalion, where he will have the entire medical care of the corps under his superintendence, his allowances in this capacity being about 450 rupees per month. In fourteen or fifteen years service, he may expect to be promoted to the rank of regimental surgeon, when, according to his medical charge being in the infantry or the cavalry, he will receive from 700 to 1000 rupees per month. After twelve or fourteen years of further service, he will probably obtain the appointment of superintending surgeon at an allowance of 2000 rupees per month, and in six or eight years more, he may look to a seat at the medical board. A certain proportion of the officers of the medical service are lent to the civil departments doing duty at civil stations, the allowance of an assistant-surgeon thus appointed being about 350 rupees per month, while those of a full surgeon vary from 700 to 1000. This, according to the observations which I was enabled to make, appears to me to be a just representation of the advantages and prospects of a service whose promises are apt to be over estimated at home. It may still be said to offer a fair field for exertion, yet the hopes it holds out are scarcely of a nature to induce medical men of high attainments to leave their native country, should they entertain any expectation of success at home. Nevertheless, having shewn the unpleasing realities of the case, India, it must be admitted, possesses great attractions to the scientific and enquiring mind, and the long list of distinguished names amid the rolls of the Company's medical practitioners shew that it affords a wide scope for the exertion of superior talent. In addition to their peculiar professional studies, medical men going out to India will do well to acquaint themselves with some branch of native philosophy; botany, and geology are especially recommended, as being likely to attract the attention of Government, and leading either to the few select appointments now existing, or to the creation of others. Officers belonging to the medical service differ in opinion regarding the expediency of carrying out an extensive library. Some consider a great number of books in the light of a burthen, it being, in many instances, impossible to convey them about, while others deem a large collection of medical works indispensably necessary; it will at any rate be advisable to carry out the most important books of reference upon the subjects connected with any particular pursuit, portability of size being a great desideratum.

Government will supply all the surgical instruments which are required, it is therefore optional with the medical officer either to furnish himself, or to be content with those that are issued for the use of the service. Should he be in the habit of making chemical experiments, it will be prudent to take with him from England every thing that is necessary for the purpose, always looking to weight and size in the selection. Scientific men belonging to this branch of the Company's servants, will find in India an unlimited field for the study of *materia medica*. Native drugs not yet sufficiently known to Europeans are in general use in the country, and the investigation of their properties may prove exceedingly beneficial to society. A short report upon the subject will be given in a succeeding page. Indeed the productions generally of a country which most unaccountably has not hitherto invited research, and which are still very imperfectly known, demand the attention of the scientific world. There can be no doubt that a great proportion of vegetable products which are now disregarded, would be found exceedingly serviceable in many of the arts and manufactures of Europe, and for the latter there is a field open to the scientific and enterprizing enquirer, of unbounded range, which would richly reward the trouble and pains bestowed upon the investigation. It would not be proper to conclude this paper without adverting to a new era opening in India for the promotion of medical science. The proceedings of the late Governor-General, Lord William Bentinck, in founding, as it were, a school of medicine in Calcutta for the instruction of natives, to be employed in the service, should receive all the praise they merit. The activity of mind sometimes carried to a fault, of a nobleman whose administration was distinguished from those of his predecessors, by the working out of the minute details of suggested improvements, which the more pressing political exigencies hitherto arising under former Governments, had unavoidably postponed, was in this instance wisely directed. The success of a measure of considerable promise at the time, has, I believe, exceeded the expectations formed of it. A spur has been given to the advancement of European science in India, in this particular branch, which it is sincerely to be hoped may extend its useful influence as rapidly as its early success has been effectual. Lectures are given, I believe, in English on the more important branches of medicine and surgery, by gentlemen belonging to the profession, to a certain number of native youths, whose previous education has qualified them to become candidates for admission to this institution. When they have attained sufficient knowledge for the trust, they are attached to the military and civil departments of the service, in the character of native doctors, two being allowed to every regiment; and these are placed under the superintendence of the European surgeon; two in like manner being appointed to every civil station. Native doctors have hitherto been useful only as compounders of drugs and dressers in hospitals, and though I believe they were found to answer these purposes admirably, their natural intelligence, aptitude to learn, amiable temper, and handiness with the sick, rendering them peculiarly fitted for these duties, few of them possessed more than the mere routine knowledge of hospital practice. Having no acquaintance whatever with anatomy, while proving very useful and even valuable aids to the surgeon, they could scarcely officiate without his direction and superintendence. Now, however, that they are receiving a regular and well-grounded education, and, as I am informed upon the best authority, that the Brahmin and Hindoo youths amongst these medical students, have so completely overcome their prejudices as to study anatomy from dead subjects by dissection, with as much ardour as any pupil of a London hospital, the time is approaching when the higher duties of the profession in the native hospitals and goals may, in many instances, be left to native practitioners thus educated. In surgical operations, the delicacy of hand, and sharpness of eye, which distinguish the natives, will, when combined with competent knowledge, render them superior even to the European practitioners. When the time arrives in which native talent will be thus made available, and all who regard the subject stedfastly consider it to be in speedy progress, a gradual reduction of the already enormous medical establishment of India will certainly be advisable. The establishment is, according to the opinion of many competent judges, much larger on its present footing than a judicious arrangement would render necessary. Many of the details could now be carried into effect by the natives, in which event the superintending duties, together with the more important departments of the service could be conducted by less than half the existing number of surgeons. The only objection to a new system arises from the manner in which it might affect the patronage of the home authorities, but here, probably, the pen becomes too discursive, a point of this nature not belonging legitimately to the subject under discussion. When, however, we consider that the Indian medical establishment amounts to seven hundred and thirty surgeons and assistant surgeons, and compare the number of these functionaries with the duties which they have to perform, and the community in whose behalf they are chiefly if not solely occupied, and then advert to the talent and capacity of the natives, we are surprised that arrangements, similar to those now in progress, should not have been adopted at an earlier period. If it be an object of importanoe to give efficiency to every department of the Indian service, by adopting improvements which experience has pointed out, and making requisite additions when the advantage is obvious, it is not less so that there should be nothing superfluous or redundant. When, on account of a change of system, or the necessity of new arrangements, situations formerly indispensable, shall no longer be required, every available opportunity should be taken to suppress them, and by this means needless expences would be reduced, and facilities given for the extension of further improvements by the judicious application of funds so acquired. With this view the medical department of India will, in all probability, be scrutinized by the home authorities. It appears to be likely, that in the first place, the medical boards as they are now constituted, and the changes and reductions which they will admit, will come under serious consideration. Secondly, the propriety of equalizing by a more just and judicious arrangement than now applies, the prospects and advantages attendant upon promotion, and the retiring pensions of the medical officers belonging to the three Presidencies will afford a subject of discussion. Thirdly, the improvement of the prospects of medical officers in India by some increase of allowances according to lengthened periods of service, without regard to promotion, will force itself upon the notice of the court: and fourthly, retiring pensions granted according to the number of years devoted to the service in India, similar to the advantages conferred upon all other military officers, but from which the medical branch has hitherto been most unjustly excluded, will undoubtedly be conceded. Though many medical men obtain very considerable eminence in their character as physicians, in Calcutta and the other Presidencies, and no small number turn the experience which they have acquired in India, to good account at home, the greater proportion who have distinguished themselves are indebted to their superior attainments in branches of science independent of their professional studies. Excepting in a few instances there is scarcely a sufficient field in the routine of medical duties, to satisfy the ambition of high-minded men, and perhaps their attention has not been sufficiently directed to the natural productions of the scene of their residence. The proceedings however of learned bodies both at home and at the three Presidencies, are now doing much for the promotion of this desirable object, and we may look especially to the labours of the medical profession for an acquaintance with the agricultural resources of India, and the capabilities of turning many of its neglected products to advantage.

CHAPTER XII.

THE MEDICAL SERVICE.

AN officer having been appointed to the Honourable Company's Medical Establishment in the East Indies, will receive at the India House printed rules, for his guidance, according to the regulations of the service, which will be put into his hands immediately after he has taken the oath of allegiance. A duplicate of the covenant to which he has subscribed his name is also furnished to him for presentation to the Town Major of the Presidency, at which he may disembark in India. Having now entered the service, it will be advisable to give serious consideration to the best method of proceeding with respect to the outfit, and the mode of going out to India. Upon enquiry at the warehouses, a multiplicity of articles will be enumerated, and a list of necessaries offered, described as being absolutely essential, many of which, however, may be dispensed with; and the catalogue reduced within narrow bounds. An ample supply of linen, comprehending white jackets and trousers, socks and towels, will comprise nearly all that is wanted for the toilette, the wardrobe already possessed being sufficient for the cold weather to be encountered on the voyage. A couple of suits of silk or some thin stuff will be useful in saving the white jeans from the damage occasioned by iron moulds, which are always conspicuous on the cotton garments worn on board ship. A Bengal correspondent concurring in the view already taken in preceding papers upon the subject of outfit, observes, that all articles of saddlery, uniform, cloth, swords, epaulettes, &c., may be omitted with advantage. These things cost a considerable sum of money, which in many instances cannot be easily spared at the moment, and there is always a risk of injury upon the voyage, while they are to be purchased at the place of destination, very frequently considerably under the price demanded for them in London. When these heavy and costly articles are withdrawn from the list, the expence of an outfit is greatly reduced, and any surplus, after providing a sum for the purpose of meeting the demands upon landing, will be advantageously laid out in the purchase of a small but choice collection of philosophical works, and a few useful surveying instruments; these should include a barometer, a pocket compass, a thermometer, a pair of reducing compasses, and a camera lucida, should the individual be an indifferent draughtsman. Such instruments will be found permanently useful, and by a prudent selection from the multifarious articles offered at the outfitters, all or part may be included without exceeding the ordinary sum spent, or rather thrown away by persons who have no judicious friend at hand to assist them with the fruits of their experience.

Another great saving may be effected by a medical officer proceeding to India, who is recommended to employ his most strenuous endeavours to secure a cabin for the voyage free of expence. This advantage is rather difficult of attainment, but as there is always a chance of success, the attempt should be made, especially by those to whom economy is an object, since, as it will be seen hereafter, a very considerable outlay will be required to set a medical officer fairly afloat after his arrival at the place of destination. Since the abolition of the commercial transactions of the East India Company, all the troops embarking for their Asiatic possession belonging to the artillery, &c., are sent out by contract, and in order to secure efficient medical attendance for these men, the Court of Directors have the power of nominating one of their own officers to take charge of them during their voyage. Should they fail, however, to exercise this privilege within twenty-one days of the time appointed for the sailing of the ship, the patronage devolves upon the owners of the vessel, who can name the party eligible for the appointment. To a young surgeon proceeding to India for the first time, the attainment of the charge is difficult, in consequence of its being sought by those who are already in the service, and who happen to be at home upon leave, all who are on the point of returning being usually desirous to avail themselves of the allowance, which, when the number of troops amounts to one hundred and fifty, will afford a sum about equivalent to the price of a cabin, thereby effecting the saving of £120 or £130. The rule which guides the Court of Directors in the selection of the person to fulfil this important duty, lessens the chance of the young surgeon who seeks the appointment, since the senior applicant is always chosen; yet as it does not invariably happen that the number of medical officers returning to India is sufficient for the charge of the troops that may be going out, the ship-owners have not unfrequently the appointment in their gift. Every medical officer therefore, as soon as he has passed the India House, should speak to the military secretary or his assistant, the gentleman holding the situation at present being exceedingly courteous and obliging, and have his name registered as an applicant for the medical charge of troops. Should he succeed, a second advantage may be gained, as the ship-owners find it to their interest to offer a cabin as the remuneration for the services of the surgeon going out in charge of the troops, for his attendance on the crew and passengers. An Act of Parliament has been passed, which requires every ship leaving England for a foreign port, and carrying a crew of more than thirty men, to take out a surgeon under a heavy penalty, while few persons would like to engage a passage for so long a voyage unless they could be assured of medical assistance during its continuance. Every vessel going to India of sufficient burthen to carry passengers is therefore provided with a surgeon, to whom if not belonging to the Company's establishment, a salary must be paid, in addition to the cabin to which as an officer of the ship he would be entitled. In an arrangement of this nature the advantage is mutual, the expence of a cabin being a very serious item to those whose finances are not particularly extensive, while the owners also affect a saving which mercantile men know how to appreciate. A young surgeon, who on going out to India for the first time, can thus provide himself with a passage, and also secure the allowance granted by Government for the charge of the troops, may be considered most peculiarly fortunate, such circumstances occurring in the commencement of his career, affording, if followed up by prudent management, the means of starting in the world clear of debt and incumbrance.

In order to claim the sum per head granted by the Court of Directors, for the medical care of their troops, it is necessary to produce a living individual, those who die upon the voyage being struck out of the muster roll. The meanness of the stipulation, which requires living evidence of medical care, and the distrust of higher motives of action than the mere desire to secure pecuniary remuneration, have been not unjustly made the subject of indignant comment. The patients suffering from fatal attacks, and dying under the hands of their medical attendant, would when the duty has been strictly and conscientiously performed, be those for whom the highest rate of remuneration should be given, but the surgeon is paid for men who have not occasioned the slightest anxiety, and deprived of his just reward for the care and attention bestowed upon cases, perhaps beyond all human power. Prevention it is said is better than cure, and the surgeons on board Indiamen are paid according to the rule of some wealthy individuals, who give fees to their physicians only while they are in good health; but while the Home Goverment thus holds its medical officers responsible for the lives of the people entrusted to their charge, it denies them the right of interference respecting the general treatment of the men while on board. The surgeon is merely permitted to insert at the end of his journal the causes, which in his opinion have led to sickness, which might have been prevented; while it frequently happens that he experiences the utmost difficulty in obtaining attention to his representations at the proper time, should he even avoid the unpleasant consequences of a collision with the ruling powers. A striking instance of the impolicy of restricting the authority of a medical officer in cases so essential to the preservation of life and health, occurred on board a vessel which left Gravesend in July, 1837, with one hundred and sixty recruits on board for the Bengal artillery. In consequence of a lamentable want of discipline and inattention to the means pointed out as necessary to secure the proper degree of air and exercise, the scurvy made its appearance by the time that the ship had neared the Cape. So greatly did the disease prevail, that seventy men were struck down with it at once, their sufferings being attended with the most alarming results. Notwithstanding this disastrous state of affairs which the surgeon had predicted in vain, he found some difficulty in procuring any advantageous change, the colonel in charge of the troops replying to his representations on the subject that two commanding officers could not be permitted. Fortunately he succeeded better by his spirited representations to the captain of the vessel, who in consequence of the threatened mortality on board, put into the neighbouring islands, and by the judicious change of diet, occasioned by the purchase of fresh vegetables, the health of the sufferers was restored.

Those medical men whose pursuits are fixed, will of course employ themselves after their accustomed manner, but young surgeons should carefully guard against the contraction of idle habits on board ship, and should they not find the duties in which they may have engaged themselves, sufficient to occupy their time, they should strenuously endeavour to find some useful mode of passing hours, which otherwise will be wearisome as well as most unprofitable. Medical men must necessarily be acquainted with many branches of popular science, and these can be brought in aid of any little incident occurring on the voyage, increasing the interest which the capture of a shark or the appearance of a shoal of sea weeds will afford. Every medical man going out to India should endeavour to qualify himself for a public lecturer, and there can be no place better adapted for rehearsals in that character, than a ship during a long voyage. By addressing an audience with whom he is well acquainted, he will acquire confidence, and be enabled to introduce a new feature in the society to which he will hereafter belong, which will be found not more advantageous to others than to himself, there being few things more distasteless to men of scientific attainments, than a want of congeniality of pursuits on the part of their associates. Though great pains are now taking to disseminate the English language throughout India, every medical officer bound to this country should apply himself diligently to the study of Hindostanee, for he will be continually placed in situations in which he will find that nothing of consequence can be expected, unless he is able to converse fluently with the people about them in their own tongue.

A surgeon going to India will find some advantage in a previous study of the treatment of the lower animals, and should not be above taking an interest in the diseases of cattle, dogs, or even birds. This knowledge will be useful to himself and to others, while the silly prejudice which has hitherto deterred medical men from stooping to things that have been considered incompatible with professional dignity, is fortunately so rapidly wearing away as not to be worth thinking about. All the cavalry regiments in India are supplied with veterinary surgeons, who by a wise regulation of the service are placed upon a footing with the other officers of the corps; the appointment being in every way rendered so comfortable that men eligible for higher branches of the profession are induced to qualify themselves for it. The advice and assistance of these gentlemen can, however, only be obtained at cavalry stations, and though natives well skilled in the management of the diseases of the brute creation may occasionally be found, scientific knowledge on the subject would be very desirable in a place where pet birds and quadrupeds of all denominations form so great a source of interest and amusement. At any rate a medical man should be supplied with a few works upon the treatment of domesticated animals, to consult upon any emergency for the benefit of himself or his friends.

The first duty of a medical officer on reaching the place of his destination, is to report himself to the town major. If bound to Bengal, he should as a matter of precaution procure a certificate from the pilot, of the date of his taking charge of the ship at the Sand Heads, for although at present the town major refuses to receive this notification as a formal report, yet there can be no doubt that it will eventually be recognized in that character, recent orders from the Home Government having expressly stated that the pay of the officers belonging to the Company shall commence from the date of their arrival at the limits of the Presidency to which they are attached. The Sand Heads are considered the sea limits of the Bengal Presidency, every officer on quitting India drawing his pay until the vessel passes out of soundings. The settlement of this question is of some importance, since four or five days, or even a week's pay may be gained when the regulation shall be fully established, meanwhile it is advisable to be upon the safe side, and to be provided with the requisite certificate. Having reported himself in person to the town major, and delivered the counterpart of his covenant, the surgeon's next duty will be to wait upon the Secretary of the Medical Board, from whom he will receive instructions to repair to the General Hospital and report himself to the surgeon of that institution. Quarters will be provided for him in the hospital, or in the south barracks of Fort William. His residence at the hospital ought, according to the regulations of the service, to be protracted to three months, but at present the number of medical officers not being equal to meet the exigencies of the times, the moment a new arrival reports himself, he is directed to proceed to the military stations in the interior, a conveyance being provided by Government for the purpose. Under these circumstances he will immediately be placed in a situation of great responsibility, and his career in consequence be fully commenced.

A correspondent from Bengal deeply interested in the subject, writes thus :—

"Young medical officers were formerly accommodated with apartments at the Presidency General Hospital on their arrival from Europe, but one room after the other has been 'taken in' by the present incumbents until the whole have been absorbed, and they are now sent to the garrison of Fort William. It would seem that great importance is attached to the attendance on the practice of the General Hospital, and it is to be regretted therefore that the distance of their residence should so far preclude their attendance as to make the following order next to a dead letter.

'*General Orders by the Right Honourable the Governor General in Council.*

'*Fort William, July* 22, 1826.

'For the purpose of enabling His Excellency the Commander-in-chief to judge of the disposition shewn by the assistant surgeons, who on their arrival from Europe are sent to do duty at the Presidency General Hospital, to avail themselves of so favourable an opportunity of acquiring professional experience. The Right Honourable the Governor General in Council is pleased to direct that the medical officer in charge of the Hospital, shall on the 1st of each month transmit to the Adjutant General of the army, a report in the following form.'

In the report the number of days he visited, and how many days he did not visit the hospital is inserted, and any other useful remark the surgeon may please to make. These gentlemen complain very much of the hardship of being obliged to attend from a distance so great as that of the Fort from the General Hospital, without being granted the usual palanquin allowance. In fact they rarely if ever attend, for at the early hour the surgeons of the hospital make their visit, no hired palanquins are attainable in the garrison, and to walk appears very hazardous. A young medical officer returning to the Fort after having performed his morning duties, was so overpowed by the heat, that he dropped perfectly exhausted; and was obliged to be supported to his quarters by two of his companions, subsequently a fever came on which brought him to the verge of the grave.

However greatly the medical service may distinguish themselves for zeal and talent in their profession, there is not one appointment of which the salary is equal to that of the lowest staff appointment of the army, and this difference is bitterly felt by all. They look on themselves as slighted and ill-used since the reductions they have experienced have been threefold that of any other branch of the service. No stimulus for exertion is therefore held out to them, and if they pursue their duties diligently, it is only out of pure love for the science which their professional habits engender. It cannot be said that their duties are light. No officers are so much exposed as the medical officers are, for in a country like India, where disease runs its course so rapidly, the most vigilant care in marking and endeavouring to arrest its progress, is required; thus, it is not unusual for the medical man in his anxiety for the well-doing of his patient, to visit him three or four times a-day."

The pay of an assistant surgeon is 120 rupees, about £10 a month, including the deductions for the Orphan Fund, Military Fund, and the Bengal Medical Relieving Fund. When sent to a full batta station he must provide himself with a residence, and will then draw 246 rupees a month, £24, which upon obtaining the charge of a corps will, as acting surgeon, be farther increased by an additional 120. The staff allowance to a full surgeon in charge of a corps is 300 rupees, when absent upon leave, and if an assistant surgeon be appointed to do the duty, Government effect a miserable saving by the withdrawal of half, the junior being obliged to perform all the work for a moiety of the pay, and in this way a very large proportion of the sepoy battalions are conducted, the poor assistant surgeons having no remedy. Such being his prospects, it will be advisable for the medical officer holding an appointment in India to carry out with him all the money that he can muster. As he quits England at a more advanced period of life, and holds upon his arrival in India a more responsible situation than the cadet, he cannot so easily submit to be content with the bare necessaries for which a young boy just entering upon a professional career may be thankful.

The Company have not, unhappily, been guided by that

wise policy which induced the crown to render its service an object of attention to able and well-educated persons, and though medical men attached to the Indian establishments have reaped golden harvests in times of war, when Government contracts fell into their hands, the service itself has never received the attention due to a subject of such vast importance to the interests of the empire. An officer* whose work upon the constitution of the Medical Department in the Honourable Company's service may not be in general circulation in England, observes, in speaking of the above mentioned contracts :—"The intelligence of the realization of such brilliant fortunes in India, was not slow in reaching all parts of Britain. Gentlemen of the first families sent their sons to study medicine, the Indian service therefore was soon filled with as able and accomplished men as were to be found in any part of the world. Indeed, such were their literary acquirements, that many were employed in the political department, while the press of India, and houses of agency, were principally conducted by them. We have proof of their medical abilities by referring to several medical works written some thirty or forty years ago by Wade, Balfour, Macklean, Fleming, Assey, Wilson, &c. But these prospects were not to continue long. In 1815, while the medical service of Her Majesty's army was undergoing great improvement by encouraging men of respectability and talent to enter it, the Court of Directors commenced to adopt the very opposite policy; and the local government notified that the contract system was to cease, and an allowance granted in lieu of it, which to those in charge of European regiments scarcely afforded a fair remuneration for length of service and laborious duties. The native regiments yielded no reward to a full surgeon, but as he pos-

* Frederick Corbyn, Esq., Senior Surgeon, Fort William, whose pamphlet on "The Constitution of the Medical Department of His Majesty's and Honourable Company's Services," is well entitled to attention.

sessed the allowance of a regiment some years previous to his promotion to that grade, medical gentlemen were still content, and men of education and respectability have continued to come out and fill up the vacated ranks. From this period it would have been prudent and sound policy to have pursued a system which had been found by experience in the King's service to be expedient, namely, that of progressively improving the situation of the medical servants of the state.

The system of Government, however, we regret to say, seems to be diametrically opposed to it: for in 1828 a most alarming blow was given to the prospects of every medical man throughout British India by a further reduction in their allowances; and though in 1830 some favourable modifications were made as regards full surgeons' allowances, still the junior members of the service were generally left on a rate of pay and allowance which barely met expences."

Upon the arrival of a surgeon in India, he will have to provide himself with a regulation tent, a horse, saddle and bridle, and his regimental uniform. He must also purchase all the articles of furniture required for his domestic establishment, cooking utensils, chairs, tables, and numerous items, which, however economical he may be, will not cost less than £150. Should he not be provided with this sum, and it will scarcely cover his expences, it must be borrowed from a house of agency, the interest on which, including insurance of life, amounts to eighteen per cent. According to a calculation made by the gentleman already quoted, Mr. Corbyn, the rate of living consisting of the following items, will amount to a sum total which it is scarcely possible to diminish:—

One sweeper, rupees per month, 5; bearers to carry a palanquin, included in the pay, 30; one Khidmutghur or waiting servant, 7; one washerman, 8; one water-carrier, 5;

one cook, 8; one scullion, 4; one syce or groom, 5; house-rent, 50; tentage and travelling expences, 75; subscriptions to the Military and Orphan Funds, 6; clothing, including bedding, 20; food, including wine on the most economical terms, 75; contingencies, postage, stationery, &c., 20.—Total 319. The expenditure consequently is greater than the receipts, and even if by the strictest attention to economy some saving should be effected, a medical officer is liable to so many removals, that he cannot follow up the plan he may have adopted, and is in nine cases out of ten involved in debt, which unless some fortunate circumstance should occur, will remain a burthen to him all his life.

There are, as it has been stated in previous chapters, appointments in the gift of Government by which a young medical man may at an early period of his service be placed in the receipt of liberal allowances, and though in consequence of the number of candidates the chances of obtaining these prizes are greatly diminished, still they serve to stimulate exertion, and to cheer the otherwise gloomy prospect. In devoting their attention to the capabilities and resources of India, medical men have now more than ever an opportunity of becoming benefactors to the country, while their own happiness will be increased by the interest which they take in its improvement. Although a medical officer may find enough, and in some instances more than enough, to employ his whole time in the execution of his duties, yet these may be judiciously blended by an endeavour to introduce the indigenous substitutes for medicines imported from foreign countries into his practice and to ascertain their true qualities. The remedies, vegetable and chymical, imported into India from Europe and South America, we learn from an authenticated report, are 203 in number, and cost the State, per annum, something less than one lac of rupees, of this sum four-fifths are expended on the twelve following articles: cinchona bark and quinine, colocynth, ipecacuanha, jalap, capavia, scammony, sarsaparilla, manna, oil of peppermint, cantharides, and rhubarb. These articles being all intrinsically cheap, it is their vast consumption, which causes their great proportionate cost, and consequently it may be inferred that for the diseases of India these are the articles essentially required, and for which it is desirable if possible to introduce and find indigenous substitutes. In educating native practitioners, according to the system which prevails in Europe, we are providing more efficient medical aid to the great bulk of the natives than they could hitherto command, but as it would be quite impossible for them to incur the expence of purchasing foreign medicines it is incumbent upon us to employ our most earnest endeavours to develope the natural resources of the country. The introduction of jalap has failed in India, the root losing its medicinal qualities when transplanted to a foreign soil, but a perfect substitute has been pointed out in a preparation easily made from the *Kaladana* of Bengal, and nothing appears to be required to bring it into general use but the efforts of scientific men, who will cast aside prejudice in the furtherance of an object so well calculated to promote the public good. Colocynth has been proved by Dr. Wallich, Dr. Burn, and Dr. O'Shaughnessy to exist in abundance in the Delhi and Kurrah districts. For ipecacuanha there are so many native representations, that nothing, observes the author now quoted, "*but a love of what is foreign*, can urge us to seek for it. The bark of the root of the *mudar*, or the root of the *untamol*, will answer perfectly for many of the uses of ipecacuanha. As an emetic we have in the *Kanoor* and *Burra Kanoor* of India, a better article than ipecacuanha or any other known remedy of this class. For capavia balsam an effectual representative—one of exactly equal power is prepared by distillation from the well known *gurjun oil* of Rangoon and Sylhet. For sarsaparilla we have at least four articles, the *ununtamul*, *gulanchee*, *China-root*, and *guozuben*, of which *the first* is in the opinion of all who have used it a more powerful remedy and a much more agreeable one than sarsaparilla itself, with the *Tarianjabam* of Arabia, and the *rooza* and other aromatic oils, we may be well satisfied, instead of mana and peppermint." Although the introduction of these remarks may not at first appear to be germane to the subject of the present paper, yet as the discussion is employing the attention of scientific men in India, it seems advisable to make those members of the faculty who may contemplate a visit to that part of the world acquainted with the topics which are at present exciting interest amid the Anglo-Indian community, and of which the reports may not be unacceptable to enquiring minds at home. As usual upon such occasions "doctors disagree" upon a point of very great importance, namely, the possibility of dispensing with the expensive importations from Peru in favour of drugs of native growth. Many persons are of opinion that narcotine substances may be employed in preventing the return of periodical fevers, and 167 cases are quoted, furnished by different medical practitioners, in which the results have proved the success of this mode of treatment, but others are anxious for the introduction of the cinchona bark tree, which, though difficult, does not appear to be impossible. The expence and trouble attending importations of the kind are very great, but active and enterprising spirits delight in overcoming obstacles which serve only to excite them to fresh efforts. The attempt it appears to produce cinchona bark in Europe, as a curiosity for the hot house, has failed, but it does not follow that equal want of success would follow its transplantation to the soil of India, either in the dry or moist part of a country so favourable to the growth of plants requiring a warm climate. It is stated that not less than 6,000 trees in full vigour would be required to supply the wants of the community, and that it would take a century at least to produce them; but there can be no good reasons why a beginning should not be made.

interesting and fashionable, and there is a fashion in every thing, as the study of geology is at this moment, there can be no doubt that the time and thoughts of a medical officer going out to India, will be more beneficially employed in obtaining an intimate acquaintance with botany and horticultural science. It is unfortunate that at a period when so many subjects of the highest degree of importance to the future welfare of India, are opening upon the minds, and engaging the attention of men who see how readily they might be turned to advantage, that their own necessities will scarcely permit them to devote a single rupee to the promotion of objects of public utility. Money is absolutely essential to carry the greater portion of plans for improvement into effect, but infinite service may be also rendered to the country at large by methods which do not involve pecuniary expence. It does not appear that scientific men have as yet endeavoured to avail themselves of the channels open for communication with the natives, by means of the newspaper or Ukhbars published in Hindostanee. A series of popular articles acquainting the respectable classes with the advantages attendant upon the cultivation of useful knowledge, and recommending them to form institutions for the purpose of acquiring the means of improving their property, would in many cases awaken a desire to benefit by the introduction of European science, and if zealously followed up might be productive of the happiest results. There is no want of curiosity or intelligence in the native character, a judicious method of imparting instruction being only required to induce the people of India to take an interest in subjects of importance to the general good, and it may be said that want of judgment on the part of their instructors, rather than any inaptitude to learn, will be the cause of every failure. When the first steam vessel made its way against the current of the Ganges, without sails or towing ropes, the natives crowded to the banks of the river overpowered by astonishment and perplexity. Upon its arrival at Benares, several Asiatic gentlemen were invited to go on board to inspect the wonders of a ship which was confidently reported to be the work of jins or demons. The weather happened to be exceedingly sultry, and a windsail had been consequently put up to conduct a current of air to the cabins below. This simple contrivance attracted the attention of the native visitants, who could scarcely be prevailed upon to give more than a hasty glance at the engines or paddle wheels, so eager were they to enjoy the advantage of a method of procuring a positive good, which they could understand. The anecdote was of course told against them, but the error seemed to belong to those Europeans who expected that natives of India, who knew nothing whatever of the new power of steam, should comprehend the manner in which it was brought into action, without any previous acquaintance with the nature and effects of machinery. It requires a considerable advance in knowledge to comprehend or appreciate complicated arrangements, and in the commencement of an attempt at enlarging the acquaintance of the natives with objects of practical utility, the most obvious points should be presented to the mind. It may perhaps require as long a period to stimulate the whole community to undertakings of great importance, as to produce six thousand full grown trees of the cinchona bark, nevertheless the seeds should be sown, and in every instance where it is practicable, the native papers made the vehicle of instruction.

CHAPTER XIII.

THE MEDICAL SERVICE.

There is an old saying which assures us that when things are at the worst, they must mend, and the medical officers of the Company's service may console themselves (convinced that nothing worse can ensue) with this comfortable expectation. Gentlemen, however, who are turning their thoughts towards India with a view of engaging in its medical service, should pause before they take a step, which under the present circumstances, will most probably lead to disappointment, and all the unpleasant feelings attendant upon a sense of ill-usage. It becomes, therefore, the duty of those who profess to offer advice and instruction to the uninformed, to place before them a more detailed account than has hitherto been given of the peculiar hardships of which they complain.

It has been but too justly remarked, that the medical servants of the Company have been subjected to the consequences of all the strange fancies which the local authorities have chosen to entertain; that little or no faith has been kept with them, no compensation given to men who have suffered serious injury from the capricious and wanton changes which have been effected, and no security offered that the future shall not resemble the past. Individual cases of the greatest hardship have occurred without meeting with the slightest attention or redress, and the contempt with which the memorials have been treated, of men who suffered, and are still suffering from the loss of appointments peremptorily abolished, the cutting of allowances, which they have been taught to consider permanent, &c., &c., shew that it is absolutely necessary that there should be some influential body established at home, in order that the interests of the service may be advocated by persons whose remonstrances could not be dismissed in the disrespectful manner which the memorials of the Company's medical officers have experienced. This subject, however, must occupy a succeeding page; at present it will be necessary to shew how imperative some institution of the kind is called for. The following statement from an officer belonging to the Bombay medical service, affords abundant proof of the invidious situation in which those gentlemen who have embarked in it, may be placed.

"Since 1817, in the regimental department of the military branch of the service, the regulations affecting the pay of officers doing duty with European troops have undergone four changes, and during the same period there have been the same number of changes in the pay regulations, for officers doing duty with native troops.

IN MEDICAL CHARGE OF AN EUROPEAN REGIMENT.

In 1817,	a Surgeon	received from	2,000 to 3,000	Rupees.
In 1821,	ditto	ditto	600 to 800	"
In 1829,	ditto	ditto	130	"
In 1831,	ditto	ditto	500 to 600	"

FOR MEDICAL CHARGE OF NATIVE TROOPS.

In 1817,	a Surgeon received	——	Rupees.
In 1821,	ditto	300	"
In 1829,	ditto	130	"
In 1831.	ditto	300	"

In the staff departments of the military branch of the service, many and great changes have been made with respect to the emoluments of appointments, the chances for promotion, and the qualifications required in candidates for appointments. For details and proof of what is here stated, reference may be made to the memorials of Mr. Kemble, Dr. Smyttan, Dr. Kennedy, Dr. Burnes, and many others. In the civil branch of the service there have been a great variety of systems, some devised for one purpose, and some for another; but all without sufficient reference to the true objects of the medical profession, while all of late invention have been framed in a spirit of sordid and sickening economy, not less at variance with the public interests, than hurtful to the pride of medical officers, betraying the meanest conceptions of the value of their duties, and the most thorough contempt for those claims, on which alone the great majority of all the Court's servants in India, are obliged to rest their hopes of advancement. The following is a statement of the changes made in the salary of a medical officer in the course of ten years.

First receipt (1820)	Rs. 500
Second ditto (1822)	380
Third ditto (1830)	150

while at Indore as an acting Residency Surgeon (in 1827) he received 100.

In the Naval branch of the service all the duty is performed by assistant surgeons, the greater number of whom abominate the sea, and consider the hardship of being employed on board the more severe, in consequence of their immediate gains being very inconsiderable, from there being no prospective rewards in this service, and on account of their feeling aware that if during their term of service afloat they should acquire nautical tastes, knowledge, and experience, such acquirements can be of no value or utility in the situations they may be destined to fill in the after period of their lives.

In all the branches and departments, the rules of patronage and promotion have undergone frequent changes; every new Governor, every new Commander-in-chief, and every new superintendent of the Indian Navy, having had his own peculiar crotchet; and though the Court of Directors, and the Medical Board, have now and then interfered, and endeavoured to introduce uniformity of rule, and to enforce the principle, that claims derived from seniority, length of service and character, are to be held paramount, still their efforts have hitherto been unsuccessful, and the consequence is, that few individuals are contented with their situations, and perhaps not one person satisfied with his prospects in the service.

The evils forming the subject matter of the volumes of unheeded memorials shelved in the India House, are attributable, chiefly to two causes. 1st. The sudden introduction of great and sweeping measures of reform, unaccompanied by provisions for granting compensation to the sufferers. 2d. Omitting fairly to adjust the scales of pay and promotion, or which amounts to the same thing, omitting to make equally applicable to all the services, one common series of unbending rules, constructed on fair principles, and calculated to exclude the operation of individual interest and caprice, in guiding to selection for appointments. One great step towards a remedy for existing grievances, would be compliance on the part of the home authorities with the prayer of Dr. Kennedy's Memorial, from which the following extract is taken :—" Your memorialist most humbly and earnestly prays, that your Honorable Court will graciously be pleased to take the unhappy circumstances of the Medical Department, under your just and humane consideration, and that, estimating the great expence of our education, the important and painful, and hazardous nature of our duties, that you will be pleased to place our ill-requited body on a footing more suitable to our rank and respectability in European society, *where the Professional is not considered inferior to the Military character*. To accomplish this, and to admit a fair comparison betwixt the Ecclesiastical, Military and Medical Establishments, your memorialist earnestly prays that your Honorable Court will cause a complete new organization of the Medical Department to be made, dividing us into classes similar to the military, and in similar proportions, as follows :—

1. A class of Surgeons to be termed Senior Surgeons, forming 7½ per cent. on the whole strength; to have the rank, and pay, and pension of Lieut.-Colonels in the Army, similar to Deputy-Inspectors and Physicians to the Forces, in Her Majesty's Service.

2. A class of Surgeons to be termed Staff Surgeons, forming 7½ per cent. on the whole strength; to have the rank and pay and pensions of Majors in the Army.

3. Regimental Surgeons, forming 25 per cent. on the whole strength, as at present.

4. Assistant Surgeons 60 per cent. on the strength, and ranked as at present, but the order in favour of Her Majesty's Service, by which Assistant Surgeons, when in charge of regiments, are ranked and receive pay as Acting Surgeons, whilst so employed, to be extended, as in justice it ought to be, to your own servants.

The number in each rank, on this classification, for the Bombay Presidency, will be 11 Senior Surgeons, 11 Staff Surgeons, 36 Regimental Surgeons, and 88 Assistant Surgeons. Total 146.

Finally, Members of the Medical Board to rank as Colonels, and Superintending Surgeons as Lieut.-Colonels, the pension of £500 being granted to the latter after four years service, and to the former on obtaining their rank, and the pension of £700 to those who retire from the Board by rotation, after four years service.

These suggested arrangements would still leave the Medical Department inferior to the Military, as it gives us so small a relative proportion of Colonels, but the unspeakable advantage which some such improvement would prove to us, would fill our hearts with respectful gratitude to your Honorable Court, and your gracious liberality, would be eventually amply repaid by the new spirit which it would generate in the service; whilst the most cursory examination of the grounds, on which your memorialist ventures to address your Honorable Court, will serve to prove that no inordinate exercise of local expenditure for the present, or of the pension list for the future, is to be apprehended.

As respects the new organization into *Senior Surgeons* and *Staff Surgeons*, forming 15 per cent. on the whole strength, their duties could be amply and honourably provided for in the three members of the Medical Board, five Superintending Surgeons (for five are necessary in this Presidency (Bombay) to obtain efficiency), and the Garrison, and Cantonment, and Civil Surgeons, and Surgeons of General Hospitals, forming a total exceeding twenty-two of staff appointments, which are at present, with the exception of the first-named, left open for selection; and as respects the emolument, and salaries suitable to the ranks bestowed, and duties to be discharged, your memorialist humbly prays, that the scale of staff salary fixed for the corps of Engineers may serve as a sort of standard by which to estimate the remuneration your goodness should consider due to the Medical Department."

Some alteration in the present state of the medical branch of the service, is by every person who has considered the subject at all, pronounced to be absolutely necessary. As it now stands it offers no inducement for men to remain in it when their labours become most valuable to the community; that is when arriving at, or nearly forty years of age, after seventeen years service. A surgeon is then entitled to his pension of £190 a year, and he will receive no more should he continue to perform duty ten or twelve years longer. Neither as the service is now constituted, has he any prospects in India, a surgeon of whatever standing, being as liable to regimental duty as he who has just been promoted. The best remedy for this unfair and impolitic state of things, would certainly be the one proposed above, namely, to constitute an intermediate rank between the surgeon and superintending surgeon, call it by any name deemed most suitable, but let it be a regular grade; standing to the surgeon, as the major does to the captain in regard to rank and emoluments in India, and in pension when he retires. The same end, if preferred, might in a great measure be attained by admitting the Company's medical officers to similar advantages in their retiring *pensions*, to those which have been conferred by successive warrants on Her Majesty's Army surgeons in *pay;* that is by increasing their pensions proportionably to length of service, allowing every man to retire on the full pay of a Queen's military surgeon *of the same standing.* The regulations profess to allow every one after the prescribed period of service to retire on "the full pay" of his rank, and that full pay has always been considered to mean the full pay of the corresponding rank in the Queen's Service. But in the case of the Company's surgeons it is not so, the full pay of the Queen's surgeons rising as high as 22s. or 24s. a day by length of service, while that of the Company never goes beyond the lowest scale of 10s. 6d. per diem. While the Government of England has seen the justice and policy of thus rewarding lengthened service, that of India has done nothing for its medical officers, and while their military brethren have received the most bountiful consideration in regard to provision on retirement, their claims have been overlooked and disregarded. The harassing nature of the duties to which the Company's medical officers may be subjected during the operations of war, or in times of famine and pestilence, may be gathered from the following extract from a letter from a superintending surgeon in Bengal. " The last accounts from the North Western Provinces of India, dated the 6th of May, from Agra, mention that small-pox committed dreadful ravages amongst the population generally. Europeans and natives during the last months having suffered from severe attacks of these complaints. Subsequently measles and influenza became nearly universal, and latterly, since the commencement of the hot weather, fevers and cholera of the most virulent character, became alarmingly prevalent. The work of death still continues; thousands and thousands have been carried off in this way in addition to the tens of thousands who have died and are dying of famine, and to render these heavy calamities still more severe, there is a great scarcity of medical men in this country, many corps being without medical officers, and even some stations; so that regiments and detachments have been obliged to march hundreds of miles without a medical officer. The surgeons who are in the country are worked to death, having often the duties of treble charges to perform, and are marched through all weathers and at all seasons from one end of the country to the other. It is therefore not surprising that they die in about a double ratio compared with the military officers of the Company's army, and that in consequence, a more than usual number are at home on furlough, or on sick leave, or with the intention of giving up the service, since no man who can possibly obtain a subsistence in his own country, will continue to slave at the expence of health and comfort, especially while his laborious, anxious, and responsible duties, in so trying a climate as India, are so ill requited. Medical servants at this time have indeed nothing to excite them to exertion. Their spirits and energies are depressed not only by the curtailments of their allowances from time to time, and more particularly by the ex-Governor General Lord William Bentinck, but by their having been denied by the President of the Board of Controul, Sir J. C. Hobhouse, the pensions for length of service in common with the military branch of the Service, which has lately been conceded to the latter. The Court of Directors, who, unhappily for themselves, and for the country they nominally govern, are as nothing compared to the Board of Controul, have it appears recommended that their medical servants should be less injuriously treated, but to no purpose, the fiat has gone forth from the Queen's Government, which decides that no remedy shall be applied to the grievances complained of. The consequence is, that there are now men who have served upwards of thirty years in the medical department of the Company's establishment in India, whose retiring pension is only £190 a year, whilst a military officer of the same army who commences his career earlier in life by five or seven years, after serving thirty-two years in India is entitled to £450 a year retiring pension. After this statement it cannot be a subject of astonishment that there is a scarcity of medical officers for the military and civil duties of the India Company's Government.

It may appear that the existing evils and their proposed remedies, are enumerated too often in the present work, and that a simple statement of the disadvantages under which the service suffers, would be sufficient for the purpose of showing its situation and prospects. A mere detail of grievances however, gathered from the numerous documents extant upon the subject, would scarcely show how deeply the medical officers of the India Company feel the wounds which have been inflicted upon them, and how anxiously they are desirous to have the service placed upon a more honourable and secure footing. Those, as it has been remarked, who have any intention of engaging in this service should be made acquainted beforehand with the state of feeling which has been engendered in the breasts of their brother officers, the universal discontent that prevails, and the chances that they may be made to suffer under the same system which has been rendered so intolerable to high minded men, conscious of merit, and indignant at the wrongs they have sustained. Many of the friends of the aggrieved, who see the absolute necessity of putting an end to the present incertitude regarding the rank which medical officers may hold after protracted length of service, and who advocate the recognition of their claims to an encreased rate of pensions, are of opinion that they should be content with such prospective boons, and not seek for compensation for previous suffering. It is said that the individuals subjected to losses are few, and that others have been benefited by the changes effected in various departments. The small number of the sufferers, will in these days of economy afford an additional plea for the compensation demanded, while no generous spirit could be wholly content with the improvement of his own prospects, while he sees those of his brother officers, or their surviving families wholly blighted. The sufferers may be few, but their wrongs are of a crying description, and such as imperatively demand redress. In the arbitrary abolition of appointments, sometimes, though for the alleged purpose of remodelling the departments, in reality to promote a favourite, no pains have been taken to place the person thus summarily deprived of an honourable employment, attended with liberal emoluments, in the position to which his services entitled him. It frequently happened that men in the full confidence of the enjoyment of a staff appointment during life, and to which their talents and acquirements were peculiarly adapted, relinquished their promotion, all claims to a seat at the medical board, &c. on the score of seniority. These men at the whim or caprice of a Governor-General, or a less justifiable motive, have been cast adrift, their only satisfaction being the assurance that they are turned out of office with characters wholly unstained, and with an unblemished reputation for zeal and ability. A sort of mockery which adds insult to injury, since the very deprivation unaccompanied by a confession that it was occasioned by corrupt motives, is sufficient to produce an unfavourable opinion of the conduct or the competency of the party thus dismissed without recompense or reward.* One of the most flagrant cases in point is that of the late lamented Mr. John Tytler, hurried to the grave by the overwhelming sense of his injuries; and whose family remain unnoticed claimants for the compensation denied to him. It has happened that gentlemen on the faith of a Government appointment at the Presidency, have established a large and lucrative private practice. The appointment is unceremoniously abolished, and the officer holding it perhaps posted to a regiment, is compelled either to do duties which he never expected to be called upon to perform again, or to resign the Service. The individual thus unworthily treated comes home to seek redress, but his representations and remonstrances, unless backed by very powerful interest, meet with little or no attention. It is thought unadvisable to interfere with the measures adopted by the local Government, even when their injustice and hardship are acknowledged and lamented. Men in office seldom possess sufficient magnanimity to admit that they have erred in their judg-

* Corrupt motives, of course, never will be confessed; no person will be honest enough to say "You are deprived of your appointment because I wish to bestow it upon a friend, or because I find you less subservient to my will than is desirable;" and as no great man is without his partisans, it will always be insinuated that though there might not be sufficient cause for direct accusation, the person in authority was justified in the measure he adopted.

ment, and if once they have sanctioned a wrong committed upon one of their servants, appeals are usually fruitless and unavailing: while the denial is rendered still more grating to the party who feels that he has supplicated as a favour the justice, which under a more defined system might have been demanded as a right.

The Indian medical service has no representative in England, no influential persons invested with authority and interested in its behalf, to urge the necessity of affording pecuniary compensation to those who have had their fortunes wantonly ruined, and their feelings recklessly outraged by men who, in the plenitude of their power, have displaced them to make way for some minion of their own. Inadequate as this compensation must be in many cases, in which time, talents, zeal, and all the feelings and energies of a noble mind, have been directed to one object; and when it is discovered that the labours of a whole life have been thrown away, and that the attention must be turned at its later period to something else; still it is all that the Court can grant, and should not be withheld. The medical service requires consideration of this kind to support its members under the pressure of their numerous axieties and cares. All would rejoice at an act of justice done to a brother officer, while the widows of men, aware how deeply the sense of injury has rankled in the breasts of their husbands, and how greatly it contributed to reduce them to their present bereavement, and to render their children fatherless, would be soothed not only by the improvement of their pecuniary resources, but by the feeling that a stigma has been removed from a valued and honoured name.

It may be said that the reputation of men who have been unjustly deprived of an appointment, is not in reality tarnished, and that the smooth speeches of the gracious personage,—who assures them, that, though the interests of the service demands their dismissal, and though he does not see any way in which he can compensate them for the loss of an employment of high trust, emolument and dignity, yet he is ready to give his testimony to their efficiency, zeal, talents, and unexceptionable conduct,—are quite sufficient to prevent society from attaching any disgrace to the party thus highly complimented. The world, however, is apt to look at the facts of the case, and to disregard the words; and in instances of the grossest injustice, whispers have gone about that there have been reasons for an apparently despotic proceeding which do not appear; every man whose wrongs have been unredressed being liable to this inference.

As one means of procuring a remedy for the grievances sustained by the medical service, it has been proposed to constitute the retired members of that body into a college, to which the charge of the Company's medical library and museum should be assigned, and also the duty of revising all orders and regulations affecting the interests of the profession in India. An administration thus composed of the retired officers of the medical service could scarcely fail to produce the most beneficial effects. In the first place it would afford employments and pursuits of the highest degree of interest to men who, on their return from India, find themselves suddenly reduced to idleness, and cut off from all communication with persons of congenial tastes and views.—Secondly, passing over other obvious advantages, the Company's medical servants in India, who would all be licentiates of this college, would be stimulated to the strongest exertions in the advancement of science, and in the collection of specimens of various products connected with its several branches. The vast accessions of treasures illustrative of natural history, acquired by the patient and laborious efforts of medical officers in India, have been scattered all over the British dominions, in consequence of there being no one single place to claim them as a right; and it is impossible to calculate upon the admirable effects which might be produced by a college instituted at this juncture by men who possess all the advantages resulting from the experience of ages.

It has also been proposed to start a retired member of the medical service as a candidate for a seat in the Direction, and to this there can be no possible objection, as it would not in any way interfere with the scheme of founding the college, rather serving to promote it; but, it should be borne in mind that the establishment of the college must prove a permanent advantage, while that derived from the election of a Director, would be subjected to many contingencies, the frail dependence upon human life being one. Unanimity being so desirable in every attempt to improve the condition of any class or body of men, the whole of the medical service should unite, since there may be a difference of opinion respecting the superior utility of either plan, in the endeavour to attain both these objects, namely, a representation in the Direction, and a college. "Why," it has been asked, "have the Indian medical service no pharmacopœia, either in England or in the scene of its duties, no libraries, no museums of natural history, of morbid and comparative anatomy, and the articles used in materia medica in India? The answer to all these questions is one and the same, because it has no college, and because in the Indian medical service there is much to create dissatisfaction and disgust, and nothing whatever 'to give spur to industry and ambition.'" It now only remains to say, that in consequence of the impossibility of existing upon the pittance provided by the Company as the pension of their medical service, the officers belonging to this department have instituted a retiring fund, of which a table, taken from the *Bombay Calender*, and printed in the Appendix, forming No. 3, will shew the advantages.

CHAPTER XIV.

DESULTORY REMARKS UPON THE OFFICE OF CHAPLAIN TO THE EAST INDIA COMPANY'S INDIAN POSSESSIONS.

THE clerical establishment of the East India Company though still very small, has been considerably enlarged of late years; and while those who have had any experience in the duties of a minister of the gospel at home, must suffer many privations, and accustom themselves to an almost totally different mode of life, still there is much to interest their minds, and employ their time in a residence in India. The salaries annexed to the office of chaplain in the Company's territories are sufficient to afford a comfortable maintenance, but nothing more; and excepting in Calcutta, the additions derived from marriage-fees is so trifling as not to be taken at all into consideration. A chaplain upon his first appointment receives about six hundred pounds a year, which is subsequently augmented to a thousand; and he may now, perhaps, look forward to some of the dignities which the Indian Church in its present constitution will confer. Indeed there seems to have been somewhat of hardship in the way in which patronage has been bestowed; and that men who have slaved in the vineyard all day should not have been chosen for the mitres conferred at home upon persons wholly unacquainted with the pastoral wants of the country. Too much praise, however, cannot be given to the home authorities for the manner in which their patronage has been employed. It is very long since a boon companion or other disreputable member of the church has been appointed to either of the three Presidencies; and the most that can now be charged against the clerical establishment of India, is in some cases a mistaken zeal, which generally speaking defeats the object which it was intended to attain.

An appointment at either of the Presidencies is a matter of uncertainty, and the chaplain upon his arrival in India is usually sent to some distant station, where he is utterly devoid of all companionship with members of the clerical profession, and can meet with few or none whose studies, tastes, and pursuits have in any degree resembled his own. A clergyman often feels very deeply the want of sympathy on the part of his associates, and in some instances the consciousness of loneliness in the midst of a crowd, induces him to retire almost wholly within himself; the presence of a chaplain at a station being frequently only known by the zealous performance of the duties of his office. There is indeed considerable difficulty in marking out the path which it is most desirable for a clergyman to pursue with respect to society. His presence at all the gaieties of a station, however innocent and harmless they might be, would tend to lessen the respect for his cloth, while his entire withdrawal from all social meetings is certainly disadvantageous; it tends in the first instance to establish a clique or religious coterie, composed of persons who make great pretensions, and who in rendering their circle exclusive, deprive the rest of the community of every opportunity of spiritual profit, not attainable by attendance at church. There can be nothing in reality more anti-Christian than the determination but too often manifested, to avoid all intercourse with persons whose religious views do not coincide with the strict ideas entertained by others belonging to the same church. It is at variance with that universal charity preached by the great founder of our religion, and which should regulate every thought and feeling of those who profess to believe in and follow his precepts. Without entering into any question concerning the misemployment of time, at balls and gaieties of any kind, it may be said that it is quite sufficient for those who have tender consciences upon such subjects, and who really believe that they are committing sin in frequenting places of public amusement, to remain away from them. But with this they are not content, they go much farther, denouncing as utterly reprobate, all who indulge in what they are pleased to term forbidden things, and doing great injury to religion by displaying it in a revolting form. They should consider that in India especially, when a complete separation takes place between those who cling to the vanities of the world, and those who have given them all up for conscience' sake, the former are left utterly without the chance of benefiting by sober conversation, since they have not, as in England, the resource offered by other professing Christians who do not carry their views quite so far. Hypocrisy in religion is perhaps much less frequent than is usually supposed, and those who have been close observers of mankind, will generally give credit for perfect sincerity to persons who voluntarily embrace a strict mode of life, not unattended with disadvantage to themselves, and certainly distasteful to others. But while they feel convinced that they are pursuing the right path, they should pity rather than condemn those who have not yet found it, and who fancy that they may be equally acceptable in the eyes of the Creator. If a clergyman possessed the means of rendering his home agreeable, and of establishing conversaziones of a serious, but not of a strictly religious nature, it would do much towards the infusion of a kind spirit throughout the society, and of inducing many to think very deeply upon subjects to which they have previously given little consideration. Hitherto the customs and usages of India have been against cheap and intellectual amusement. Dinners and suppers have only been thought worthy of attendance, but no persons could with a better chance of success introduce tea parties, in which science, astronomical and botanical science especially, and natural history, might be brought in aid of an exposition of the wonderful works of God. Clergymen in India should not disdain those popular arts which would render their society courted, and which, without compromising themselves in any way, or derogating from the character which it is their duty as well as their interest to preserve, would prevent the estrangement between themselves and the gayer portion of their flock which forms at present so great a barrier to religious improvement. A microscope on an extensive scale, and a few of those amusing experiments in chemistry, which tend so much to the advancement of science at home, together with the developement of the natural productions of India, would blend instruction and entertainment very judiciously together; and ultimately prove highly beneficial in exalting the pursuits of the young and idle, and bringing forward many of the neglected treasures of the richest soil in the world.

The Padre, as he is called in India, is always a personage whom the natives are inclined to regard with very great respect; all castes and classes, both of Mahomedans and Hindoos, are highly religious people; and nothing so strongly tends to exalt the European character in their eyes, than attendance at public worship, in an edifice built expressly for the purpose, a church worthy of the notions they themselves entertain of the great Creator of the world. They look up to the officiating clergyman as a man whom they would feel inclined to reverence, and there can be very little doubt, that had the life of the late lamented Bishop Heber been spared, his example would have produced the most beneficial results to the community at large. It would require perhaps the talents as well as the zeal of that amiable and accomplished man, to effect the object for which he was so eminently qualified: but though few may be equally gifted, his example should be followed by all, who to the learning necessary to their profession, possess cultivated minds. The house of the clergyman should be the resort of Mahomedans and Hindoos, Jew and Gentile, and he should especially endeavour to induce the higher classes of natives to attend at all the social meetings held there.

A clergyman soon after his arrival in India has the mortification to discover that he cannot make converts of his own servants, and that unless he should be content with an inferior class of domestics, and run the risk of being compelled to support them whether they turn out well or ill, he must be content to have pagans and infidels about him. It is useless to try to begin with the lower and uneducated classes of adults, and hitherto little or no attempt has been made to effect the conversion of the higher orders. The first step would certainly be to conciliate them, to enlarge their minds, to direct their tastes to higher objects than those which have hitherto occupied both; and to show the character of the Christian pastor in its brightest point of view. Natives of rank would be proud and pleased by any attention upon the part of the Padre, who, if well-versed in the language, would have frequent opportunities in adverting to the Scriptures, to sow good seed, and without any formal pretensions to the character of a teacher, would in all probability do much towards effecting the end in view. The small progress, which notwithstanding the zealous efforts of numbers of pious men, Christianity has hitherto made in India, shows that there is some defect in the system. There is a wide field open for the labors of those who earnestly desire to confer the inestimable blessings of the gospel upon men whose gross religious delusions lead to an incalculable sum of misery and crime. Amid the studies of a clergyman he will strive to acquaint himself with the manners, habits, character, and wants of the people; with the view of rendering the labors of the missionaries belonging to the Established Church, useful. The large military stations in India are some of the last places in which religious instruction can be entered upon with a fair chance of effecting good amongst the native population, who are generally speaking, satisfied with their own condition and averse to change. It is in the hilly and wild districts, amid persons in a more barbarous state, ignorant of many of the useful arts cultivated in the plains, and unacquainted with the value of the natural products of the soil, and with the means of turning them to beneficial account, either as articles of merchandize or of home consumption, that the labors of the missionary would most avail. Men sitting themselves down in the midst of such a community, who would begin by ameliorating the condition of these wretched people, starving in the midst of wealth, and who die of hunger in a country where corn would abound, and which is teeming with oil, would become the benefactors, and ultimately the saviours of whole districts. The influence of the Brahmins which is so strongly felt in the more civilized parts of India, becomes faint and weak in these remote and uncultivated scenes, the people are free from the prejudices of caste, and ready to embrace a religion which comes recommended to them by practical good. Even if the expectations entertained upon the subject of the conversion of these miserable races, should be too sanguine, how can Christian missionaries be better employed, than in a work of so much charity towards their less fortunate brethren, degraded nearly to a level with the beasts of the field, wholly on account of the absence of all instruction from persons qualified to direct their labors. If settled down in some convenient spot upon the borders of these desolate regions, for the places inhabited by wild Bheels, wild Gonds, and the nearly equally savage population of the Kole country, would perhaps be untenable to an

European; means would easily be found to establish a communication with the interior, and in a very short time the advantage resulting from the advice and assistance of a superior mind, would be discovered and appreciated. In many places the most common arts are unknown, and in others, in which the soil more niggard, denies sustenance to a scanty and stunted population, the science of more advanced nations could be brought in aid of the coal and iron which they afford. No one should neglect or despise a beginning however small; the rapid extension of the potatoe in the Himalaya mountains, shows how much good a single individual may effect, and though the resident clergy cannot themselves make pilgrimages to these remote scenes, they may acquire very considerable knowledge concerning them for the purpose of animating the zeal of missionaries already in India, or who may be willing to turn their steps from Great Britain to the East. It is astonishing that so little has been attempted in the Himalaya, which, while it would afford a delightful residence to European families, offers a field of the highest promise for the labors of the missionary. It may be safely said that in these splendid territories, ignorance is the sole drawback to human happiness. They have now become the resort of the gay and idle portion of the Anglo-Indian community, who intent only upon their own interests and convenience, care not how much they deteriorate the native character by encouraging its cupidity. It is therefore the more incumbent upon those who have the good of mankind at heart, to do their utmost to counteract the evils which have already resulted from intercourse with Europeans, not entered upon by the latter with any benevolent view for the improvement of their less fortunate brethren.

To return to the situation in which a clergyman feels himself placed, when performing the duties of a chaplain in

India; one of the great difficulties which he has to encounter, arises from the offence which is so frequently taken at the tone of a sermon. A clergyman preaching before a large and mixed congregation, may lash at vice with the hope of awakening the attention of the sinner to a sense of his delinquencies, without making him the mark of public reprobation. In small societies it is different; however general the censure may be, it is invariably supposed to be purposely levelled at some person, known or suspected to have an inclination for the species of criminal indulgence alluded to; and the clergyman is very unjustly considered to have exceeded his duty in thus directing attention to an individual who has provoked his censure. It would be impertinent to offer any advice upon the subject, and the fact is only stated to shew the necessity of some caution upon a point of great importance, since of course it will be the object of every clergyman to benefit the flock placed under his care, and this cannot be effected without great consideration respecting the means to be employed. The "ears polite" to which the sermon is addressed, may be for ever closed by some inadvertent sentence twisted into a personality, and though it behoves a clergyman to be fearless in the execution of his duty, he will do well to avoid all unnecessary display of severity, and to invite and persuade, rather than revile and condemn.

A clergyman should possess a good library of the best theological works, both for the advantage of himself, and of others; for he may find himself involved in arguments and subtleties which it will require all the wisdom contained in these volumes to refute. Well educated natives are fond of entering into religious disquisitions, and it is of great importance that they should find persons able and willing to answer all their questions, and who they discover to be well versed in their own peculiar tenets, and inclined to treat the subject with temper. Of all the causes which have retarded the spread of the Christian religion in the east, mistaken zeal has been the most active.

There are many persons in India who feel the most earnest desire to see the total overthrow of those revolting superstitions, which chain down the human mind, cherish all that is evil, and which are supported by rites and ceremonies abhorrent to every true Christian; but who do not join in the outcry raised concerning what is called British encouragement of idolatry. It is perhaps very difficult for persons who have never been in India, to discriminate between the actual sanction of idolatrous practices, and the necessity of keeping the peace upon occasions of religious ceremonies. Interference with the prejudices of the natives, and especially those respecting the forms prescribed by their creed, would be highly impolitic, and even dangerous; and though possibly in the desire to conciliate, some of the authorities of India may have inadvertently given reason to suppose that they believed in the pretensions put forth by the Brahmins in favour of their gods, in general we have confined ourselves to bare courtesies, which cannot convey any impression of the kind. The Hindoos and the Mahommedans go much farther in the respect which they pay to our religious festivals, and no one can accuse them of regarding the Christian religion as superior to their own. Were they as well acquainted with the circumstance of our keeping Easter, they would come with their offerings; but Christmas is the only festival belonging to the Protestant church of which they are at all aware, and every European resident finds his house adorned with garlands upon that day. Large trees, plantains especially, are taken up by the roots, and stuck in the ground close to the pillars of the verandah, which are wreathed in festoons with flowers and fruit. Should the plantains take root, and flourish, it is considered to be a lucky omen, and they are anxious to afford us all the advantage of it. The Ayahs delight in dressing their ladies for church, and the other servants attend upon the equipages with great alacrity, the whole surrounding community shewing by every means in their power, their willingness to evince their respect for a day celebrated by us in commemoration of the great event to which we owe our salvation. For myself I am not ashamed to say, that the first Christmas day which I spent in India, was ushered in by a flood of tears. When I saw the house decorated with garlands, and the servants coming with flowers in their hands as gifts, and making more than their usual number of salaams, I was deeply affected by being thus saluted by pagans, in a pagan land. The guns which we cause to be fired at their festivals are nothing more than a return for these gracious offices, and are considered exactly in the same point of view. The omission of these acts of civility on the part of the authorities will be attributed by the natives to the cabals of the missionaries, to whom they are quite ready to impute a design of inducing the Government to interfere with the religion of the country, and the consequence will be increased hostility towards a class of men, who might, if their zeal was tempered by discretion, render themselves eminently useful. So much good might be done in India by the missionaries, if they would only pursue the most obvious means, and content themselves with instructing the multitudes who are willing to learn; that it is lamentable to see time wasted and money misemployed in raising a senseless clamour at home, about things with which we have no earthly business; and which will give occasion to enemies to say, that we only create this outcry to conceal our want of success in the progress of conversion.

The grand error which the Christian rulers and residents in India have committed, is their neglecting to shew that we have a religion. There are so few outward observances connected with our simple form of worship, and so few festivals to attract the attention of strangers, that it is the more incumbent upon us to build churches in order to convince the natives of India, that we believe in the existence of a God. All persons who have considered the subject at all, and who have had opportunities of becoming acquainted with the impression it has made upon both Mahommedans and Hindoos, deeply lament that we should continue to manifest such culpable indifference towards a point of the very highest importance, both as regards our own spiritual wants, and the good opinion of the people whom we govern. Dr. Spry in his excellent work, "Modern India," particularly adverts to the prejudice occasioned by this culpable neglect; he tells us that in conversation with respectable natives, he has been frequently asked whether his nation had any places set apart for religious worship, and was assured that the English could have no veneration for God, since they shewed more regard to the erection and decoration of their domestic dwellings, than to the building of temples for his honour. "How is it," continues Dr. Spry, "that after years of labour on the part of the Parent Society, in the selection of devout, zealous, and intelligent missonaries to preach the gospel in our Indian empire, that the cause has made such little progress? It is because they have no decent or respectable place of worship to which they might invite their benighted brethren, and which would afford suitable accommodation to the better classes, who, if wrought upon to admit the truth of revelation, would induce their inferiors to follow their example. In order to make an impression upon the minds of the ignorant of all nations, the spirit of religion must be supported by an observance of external rites; and with the idolatrous people of Hindostan this necessity is paramount." The scarcity of Christian churches in India was sensibly felt by the late excellent Bishop Heber, and every clergyman who has followed in his steps laments with equal sincerity the difficulties thrown in his way by the want of a suitable edifice for the performance of divine service. It will scarcely be credited, that in a large station like Cawnpore, there is no such thing; an old bungalow has been fitted up at one end of the cantonments for the purpose of affording accommodation to the Europeans located in that vicinity, while the riding school of a dragoon regiment effects the same object at the other end of the lines. To a devout Christian it is a subject of indifference where he offers up his praise and thanksgiving to the giver of all good, and in Christian countries it matters little how lowly and humble the edifice may be which is devoted to the service of the Creator; but in India the case assumes a different aspect, and if we had studied how to degrade our religion in the eyes of the natives, we could not have done it more effectually than by performing divine worship in a stable.

Another serious drawback to the happiness of a clergyman in India, is the want of pastoral care. In England he usually forms the connecting link between the rich and the poor, he is personally acquainted with the humblest of his parishioners, and finds one of his greatest pleasures in sitting down in the poor man's dwelling, and imparting to him consolation and instruction. The barracks of European soldiers form a poor substitute for the cottage of the rustic laborer, or the chamber of the mechanic; and many clergymen have found it more advisable to invite those who manifest any desire to listen to him, to attend at his own house, than to visit them in their noisy barracks, where his presence is considered an intrusion. The fluctuating state of society in India, and the difficulty which the majority of the Company's servants find in making their allowances meet their expenditure, prevent a clergyman from the performance of many works of charity and utility. He cannot interest his auditors in subjects which he may consider to be of deep importance, they are here to-day, and gone to-morrow; they will never see the fruits of their own exertions in the good cause, and perhaps cannot afford the pecuniary supply necessary to carry them into effect. Nevertheless something may be done. A school for the support of destitute children of all castes and denominations, ought to be established at all large stations, similar to that which has succeeded so well in Calcutta. Many of the ladies belonging to the station might be induced to exert themselves in the good cause, and to promote, if not to teach, those useful arts which will enable the female portion to earn a respectable subsistence in after life. The children belonging to the Free School in Calcutta, were found very expert in making lace, the slender delicate fingers which characterize a native being particularly adapted for the purpose, while little ornamental works made at the school, and assisted by the ingenuity of its patronesses, would form the material for a Fancy Fair, an appropriate jubilee for the cold weather.

The life of a clergyman in India it will be seen affords sufficient employment both mental and physical, and generally speaking, there is no want of energy and enterprise on the part of those who perform the duties of the holy office in our Asiatic territories. But however usefully and laboriously employed, as it has been before remarked, the existence of a chaplain is apt to become too much isolated, too exclusively devoted to a small circle, who withdraw themselves from their fellows, and neither visit nor receive visits from those who differ from them respecting the sacrifices of social enjoyment alleged to be required by the Christian religion. It is of the utmost consequence, and therefore no apology need be made for the repetition, that the young and idle should not be driven from the house of the clergyman by injudicious severity, or that in the dearth of all comparatively innocent amusements, they should be compelled to resort to drinking and gaming as the means of producing the excitement so necessary to support life in exile; while to exhibit religion under a stern and sullen aspect, is to counteract the great design of the Creator, and pervert the blessings which he has showered upon man. An acquaintance with astronomical science would, as has been previously stated, be the means of attracting all those Europeans who possess enquiring minds, to the house of the person who should endeavour to elevate their pursuits, while the natives would find the greatest attraction in a telescope. In social meetings established for the purpose of inquiry into the most popular branches of philosophy, there could not possibly be any offence, and they would afford innumerable opportunities of awakening feelings which other methods have failed to arouse. It is indeed rather extraordinary that nothing of the kind has hitherto been attempted by either of the two learned professions, stationed in the Provinces of India, and that the medical fraternity particularly should not have enlisted the intelligent portion of their acquaintance in the cause. In England nearly every parish now boasts its literary and scientific institution, yet scarcely anything of the kind has been thought of in a scene so well calculated to afford subjects of discussion of the highest interest, and while Calcutta may be called a hot-bed of science, there is no institution for its promotion beyond the seat of Government.

No person who has remained for any lengthened period in India, can have failed to observe that one of the greatest drawbacks to happiness to the residents, is the want of profitable employment. Professional duties occupy a considerable portion of the time of many of the military, and nearly all of the Company's civil servants; but still the great bulk of the Anglo-Indian community have literally nothing to do. Ennui consequently prevails, and conversation being limited to a few topics, gossip and scandal become paramount subjects of interest. Very little variety in the shape of mere amusement is attainable, it is seldom possible out of Calcutta to get up anything like good music, the accomplishment, owing to various adverse circumstances, being little cultivated. Science seems to be the natural resource, and if pains were taken to render it entertaining as well as instructive, it would speedily become exceedingly attractive. In England the galleries devoted to practical science are crowded with women and children, who take the strongest interest in all that is going on, the most distinguished philosopher not disdaining to lead the mind to higher studies, by the exhibition of toys and playthings. In this manner science might be made to supply the desideratum so much wanted in India; for curiosity once awakened, would be ever craving for something new. As a beginning, the establishment of Horticultural Societies at large stations, on the same plan as that of Calcutta, would doubtless conduce very strongly to the general improvement. Native gardeners stimulated by the hope of prizes, would exert themselves in the production and dissemination of the finest varieties of fruit and vegetables, while an institution of this kind might be easily extended, and would naturally lead to others equally beneficial. No large station in India should be without a public garden, and nothing would be less difficult than to find a piece of ground well adapted for the purpose, and already furnished with ornamental buildings, tombs, or pavilions, which might be converted into libraries or museums. A menagerie attached to this garden for the reception of zoological specimens from the neighbouring, or more distant districts, would add a very attractive feature, and in all probability induce the wealthy portion of the natives to subscribe towards its maintenance. During the cold weather the exhibition of flowers and fruits might be rendered still more interesting by the addition of a Fancy Fair, for the sale of the products of feminine ingenuity. This experiment has been successfully tried in the

Hill districts, and there is no reason why it should not be made during the cold season at every station in the North-Western Provinces, the proceeds being appropriated to some useful purpose. Fancy Fairs would be the means of bringing the Anglo-Indian community together for the furtherance of a national object, and afford a point of union with the natives which it is always advantageous to establish. Such an institution, if properly conducted, might, and doubtless would, lead to the most desirable results. It would not be difficult to add some new feature, popular lectures upon chemistry, or meetings for the purpose of developing the internal resources of India; correspondents of the learned societies of Calcutta would read their communications to an attentive audience previous to their dispatch, and the spirit now confined to a comparatively few learned persons, would be generally diffused throughout the whole community.

Hitherto little or no attention has been paid to the best means of conciliating the respectable classes of natives, and of establishing a bond of intercourse between them and the Europeans resident in the country. Many circumstances have combined to prevent the association of persons who entertain strong prejudices against each other, and have at present few, if any, tastes in common; nor would it be possible while Mohammedans and Hindoos remain so scrupulous regarding their food, to induce them to join circles, meeting apparently for the sole purpose of eating and drinking. The time however is approaching in which Anglo-Indians will see and feel the necessity of making some endeavour to cultivate the good opinion of the native society to whom they must look for the greater portion of the pecuniary means necessary for the carrying on of every undertaking of extensive utility. It is time that something should be done for the general improvement, since the eyes of Europe are now fixed upon India, and its British residents will find no sympathy in their prejudices, no participation in the narrow mindedness which has hitherto influenced the conduct pursued towards the native inhabitants, who cannot remain much longer in their present position. There are no persons whose examples and precepts would do more towards the establishment of friendly intercourse, by means of agreeable and rational amusements, than the clerical servants of the Company. Chaplains not being liable to such frequent changes of residence as individuals belonging to other branches of the service, and having also the advantage of appointments at the principal stations, can by the comparative permanency of their abode, effect many useful objects which others less happily circumstanced might vainly attempt. Even if it should not appear desirable to take a very active part in the undertakings that might involve discussions foreign to their sacred calling, still by affording at their own houses the opportunity of mental improvement, the chaplains of India would confer an incalculable benefit upon society. The want of public libraries is severely felt in all large stations, the regimental and other book clubs which are numerous, not embracing works required by the student, who has higher objects in view than the mere passing away of time. All persons therefore who would interest themselves in the formation of a library, which should comprise the standard works upon subjects connected with useful knowlege, would be public benefactors, and though the commencement of such an undertaking might be attended with many difficulties, if zealously pursued it must ultimately succeed. It is indeed rather surprising, that so very few establishments of the kind are to be found throughout the provinces of India; but if the same activity upon the part of the lovers of science should be manifested, as that which characterizes the sporting world, who keep up packs of hounds at an enormous expence, build theatres, and run horses, there can be no doubt that it would be attended with the same success. Members of the two learned professions, for law according to its accceptance at home has no representatives beyond the Presidencies, the clerical and medical servants of the Company, should therefore assiduously unite in inculcating the necessity of taking some steps to redeem the Anglo-Indian character from the imputations of an apathetic neglect of the means they possess of emulating the progress of improvement at home.

CHAPTER XV.

THE OVERLAND JOURNEY.

THE length of the voyage to India has been the principal, if not the only cause which has prevented travellers, anxious to make themselves acquainted with foreign countries, from visiting the Company's Asiatic territories. Yet even with this drawback it is scarcely possible to account for the apathy manifested towards scenes of the highest degree of beauty and interest, full of every thing that can delight and expand the mind. Whether we regard its antiquities, its rich products, or the various races of people spread over the vast surface of this splendid empire, we find almost boundless fields for research;—an inexhaustible source of intellectual enjoyment. In all other countries of Asia, India is celebrated for its umbrageous groves and sparkling waters; the trees and rivers which offer all of shade and refreshment, which enter into the national idea of paradise. The greater portion of the Peninsula may be traversed with ease, and the trifling difficulties to be encountered in Malabar and less accessible places, are merely sufficient to enhance the excitement of the journey. Since the occupation of the Himalaya mountains, the Neilgherries, and other hill districts, the climate, represented as so formidable, has lost all its terrors. By properly timing the arrival in India, no inconvenient degree of heat need be sustained, and in the Northern Provinces especially, the weather will be found most delightful, the air being bracingly cold, while the sun shines brightly from a sky without a cloud. Even in Bengal the whole day may be passed out of doors with no other shelter than an umbrella, and this season lasts from the middle of October, until the commencement of March; while in the Upper Provinces the great heats do not set in until April. There is therefore ample time permitted to travel leisurely throughout the most interesting parts of the plains, the hills affording a delightful retreat during the hot season. Notwithstanding all these advantages, the list of persons travelling through India merely for the gratification of laudable curiosity, or in the prosecution of some scientific pursuit, is so scanty that we are at a loss to understand how it could possibly happen that while all other practicable parts of the world should have been absolutely overrun by English tourists, so few should have bent their steps towards a country which may truly be termed the cradle of European science. Lady Hood is the only English lady who penetrated the interior for the sake of making herself acquainted with the interesting features of the country; Lord Valentia one of the few, perhaps, the only Englishman unconnected either by public duties or commercial enterprise, who paid it a visit; the catalogue of foreign names is not much longer, while, considering the vast number of intelligent persons attached to the British civil and military service or to whom India has been the scene of mercantile speculation, it is still more astonishing that the country should remain a sort of *terra incognita* to the greater number of English readers. Without in the slightest degree desiring to lessen the merit of the numerous valuable works which we possess concerning the British territories in the East, and which if extensively perused, would afford ample information concerning nearly all that is curious or interesting in those singular and magnificent provinces; it must be admitted that until Bishop Heber entered the field, no writer ever strove to make the subject universally popular. Ponderous quartos were brought forth, which absolutely alarmed the reader, and so paralyzing was their effect, that it may be safely asserted that notwithstanding the exciting nature of the subject, a single number of the "Bengal Sporting Magazine" would attract much greater attention at the present day than the splendid volume of Captain Williamson's "Wild Sports of the East," which has never found its way into general circulation. The associations connected with India, if we except the prevailing notion, that gold was a drug, principally consisted of heat and tigers; the alternations of climate, the extraordinary degree of cold experienced in some parts of the country during several months of the year, never being mentioned as circumstances favourable to the European traveller. Bishop Heber's work has been succeeded by many others of a similar character, and it may be hoped that such men as Mr. Scrope will be induced to go out to India by way of varying the sport of deer stalking, with a little tiger shooting, or buffalo hunting, which is still more exciting. It would then be seen that, although rich in exterior attractions, India is in fact a very poor country, its treasures being now inaccessible to its inhabitants, on account of their poverty; and that European capital, and European science, are required to open those mines of wealth which it possesses, and which have been overlooked or disregarded for ages. The outward show and splendour of style of living in India, has blinded the greater number of persons to the truth; so far from being able to afford encouragement to useful or elegant arts, few of the Anglo-Indian population have any money to spare after the necessary expenditures of their households have been defrayed. The natives also, with few exceptions, if sufficiently wealthy to assist in those public improvements which the advanced state of civilization in India would seem to demand, have not been made to comprehend their utility, and every observant traveller who perceives the wants of the country, and can point out the methods by which its rich products, its coal and iron, and dyes and drugs can be rendered available, will, by attracting public attention to the scene, confer an inestimable benefit upon millions now languishing in the most sordid poverty. That the higher classes of natives of India will gladly turn any capital which they may possess to account, there can be no doubt; only once acquaint them with the method in which they may best benefit their estates. The immense numbers of public buildings reared all over the country by private individuals at their own expence, shew that liberality and enterprise are not wanting, and that there would be little or no difficulty in persuading them to devote both to useful purposes. Inland steam navigation will doubtless prove the means of inciting the native population to great activity; and when they find Europeans settled amongst them, and deriving great advantages from commercial and agricultural speculations they will follow the example, and exert their utmost endeavours to share in the benefit. A spur is now required to the enterprise of Great Britain which hitherto has only seized upon temporal and merely personal advantages, and overlooked the great truth, that in making India rich, in encouraging its manufactures, we shall create wants which will induce its multitudinous natives to supply themselves with foreign products, and that when rendered cheap enough to be extensively purchased at home, the demand will be so great for sugar, &c., that however immense the supply, there will be little left for exportation. Give him the means, and the poor native will indulge in the sugar on which he fattens, will clothe his body in decent garments, and add to all his household effects; while those of a higher class will begin to adorn their houses, and decorate their persons with articles from the warehouses of European capitalists. The natives of British India have remained unchangeable in their habits, because no motives or temptations to change have been offered them. It is not by glutting their bazaars with foreign commodities for which at present they scarcely know the use, that we can induce them to take our manufactures. They must first be enabled to indulge freely in native luxuries, to perceive that their own interests are involved in the improvement of their property by the introduction of novel methods of cultivation, &c., by employing the coal and iron which, connected with the new power now brought in aid of skill and enterprise, offer boundless sources of wealth. It is indeed to this new power that we must look for the regeneration of India. The country is now open to us, and its resources have been made known by the surest guides, the scientific societies which both in the Peninsula and at home, have been so usefully and honourably employed in developing the capabilities of our magnificent eastern empire. Still a great deal remains to be done, which might be effected by tourists. The Anglo-Indian community have hitherto resembled the natives in the sameness of the routine established amongst them. There is nothing like variety in their pursuits, habit in some instances perhaps, occasioned by necessity, has chained them down to a dull round of vapid amusements, in which there is neither interest nor novelty. What an impetus would be given to society, by the transit of an invalid duchess, who labouring under some nervous ailment, brought on by too much luxury at home, would derive more advantage from an overland journey to the Himalaya, than by pilgrimages to the theatres of the most celebrated quacks of Europe. How many objects of interest and attraction, would a rich and intellectual lady find in her tour throughout the country, and how efficiently might she aid the few persons of wealth and rank which she would find there, who would willingly set many improvements afloat, could they find means to make a commencement. The observations also of persons fresh from Europe, bringing with them its latest fashions, not merely of dress or ornament, but of thought and feeling, would do much towards the creation of new ideas. Persons who go out to reside in India and who belong to either service, are expected to fall into the common routine, but a traveller, being a sort of lion, would obtain more influence, his tastes would be consulted, and his suggestions would, if not immediately adopted, prove the precursors of many beneficial changes.

The comparative accessibility of India by means of the Overland Journey, will, it is to be hoped, induce many wealthy and intellectual persons, to visit it in quest of amusement; while it offers to those whose duties call them to the British territories, a most delightful alternative to the long and tedious voyage. The route recommended by Mr. Waghorn, to whose unceasing perseverance the public is mainly indebted for the facilities of the new plan, is from London to Marseilles, and thence by the French steamer to Egypt. He informs us in a pamphlet which he has published for the guidance of travellers, that he found that this journey might be accomplished in a manner combining comfort, amusement, and expedition. Even in the winter he appears to think this route preferable to the voyage from Falmouth, inasmuch, as the traveller escapes the horrors of the Bay of Biscay. Should dispatch be a desideratum, it may be better attained by a journey which admits of the speed of a courier; while under circumstances of less exigency, the traveller will have an opportunity of remaining long enough at Boulogne, Paris, Chalons, Lyons, Marseilles, Leghorn, Civita Vecchia, Naples, Malta, Syra, and Alexandria, to see what is best worthy of observation in all. Persons desirous to proceed by Mr. Waghorn's directions, must first apply to Captain Grindlay, No. 16, Captain Barber, 64, Cornhill, or Stocqueler and Co., 5, King William Street, at least a week previous to their projected departure, and intimate their intention of proceeding to Egypt *viâ* France.

Those gentlemen will afford the necessary information, and the aid of their establishments in facilitating the arrangements. Personal application for passports are to be made at the French Passport Office, No. 6, Poland Street, on one day, and on the following the party thus applying, will receive the document, gratis. Forty pounds will cover the expenses to Egypt, a journey which if performed with due attention to economy, may be accomplished for thirty, while second class passengers, who may wish to adopt a still more frugal plan, can get to Alexandria for twenty-five pounds; and thence on to India for seventy pounds more. Captains Grindlay and Barber forward the baggage to Mr. Waghorn's agent, and send one of their clerks to the Commercial Steam Packet Company's Offices, Fish Street Hill, to book the places for cabin passengers in the next packet to Boulogne, to which place the fare is twelve shillings. These packets usually start an hour before high water, and arrive in Boulogne in about twelve hours. On landing, the party is recommended to proceed to the Hotel de Londres, kept by Boutroy, where excellent accommodation is to be found. A seat in the *coupé* of the diligence to Paris is forty-two francs, and the time occupied twenty-five hours. Should the traveller remain more than a day or two at Paris, Mr. Waghorn recommends the boarding house of Mrs. Mills, No. 11 Bis, Rue des Capucines, and for a shorter sojourn, Meurice's Hotel. Places by either of the two routes to Lyons are booked at Messrs. Lafitte, Caillard, & Co., Messageries Royales, and should always be secured some time beforehand, since they are much in demand, for the *coupé* especially. It will be necessary to get the passport signed for Marseilles. One route to Lyons is performed entirely by the diligence, and occupies three days; the other by the diligence to Chalons sur Saone, and thence by the steamer to Lyons. The Hotel du Parc, kept by Monsieur Preta, is a great resort of the English; and the traveller, who arrives in two days from Paris to Chalons, will have the option of remaining, or proceeding immediately by one of the steamers which start twice a day—at four and seven o'clock, P. M. A pleasant trip of ten hours on the Saone, brings the steamer to Lyons, for which the passage money is twelve francs. If in summer, it is recommended to proceed down the Rhone, by steamer to Avignon, in preference to taking the diligence direct to Marseilles. By the Rhone the passage will occupy twelve hours, at the rate of thirteen miles an hour, including stoppages; for although the distance is one hundred and fifty miles, the current is full five or six miles in favor of the passage all the way, during which the boat passes under at least thirty bridges, chiefly on the suspension principle, while the views of the surrounding scenery are most delightful. The passage-money from Lyons to Avignon is fifty francs. The house which Mr. Waghorn recommends at Avignon as a most comfortable one, is the Hotel de l'Europe, whence he informs us diligences start three or four times a day for Marseilles, the fair being sixteen francs. One of these diligences starts at 6 P. M., about an hour after the arrival of the first steamer from Lyons. "I should here observe," continues Mr. Waghorn, "that the French Government steamers leave Marseilles on the 1st, 11th, and 21st of each month, at five P. M., and as they are usually very full of passengers, particularly in summer, care should be taken to secure berths beforehand, which may be done through my agents at Marseilles, Messrs R. Gower and Co., on application to Mr. Wheatley, at my office, No. 71, Cornhill, London. The whole fare is required on securing a berth, one half being forfeited if the party do not proceed (see Tables onwards), this may be arranged at Mr. Wheatley's previous to starting thence. A more delightful trip, than that offered by these packets, particularly in summer, can scarcely be imagined; the passengers being so often in port and ashore, that the voyage rather resembles a cruize of pleasure. On arriving at Alexandria, the traveller on presenting a letter from Captain Grindlay, or Mr. Wheatley, to my agent at that place, will be provided with a faithful servant, who will act as his guide, and safely conduct him to my agent at Cairo, to whom a letter of introduction can be given. On the traveller's arrival at Cairo, where every comfort will await him, he will visit the Pyramids, the Citadel, Caliph's Tomb, Joseph's Well, &c. &c., where camels, dromedaries, tents, &c., with horses and donkeys and all other requisites, if ladies and children be of the party, will be procured for his journey to Suez, a distance of eighty-four miles. On the other hand, should he desire to visit Thebes, boats will be procured for him through the same channel. The traveller need be under no apprehension of robbery or molestation in any shape; his person and property being as safe as in a journey through England. The mails to India leave Suez for Mocha, regularly every 3 days after their arrival at Alexandria, by the Falmouth line of steamers; and with these mails, the traveller may proceed to Mocha, where steamers and all other vessels to India are in waiting. There is so much in the way of antiquities to interest the traveller in the vicinity of Cairo, that he will be amply rewarded for his stay there, until the departure of the next month's mail from Suez. Passengers going to Thebes will find opportunities every three or four days at Cosseir, to proceed thence in the native boats of the Red Sea to Juddah, whence my agent will forward them to Mocha, to proceed by the conveyance which will take the mails on to India. The steamers from Suez will always call for passengers, &c., at Cosseir and Juddah, on their way down the Red Sea. Passengers to India are of course aware, that the *Hugh Lindsay* has been ordered by the Honorable Court of Directors to go between Suez and Mocha, and the *Atalanta* and *Berenice* to go between Mocha and India; and that thus steam navigation between England

and India is rapidly advancing to a system by this route. As servants may not always be ready on the spot at Alexandria, it would be advisable for passengers to apprize my agent at that place, through Capt. Grindlay or Mr. Wheatley, of the opportunity by which they are proceeding thither, and what accommodations they will require on their arrival, when they will find every thing prepared for them; and as a guarantee against any loss which may accrue to my agency, in providing for passengers who may be prevented from proceeding, a deposit in advance of ten pounds with Captain Grindlay, or Mr. Wheatley, will be required. Passengers may of course take any quantity of luggage they please. They will require a canteen proportionate to their number. Sovereigns are the best form in which they can provide themselves with money, and should they not care to burthen themselves with any sum beyond the forty pounds required to defray expenses to Alexandria, any surplus can be paid into the hands of Mr. Wheatley, who will give a receipt for it, and an order upon myself in India for the amount. Beds being furnished in the French steamers, it will be well for the passengers to provide themselves with ticking for beds and pillow cases, which they can have stuffed with cotton at Alexandria, by which method the expence and annoyance of carrying bedding from England, will be avoided. The wants of passengers being so various, it is impossible to fix a charge for travelling through Egypt under my agency; the only method is for the parties to pay for what they may respectively require. English hotels, as well as lodging houses, are established at Alexandria and Cairo, and houses both furnished and unfurnished, may be obtained by those who prefer them. English medical men are also practising at both places."

In a M.S. note appended to a copy of Mr. Waghorn's Guide, obligingly furnished by Mr. Wheatley, for the purpose of rendering the overland communication to India more extensively known; it is stated that Mr. Waghorn has recently opened a boarding house at Suez, under the superintendence of an Englishman, where passengers will find every comfort. "My agent," continues our authority, "at Boulogne will require a fee of 10s. 6d., for receiving and taking charge of the luggage, and a similar fee will be received by Messrs. R. Gower and Co., of Marseilles, for securing each passage on board the steamer. The passage money from Marseilles to Alexandria, should be paid in London, to Mr. Wheatley, for which he will give a receipt, at the same time writing to Messrs. Gower and Co., to secure and pay for a place in the steamer. The fees payable in Egypt, are five per cent on the cost of what the passenger may there require, and these fees which constitute the only profit of the agency, are more than compensated to him by the difference between the prices at which the agency can supply his wants, and those at which he could purchase the articles himself. Publications on Egypt, Syria, Palestine, Nubia, and Arabia, &c., as well as wine, spirits, beer, &c. &c., may be obtained on application to me or my agent at Cairo. Captain Grindlay being in constant communication with me, will at all times be in possession of the latest news from Egypt, and will be enabled to give every information as to the steamers, the locality of the plague, and all other matters which may be interesting to travellers." Those persons who can afford the luxurious conveyance by wheeled carriages across the desert, may proceed to Suez in vehicles adapted to the purpose, water being previously sent on for the horses. Bungalows are either built, or building for the accommodation of travellers, who may be unwilling to incur the fatigue of a journey without rest, under a roof, upon the road; and every day will render the route more smooth and agreeable. At present it is traversed by ladies and children without difficulty, and there is a project on foot to open a hotel at Cairo of the most splendid description.

It will be seen by the very copious extracts taken from Mr. Waghorn's Guide, that he strongly advocates the route from Marseilles, in preference to that by Falmouth, as being cheaper, more pleasant, and expeditious, and consequently the best. Mr. Wheatley who has most kindly afforded his assistance in adding to the information already extant upon this interesting subject, has forwarded the Table of Expences (annexed); £125 he informs us will cover the whole amount, per steam from London to Bombay, *viâ* Marseilles; but at least fifteen pounds more is required by passengers proceeding by Falmouth; that the former is the more expeditious not a doubt can exist, twenty or twenty-one days being the time occupied between London and Alexandria, while the latter averages ten days more. The French Government have it in contemplation still further to shorten the time, by having a direct line of steamers to Malta, instead of touching at the ports of Italy, by which a saving of three days will be effected. From Alexandria to Cairo, two days and a half are required, passage boats along the canal to Atfieh and then by the Nile, being the ordinary conveyance. Camels are always in readiness at Cairo, and the time occupied in crossing the desert to Suez, two days more, so that including all stoppages, passengers can be transported comfortably in six days.

The expence from	London to Marseilles is ..	£10	0	0
"	Marseilles to Alexandria ..	25	0	0
"	Alexandria to Suez	10	0	0
"	Suez to Bombay	80	0	0

It is necessary that all passengers should receive a letter of introduction to Mr. Waghorn's agent at Alexandria, from his London Office, 71, Cornhill, in order to secure to them his services or those of his agents in Egypt. There is nothing at present to prevent the practicability of this route at all seasons of the year, except the boisterous weather, which at particular periods must be encountered in the Red

Sea, and against which no vessel of less burthen than the *Great Western*, &c., can at all times contend: but it is not because at the commencement of this grand undertaking, we do not possess the whole of the gigantic means necessary for its full completion, that we should despair of gaining them at last. Taking into consideration the rapid strides which improvements are making in these days, and the value of the raw and manufactured products (tea and sugar) which in a short time may be ranked amongst the exportations from India, we may look forward to the most magnificent results:—steamers of the largest burthen on the Red Sea, and a railroad from Bombay to Calcutta. The practicability of the latter measure cannot be doubted, there being no obstacles which skill and perseverance could not overcome, while the wealth and intelligence of India, once brought into action, would suffice for any achievement. Notwithstanding the inducement which the Overland Journey to India holds out for visitants to proceed thither by the route now described to Bombay, it does not appear that anything has yet been effected for the accommodation of strangers at any public establishment opened at the latter named place. Calcutta has long boasted several excellent hotels, in which every comfort is provided at a moderate expence, while at the other Presidencies, demand must still be made upon private hospitality. This, it must be said, is always most cordially extended to those who come properly recommended. Of course the rich and great, travelling through India for pleasure would always find the best houses open to receive them, while scientific travellers would always be welcomed everywhere. There are other classes of persons, however, who might require accommodation at an hotel, and who could not fail to be astonished to find no house of public establishment open to receive them at a place like Bombay; but no doubt this desideratum will be supplied very shortly.* Although the cold season in the Bombay Presidency is not so bracing as in the N. W. Provinces, the weather admits of pleasant travelling after the rains have dried up, and there are few portions of the whole Peninsula which contain an equal number of places of interest and antiquity; it is to be hoped therefore, that fewer persons will in future stop short in Egypt. The establishment of steam navigation upon the Indus will enable the traveller to reach Loodiana in the most easy and agreeable manner, avoiding all the fatigue of a bad journey from Bombay to the Himalaya, which will now be as easily approachable as many places on the continent.

It is unnecessary to dilate upon the grandeur and novelty of the scenery afforded by the highest and most magnificent mountains in the world, since the splendid hill districts of India have employed many pens, and many pencils; and though of comparative late discovery, their beauties are more extensively known than those of the plains. The climate is delightful, any degree of temperature being attainable in the course of a few hours, summer heat being found in the valleys, while eternal winter reigns upon the snow clad peaks. Already there are roads formed to the frontiers of China, and in a short time there can be little doubt that the sources of the Ganges and Jumna, at present very difficult of access, will be rendered practicable to every visitant.

* It is understood that hotels are now building in Bombay.

JOURNEY FROM LONDON TO BOMBAY viâ FRANCE AND EGYPT, 1838.

WEDNESDAY, *April* 4.—Departed per *Steamer* from London Bridge, at 7 A. M., and arrived the same day at Boulogne, at 6 P. M. Lodged at Hotel de Londres.

SATURDAY, *April* 7.—Left Boulogne at 9 A. M. per *Diligence*, and arrived at Amiens at ½ past 9 P. M., hotel, where the Diligence changed. I might have gone direct from Boulogne to Paris, had it suited me.

SUNDAY, *April* 8.—Left Amiens at 6 P. M., per *Diligence*, and arrived at Paris, at 8 the next morning. At Paris lodged, at the Hotel de Lisle et d'Albion, Rue St. Thomas, du Louvre.

WEDNESDAY, *April* 11.—Left Paris per *Diligence*, at 7 P. M., for Chalons sur Saone, (by Troyes and Dijou, but I ought to have gone by Auxerres) and arrived there at 3 on Saturday morning. Staid a few hours at Dijou. At Chalons lodged, at " Les Trois Faisans.

SUNDAY, *April* 15.—Left Chalons per *Steamer*, on the Saone, at 5 this morning, and landed at Lyons at ½ past 2 in the afternoon. Lodged at Hotel du Parc.

TUESDAY, *April* 17.—Left Lyons per *Steamer* on the Rhone, at 5 A. M., and landed at Avignon at 5 in the evening. Dined there at the Hotel de l'Europe, and at 8 the same evening left per *Diligence* for Marseilles; arrived there about 10 the next morning. Lodged at Hotel Branrau.

From London to Marseilles, 14 days, including stoppages, viz. 2 days at Boulogne; 1 day at Amiens; nearly 3 days at Paris; 1 day at Chalons, and 1½ day at Lyons. The weather between London and Marseilles, was on the whole fine and mild.

SATURDAY, *April* 21.—Embarked at Marseilles, at 5 P. M. in the Steamer *Minos*. Arrived at Leghorn early in the morning of the 23rd; at Civita Vecchia the next morning; at Naples the next morning; and anchored at Malta, at 9 A. M. of the 27th, being the sixth day from Marseilles. We staid a few hours at Leghorn and Civita Vecchia, and landed there, but were not allowed to land at Naples. Fine weather and smooth sea generally all the way. Hotels at Malta, Morells, and the Clarence.

SATURDAY, *April* 28.—Left Malta per French Steamer, *Rhamses*, at 5 P. M., and anchored at Syra at 8 A. M., on Tuesday, the 1st May. Embarked the same day on board the French Steamer *Dante*, for Alexandria, and arrived there about 2 in the afternoon of Friday, the 4th May, being the thirteenth day from Marseilles. Hotel de l'Europe (the French Hotel) at Alexandria, and Hill's Hotel there, are both good.

MONDAY, *May* 7.—Embarked on the Mahmoodee Canal, about 5 in the evening, reached Atfee between 2 and 3 the next day. Embarked there on the Nile soon afterwards, and arrived at Cairo at noon, on Friday, the 11th May, having seen four nights and 3½ days in coming from Alexandria, which is considered a good voyage at this season. Paid 70 piasters for a boat from Alexandria to Atfee, and 250 for one from Atfee to Cairo. These boats afforded the room for two persons. One pound English money is equal to 97 or 98 piasters. Hill's Hotel at Cairo.

SATURDAY, *May* 12.—Left Cairo at 5 P. M., and arrived at Suez on Tuesday, (the 15th) at 8 A. M., having been three nights and two days in performing the journey. Travelled at night. There were three of us, and each person had a donkey, and a dromedary for his own use, and one camel for baggage. Scarcely used the dromedary. We paid Mr. Waghorn 50 dollars each, for providing donkeys, dromedaries, a small tent, eatables, wine, servants, and everything required for the journey. In crossing the desert, the heat during the day-time was great, and at Suez it was still greater, both during the night and day.

FRIDAY, *May* 18.—Embarked at Suez on the *Atalanta* Steamer, the evening of the 18th May, and arrived at Mocha on the 25th. Fine weather from Suez, and smooth sea. Heat extreme.

MONDAY, *June* 4.—Anchored at Bombay about 1 in the afternoon. Weather fine from Mocha, and sea smooth till within a day or two of Bombay, when there was more swell, but nothing remarkable.

Sixteen and a half days from Suez to Bombay.

Sixty-one days from London to Bombay.

The French steamers are all exactly similar, and afford comfortable accommodation for passengers. For first class passengers, there are eight cabins at the side of the saloon, each containing two beds, one above the other, and one cabin containing 4 beds, besides a saloon with six beds for ladies.

As regards money. Sovereigns are the most convenient and advantageous in the shape of coin, throughout the journey. Bankers circular bills, of £25 each, are better.

EXPENDITURE ON JOURNEY TO BOMBAY *viâ* EGYPT.

Steamer, London to Boulogne	0	12	0
Sundry expences on board, landing, &c.	0	16	2
Hotel Bill, Passport, &c., about	2	0	0
Diligence to Amiens, &c.	1	0	0
Hotel Bill, &c.	0	13	0
Diligence to Paris, &c.	0	19	2
Hotel Bill	1	13	4
Diligence to Chalons, &c.	2	12	6
Hotel	0	15	10
Steamer to Lyons, &c.	0	7	6
Hotel	0	17	1
Steamer to Avignon	1	10	10
Diligence to Marseilles, &c.	0	17	2
Steamers from Marseilles to Alexandria	21	3	6
Passport, &c.	0	18	11
Hotel at Marseilles	1	8	2
Table, &c., between Marseilles and Alexandria...	5	12	0
Hotel, &c., at Alexandria	3	3	0
Mr. Waghorn's Bill for supplies, &c., on the Nile	2	2	2
Servants Account ditto	2	16	2
Boat hire on the Nile, &c.	3	7	2
Servant, &c.	2	13	0
Mr. Waghorn, 50 dollars for all requisites for the journey from Cairo to Suez	10	4	0
Sundries	0	12	1
Expences at Suez about	2	5	0
Passage Money, Suez to Bombay, Rupees 800, or	80	0	0
Servant to Bombay, &c., say	3	0	0
	£153	19	9

Left London 4th April, arrived at Bombay 4th June, 1838. Was 2 days at Boulogne; 1 day at Amiens; 3 days at Paris; 1 day at Chalons; 1½ day at Lyons; 4 days at Marseilles; 1½ day at Malta; 3 days at Alexandria; 1 day at Cairo, and near 4 days at Suez.

APPENDIX.

I.

List of Outfit referred to in Chapter V.

1. One suit of evening dress cloth clothes, best, of light but good materials—One morning ditto. 2. A cloth jacket—Six camlet jackets—Six pair trousers ditto—One and a half dozen white jean ditto—Waistcoats (fancy or white) one dozen. 3. Stocks, black, half a dozen—Of sorts, half a dozen. 4. One best hat—Two cloth caps. 5. Four pairs of shoes—Two ditto boots. 6. Socks, white cotton, four dozen—Worsted, or lamb's wool, one dozen. Amid many good outfitters, Thresher and Glenny, 152, Strand, may be recommended as especially excellent, and the young civilian, if dissatisfied with the above meagre list of mere necessaries, may at their establishment see and be supplied with every article for comfort and luxury.

II.

Outfit for a Cadet to Bengal or Madras.

Six dozen calico shirts—Four dozen of cotton half hose—One dozen of worsted ditto—Twelve pair of sheets, each three yards long, and two widths of calico—Twelve pillow cases—Six pair of musquitoe drawers, to sleep in—Twelve pair of drawers—Three dozen pocket handkerchiefs—Six black silk military stocks—Two black silk neckcloths—Four dozen cotton towels—Twelve pair of cotton gloves—Six pair of white kid gloves—Six pair of white doeskin gloves—Two jackets of blue merino, and two trousers of gambroon, to wear at sea—Six white jean trousers—Six white jean waistcoats—Enough white jean to make in India twelve jackets, twelve trousers and twelve waistcoats of the regimental form—Blue military cloak. All the things to be packed in bullock trunks of the largest size.

A saddle and bridle—Shako-Plate can be altered after cadet is appointed to a regiment—Sash—Buff belt—Black leather sword belt—Regulation sword—Sword knot—Cot and screws, with mattress, and pillows—Blankets, and white quilt—Combs, and brushes of all sorts—Cabin wash-hand stand—Pewter basin, bottle, beaker, &c.—Cabin-chair—Looking-glass, with slide—Brush case, complete—Six pounds of wax candles—Cabin lamp, with sliding shade—Three pair of boots, rather thin—Two table-spoons—Two dessert spoons—Two tea-spoons—Two silver forks—Twelve knives and forks, six large, and six small—A metal teapot—Pair of silver muffineers.

To be procured in India, after Cadet is appointed to a Regiment.

Regimental dress coat, price in Calcutta, 10*l.* 10*s.*—Ditto shell jacket, 7*l.* 7*s.*—Regulation blue surtout, 7*l.* 10*s.*—Regimental pantaloons, 3*l.* 8*s.*—Regimental epaulettes, with facing stripe, 7*l.*—Forage cap, 3*l.* 3*s.*—Regimental breast-plate, uncertain—Regulation tent, 30*l.*—Cooking pots and pans, tea-kettle, spits, &c.—Chairs, table, and tea-trays—Bed, and musquito curtains—Brass wash-hand basin—Butter-pot—Milk-pot—Plates and dishes—Teacups and saucers, tumblers and wine glasses. These may be taken from England, and arranged in small canteens, as a bullock load.

The cavalry cadet going out to Bengal, must in the event of providing himself, take blue cloth for jackets, which is the undress of that army.

It has been suggested, that out of the six dozen shirts, two or three dozen should be of a superior quality, with fine linen fronts and collars. If the cadet be a careful personage, this arrangement will prove advantageous, otherwise the best may be lost and destroyed, and the worst retained. Should the friends of the cadet approve of the advice given by the Madras authority, backed by one of the correspondents from Bengal, blue cloth, sufficient for a military frock coat, scarlet for uniform coat, shell jackets, and cloth for pantaloons will be taken out from England, and made up by a native tailor, instead of being obtained in Calcutta from an European house, according to the instructions afforded in the above list. Considering the advice of both parties to be equally worthy of attention, I have recorded their different opinions, leaving it to the reader to make his own option between them.

Flannel is a very useful article in India, and if taken out in the piece, should be employed as a wrapper round the more valuable items of the baggage, which will be materially benefited by its assisting to exclude the air, and preventing the injurious effects of a damp atmosphere.

The uniform of the artillery being precisely the same as that of Her Majesty's forces, the objection to making up the regimental coat., &c., in London, will only refer to the contingency of a probable increase of bulk of the party during the passage out.

III.

The object of this fund is to provide the means to enable the seniors of the Medical Service to retire. It offers annuities of £300, or the value of annuity in money, to such medical officers as have completed their period of service. One annuity is available yearly through the Honorable Company's Treasury, and when the fund is able to offer an annuity or its equivalent, the offer is made to the senior on the list, and in succession downwards, until it is accepted. The individual must resign the Service within three months after acceptance, or forfeit one year's annuity or 3,000 rupees.

The monthly subscriptions are as follows :—

	In India.		In Europe.		
			£.	s.	d.
Members of the Board	Rs. 70	0	3	10	0
Superintending Surgeons . . .	50	0	2	10	0
Surgeons	25	0	1	5	0
Assistant Surgeons of two years . .	15	0	0	15	0
Assistant Surgeons under two years .	10	0	0	10	0

Donations are as follows on Promotion.

To the Medical Board	400 Rupees.
To Superintending Surgeon	200 "
To Surgeon . , ...	100 "

To entitle the subscriber to the annuity, he must pay to the fund, if a surgon, one-third the value ot the annnity ; if a superintending surgeon two-fifths.

If a member of the Board of not more than two years' standing, one-half.

If not more than three years, three-fifths.

If not more than two years, two-thirds.

In the fifth year of his service in the Board he must pay the full value of the annuity, credit being always given to the annuitant for his contributions, with compound interest at six per cent.

Should the fund be able to afford annuities or their value in money in addition to the one annually through the Government Treasury, the same regularity of payment of such annuities is guaranteed by the fund. The annuities are valued by a table similar to that used by the civil fund.

Subscribers retiring after seventeen years service are not called upon for any farther subscription until, by accepting the annuity, they are required to pay up the price fixed for their particular rank ; and members of the medical board may withdraw from the fund with their net contributions at the end of their second year at the board, giving up all future claim to benefit.

The fund is managed by a committee of seven subscribers at the Presidency, who choose their secretary from among the subscribers; three members go out annually by rotation, and three are chosen by the votes of the subscribers. Two-thirds of the votes are necessary to carry a point, and six weeks are given for the return of the votes.

IV.

PRESIDENT—MAJOR FRITH.

MEMBERS.

1st Lieutenants Emly, Humfrey, Jervis, and Macdonald.

The court having met pursuant to orders, the president submitted a letter from Captain Tennant, Assistant Adjutant General of Artillery, dated 18th of June, conveying a copy of a letter from the Secretary to the Military Finance Committee, for the information and guidance of this committee, which was read accordingly, and proceeded to the examination of bills and vouchers, and every obtainable evidence in order to make true and just calculations, agreeable to the tenor of the above letter of instructions. The result of their labours is as follows:—

1. After a most minute and careful examination of the bills of several officers of regiment, as well as the bills which are appended to this report, the committee have taken the averages as the best data they could obtain, for making their calculations and for drawing up their present report, in accordance with the instructions before them.

2. This estimate (No. 1) contains the particulars of the absolutely necessary monthly expences of a second lieutenant of artillery, stationed at Dum-Dum; the amount is calculated upon the lowest possible scale of expenditure consistent with the respectability of an officer.

3. The committee are not aware that there is any item in this estimate that requires a particular explanation, unless the allowance for house-rent may be considered too high, which arises from there being only four houses at the station, which let for less than eighty rupees each per month, all the rest averaging considerably

above one hundred rupees each per month, as will be seen by the list in the Note.*

4. The committee also consider it necessary that every subaltern should have a set of servants (as detailed in the estimate No. I) to himself, as he is frequently sent into garrison on his tour of weekly duty.

5. From this estimate (No. 1), it will be seen, that after paying the necessary and unavoidable expences for the month, the second lieutenant has a surplus remaining of sicca rupees 8 3 11, from which he is to pay the monthly proportion of charges, contained in the estimates No. 2, 3, 4, 5, 6, and 7, amounting in the whole to sicca rupees 75 14 1 per month, whereby the second lieutenant incurs a debt every month of sicca rupees 67 10 2.

6. The committee have not allowed any charge in the foregoing estimate (No. 1), of a palanquin and bearers, though they deem such a conveyance indispensably necessary for officers, who have to perform the duties detailed in the Note† during the course of

* List of houses and their rents.—2 of 50, 1 of 64, 1 of 74, 6 of 80, 1 of 84, 2 of 90, 5 of 100, 5 of 150, 1 of 160, 1 of 300 rupees each per month. Total.—25 houses at the station.

† One officer of each company to attend at the barracks at 8 o'clock, to inspect the breakfasts, and at 1 o'clock the dinners, daily.

To attend battalion, regimental and general courts-martial, courts of enquiry, &c., &c., which meet at the mess house between the hours of ten in the morning and three in the afternoon.

Young officers to attend all courts-martial and courts of enquiry during the first six months after their joining.

The orderly officer of the battalion to wait on the commanding officer daily at 10 o'clock, and attend daily at 12 o'clock to see the liquor served out.

Sicca rupees 64 12 16.

Lieutenant Colonel Dundas, from Dum Dum to Nusseerabad.

Captain Debrett, from Dum Dum to Agra.

Major Playfair, from Dum Dum to Berhampore, on general court-martial.

Lieutenant Dalzell, from Dum Dum to Berhampore.

Lieutenant Mallock, from Dum Dum to Cuttack.

the day, and to the performance of which they are under the necessity of walking, from some bungalows situated at a distance of not less than a mile, to the inevitable destruction of their health, while at the same season no European soldier is allowed to go out of his barracks from the hour of nine o'clock in the morning until five o'clock in the afternoon. The above prohibitory order clearly evinces the danger of exposure, in the heat of the day, but to which the subaltern officer is daily exposed; and if any proof were necessary to corroborate the opinion of the committee on the necessity of such a conveyance, they have only to state the fact of an allowance of rupees 30 6 per month being granted to assistant and veterinary surgeons while with their corps to provide such a conveyance to protect them (in the performance of their duty) from the baneful effects of the climate.

7. By these estimates it will be seen that the monthly expences (together with the monthly proportion of those of less frequent occurrence) of a second lieutenant on full batta and full tentage at Dum-Dum, with all the advantages of a mess establishment, exceed his monthly pay and allowances by sicca rupees 67 10 2; if such be the fact in this situation, it is not difficult to divine what will be the result when marching, with an increased establishment of servants, wear and tear of camp equipage and cattle, more clearly defined in estimate No. 8, viz., an increase of monthly debt (as per Note), and that this is really and truly the case, is established by the fact, that with very few exceptions, there is not a single subaltern officer in the regiment, from the senior first lieutenant down to the junior second lieutenant, that is not, in some degree, involved in pecuniary difficulties. It may probably be considered unnecessary to keep up a full marching establishment of this station; it is indispensably necessary however to be provided with the means to obtain it, at the shortest notice, for officers of all ranks in the artillery are liable to move at all times and seasons,

---

Lieutenant White, from Dum Dum to Assam.

Lieutenant Campbell, from Dum Dum to Dacca.

Captain Counsell, from Cuttack to Keitah.

from one station to another, frequently at remote distances, and of which the committee need only adduce a few instances of late occurrences as a proof.

8. During the time the officer is absolutely marching, his monthly expences will be reduced sicca rupees 40 (house rent), but this expence will recur on his arrival in cantonments, in addition to his marching establishment, making a total deficit per month of sicca rupees 132 7, with the interest accruing thereon.

9. With references to the expences of a first lieutenant the committee see no reason to alter the rate of the estimates already made for a second lieutenant, although it may reasonably be admitted that officers who have been in the service from 7 years, the junior first lieutenant to above 17 years, the senior would require a little more comfort and convenience, rendered necessary, not only from a longer residence in the country, but also to enable those, having charge of companies, more effectually to discharge the duties consequent thereon, as well as to preserve the books and documents belonging thereto.

10. The committee beg to refer to the estimate No. 9, to shew the actual difference between the expences and receipts of a first and second lieutenant, in which it will be seen that even a first lieutenant who receives sicca rupees 50 per month more than a second lieutenant, exceeds his monthly receipt by sicca rupees 19 15 11, on full batta and tentage, at this station, and by sicca rupees 84 12 9, with the addition of his marching establishment.

11. The committee now beg to submit for attention the fund necessary for a young man's first outfit, before he has received a farthing of pay, amounting to no less a sum than sicca rupees 1,417 15 1, as will be seen by the particulars detailed in the estimate No. 2, the greater part of which, if not the whole, is generally borrowed from some of the houses of agency in Calcutta, with an appendage of interest and insurance, that, combined with the monthly accumulating debt already stated, creates one of such a magnitude, that no exertions or privations on his part, to the latest period of his service, can ever enable him to discharge.

12. In the foregoing calculations, no allowance has been made for contingencies of any kind, such as books, postage, &c., &c.

13. The committee in closing their report, need hardly remark, that if such be the prospects of subaltern officers who are unmarried, how much more appalling must be those of one who has a wife and family to maintain.

W. H. L. FRITH, Major, President.

G. EMLY, 1st Lieutenant
J. H. JERVIS, ditto
H. HUMFREY, ditto
J. H. M'DONALD, ditto
} Members.

***ESTIMATE** No. 1, shewing the monthly expenditure of a second lieutenant of artillery at head quarters of the regiment.*

House rent				40	0	0
Mess bill, including mess wines				70	0	0
Share of breakfast expences				16	0	0
Contingencies. Blacking, pipe-clay, oil, candles, soap, mussala, stationery, &c.				10	0	0
1 Bearer	6	0	0			
1 Kidmutgur	7	0	0			
1 Mussulchee	4	0	0			
1 Dhobee	6	0	0			
1 Sweeper	4	0	0			
1 Saics	5	0	0			
1 Grasscutter	3	8	0			
½ a chokeydar	2	0	0			
1 Bhisty	4	0	0			
2 Days' ticca tailor	0	8	0			
				42	0	0
Feed and keep of horse	....			7	8	0
Military fund	3	0	0			
Orphan ditto	2	13	11			
Regiment ditto	3	8	0			
Church ditto	1	0	0			
				10	5	11
Total monthly expenditure, S. Rs.				195	13	11

***ESTIMATE** No. 2, shewing the outfit required by a second lieutenant of artillery on his first joining head quarters.*

1 Dress coat	165	0	0		
1 Shell jacket	48	0	0		
1 Epaulette	60	0	0		
1 Shako	120	0	0		
1 Cross belt	20	0	0		
1 Black waist belt	22	0	0		
1 Breast plate	16	0	0		
1 Gorget	24	0	0		
1 Sword	75	0	0		
1 Sword knot	18	0	0		
1 Sash	30	0	0		
1 Blue frock coat	70	0	0		
1 Pair blue dress trousers	70	0	0		
1 Pair undress trousers	40	0	0		
1 Pair white kerseymere ditto	36	0	0		
1 Forage cap	32	0	0		
12 White jackets	96	0	0		
12 Ditto trousers	96	0	0		
6 Ditto waistcoats	27	0	0		
3 Pair boots	30	0	0		
2 Pair shoes	8	0	0		
1 Cloak (regimental)	110	0	0		
1 Silk waistbelt	12	0	0		
3 Pair leather gloves	10	8	0		
1 Pair buckles	10	0	0		
2 Pairs silk stockings	16	0	0		
2 Stocks	14	0	0		
Amount of furniture outfit, vide Estimate, No. 6	234	6	0		
Do. horse, &c., vide No. 7	315	0	0		
Fees on commissions	35	12	5		
Mess entrance	90	0	0		
Total expence of outfit, sicca rupees	1950	10	5		
Deduct a credit of £50 exchange, 1s. 10½d. per rupee	533	5	4		
Leaves a balance to be borrowed of	1417	5	1		
Interest and charges on which at 12 per cent. per annum	170	0	0		
Total	1687	5	1		
Or monthly				14	4

ESTIMATE No. 3, shewing the annual expenditure of a second lieutenant of artillery.

Article	Rs.	As.	P.	Rs.	As.	P.
1 Shell jacket	48	0	0			
1 Sword knot	18	0	0			
1 Pair undress trousers	40	0	0			
1 Forage cap	32	0	0			
6 White jackets	36	0	0			
6 Pairs white trousers	36	0	0			
4 Pairs boots	40	0	0			
6 Pairs leather gloves	24	0	0			
9 Shirts	45	0	0			
6 Flannel banyans	24	0	0			
12 Pairs stockings	8	0	0			
2 Pairs silk stockings	16	0	0			
4 Socks	8	0	0			
12 Pocket handkerchiefs	9	0	0			
12 Hand towels	5	0	0			
6 White waistcoats	24	0	0			
3 Pillow cases	3	0	0			
1 Pair sheets	8	0	0			
Annually Sicca Rupees	424	8	0			
Or monthly				35	6	0

ESTIMATE No. 4, for those articles which require renewal every three years.

Article	Rs.	As.	P.	Rs.	As.	P.
1 Dress coat	165	0	0			
1 Epaulette	60	0	0			
1 Shako	120	0	0			
1 Black waistbelt	22	0	0			
1 Blue frock coat	70	0	0			
1 Pair blue dress trousers	70	0	0			
1 Pair white kerseymere ditto	36	0	0			
Total Sicca Rupees	543	0	0			
Or monthly				15	1	0

ESTIMATE No. 5, articles which require renewal every seven years.

Article	Rs.	As.	P.	Rs.	As.	P.
1 Cross belt	20	0	0			
1 Breastplate	16	0	0			
1 Gorget	24	0	0			
1 Sword	75	0	0			
1 Sash	30	0	0			
1 Cloak	110	0	0			
1 Pair buckles	10	0	0			
1 White silk belt	12	0	0			
Total Sicca Rupees	297	0	0			
Or monthly				3	8	7

ESTIMATE No. 6, outfit, furniture, &c., &c., for a second lieutenant on his arrival.

Article	Rs.	As.	P.	Rs.	As.	P.
1 Camp table	12	0	0			
2 Chairs	7	0	0			
1 Bedstead, mattress, &c.	30	0	0			
1 Bedroom table	7	0	0			
1 Set cooking utensils	40	0	0			
Breakfast Service. 4 cups and saucers	3	0	0			
Breakfast Service. 1 Tea-pot	5	0	0			
Breakfast Service. 1 Coffee-pot	1	0	0			
Breakfast Service. 4 Egg cups	3	8	0			
Breakfast Service. 1 Sugar pot	1	4	0			
Breakfast Service. 1 Milk jug	1	0	0			
Breakfast Service. 1 Butter pot	4	8	0			
Breakfast Service. 1 Tea-kettle	4	0	0			
Breakfast Service. 1 Slop basin	0	12	0			
1 Candlestick and shade	10	0	0			
1 Basket for ditto	1	6	0			
4 knives and forks	8	0	0			
Dinner Service. 2 Curry dishes	6	0	0			
Dinner Service. 4 dishes of sizes	5	0	0			
Dinner Service. 4 Hot water plates	6	0	0			
Dinner Service. 4 Plates	1	8	0			
Dinner Service. Glass. 1 Muffineer	1	12	0			
Dinner Service. Glass. 1 Salt celler	1	0	0			
Dinner Service. 4 Tumblers	4	0	0			
Dinner Service. 4 Wine glasses	2	0	0			
Dinner Service. 1 Corkscrew	0	12	0			
1 Brass chillumchee and stand	7	0	0			
1 Angerty	2	8	0			
4 Table cloths	12	0	0			
6 Napkins	2	0	0			
Plate. 1 Set silver spoons and forks, two of each	40	0	0			
1 Chatta	1	8	0			
1 Lantern	1	8	0			
Total Sicca Rupees	234	6	6			
Renew once in five years will give monthly proportion of				3	14	0

ESTIMATE, No. 7.

Article	Rs.	As.	P.	Rs.	As.	P.
A horse	250	0	0			
Saddle and bridle	65	0	0			
Sicca Rupees	315	0	0			
Allow renewal once in seven years gives a monthly proportion of				3	12	0

ESTIMATE No. 8, shewing the additional expences incurred by a second lieutenant of artillery when in the field.

Purchase of a regulation tent complete	350	0	0			
Ditto three camels	300	0	0			
Do. one pair camel trunks	45	0	0			
Do. camel gear	30	0	0			
Do. two pairs of bangies..	14	0	0			
Total cost, Sicca Rupees	739	0	0			
Allow renewal once in seven years, will give a monthly proportion of	8	12	10			
Additional expence. 1 Sirwan	6	0	0			
2 Bhangy bearers..	8	0	0			
1 Classy	5	0	0			
1 Cook	7	0	0			
Keep of camels ..	16	0	0			
Table expenses ..	14	0	0			
Giving a monthly expenditure of				64	12	0

ESTIMATE. No 9, shewing the expences incurred on becoming a first lieutenant of artillery.

Fees on Commissions { King's	15	0	0			
Comp.'s.	17	14	11			
Donation to military fund	180	0	0			
Sicca Rupees	222	14	11			
Difference of subscription. { Mility. fund	2	0	0			
Regtl. ditto	0	8	0			
Additional when 1st lieut. monthly				2	8	0

ABSTRACT shewing the aggregate amount of the monthly expenditure of a First and Second Lieutenant of Artillery.

	Second Lieutenant.		First Lieutenant.	
	At head quarters.	Detached.	Head quarters.	Detached.
Regular monthly expences, estimate No. 1 ..	195 13 11	105 1 11	193 13 1	195 13 11
Average ditto ditto, vide estimate No. 2 ..	14 4 0	14 4 0	14 4 0	14 4 0
" " 3 ..	35 6 0	35 6 0	35 6 0	35 6 0
" " 4 ..	15 1 0	15 1 0	15 1 5	15 1 0
" " 5 ..	3 8 7	3 8 7	3 8 7	3 8 7
" " 6 ..	3 14 6	3 14 6	3 14 6	3 14 6
" " 7 ..	3 12 0	3 12 0	3 12 0	3 12 0
" " 8 ..	0 0 0	64 12 10	0 0 0	64 12 10
" " 9 ..	0 0 0	0 0 0	2 8 0	2 8 0
Total monthly expenditure, Sicca Rupees	12 12 1	336 8 10	274 4 0	239 0 10
Monthly receipts .... Sicca Rupees	1 1 10	204 1 10	254 4 1	254 4 1
Average expenditure above receipts	10 10 2	132 7 0	16 15 11	84 12 9

W. H. L. FRITH, Major,

President.

In the above document we find the total average expenditure of a subaltern officer of the foot artillery, stated on the honour and integrity of a committee of officers, to amount to 339 10. The military assistant surgeon is not only subject to every expence incurred by the lieutenant, but to much greater as we have already proved. Our estimate of an assistant surgeon's expences amounted to 321, or 18 rupees ten annas less than that stated to attach to an officer at Dum-Dum. If such be the expences of the medical and military officer cantoned near the Presidency, what must they amount to at a distance, where all European articles are to be purchased at double the cost at which they are obtained at the Presidency? Moreover, if 339 rupees be the monthly expence of the bachelor, what must it amount to should he marry and have a family? We now come to any objections which may be made against our calculations and statements, from which we inferred that the superintending surgeon has to pay the debts of the assistant surgeon. If our statements be attentively examined from the commencement, we are satisfied no such objection will be maintained. Our statements are at least corroborated by the opinion of the committee to which we have already adverted.

The committee observes that the amount of outfit "*is generally borrowed from some of the houses of agency in Calcutta, with an appendage of interest and insurance, that, combined with the monthly accumulating debt already stated, creates one of such magnitude, that no exertions or privations on his part, to the latest period of his service, can ever enable him to discharge.*" In the event of its being advanced that the medical department is better paid than the military, we would, disclaiming all invidious feelings, proceed to prove the contrary; viz., that the military officers of the Bengal army enjoy actually superior advantages. Out of 1,980 military officers, 297, or 1 in 61, are field officers, and are on the receipt of regimental pay and allowances far superior to those of surgeons. Out of 350 medical officers, 12, or 1 in 29, rank with field officers, and draw allowances superior to those of regimental surgeons. Out of 495 captains, 159, or 1 in 3, hold staff appointments with extra regimental allowances. Out of 120 surgeons, 10, or 1 in 12, hold staff appointments with extra regimental allowance.

Besides these, six hold staff situations at the Presidency, on allowances less than those of regimental surgeons. The sum total of medical officers on the establishment is 350; out of these 12 comprise the higher grades, viz., three members of the board, and nine superintending surgeons; the rest, amounting to 334, have rank, pay, and pension of captains and lieutenants respectively. All regimental and other staff maintain a moiety of staff allowances when absent from their corps or appointments, on sick or other leaves; but not so with the medical officer whose allowances are forfeited instantly on quitting his regiment. From the facts here stated, it is clear that the situation of a medical is inferior to that of a military officer.

In order to prove that, from the circumstances to which we have alluded, the medical department is involved in great pecuniary difficulties, we attended at the insolvent court; and with our own hand noted down from the schedules of the different houses of agency which have failed, the number of the medical men on the debtor's side. In some of the schedules the profession of individuals is not mentioned opposite their names, and consequently we could not obtain the whole; but those specified amounted to 165. If we take into consideration those not distinguished by professional designations in the schedules, as well as those not mentioned in them, being indebted to friends and other persons, it will be obvious, that in India there are but a few medical men out of debt. Can it be advanced with justice against so large a body of respectable professional men, that their debts have arisen from imprudence or extravagance? We are satisfied it will be allowed by every candid reader that it cannot. To one estate alone the number of medical men in debt amounted to 52, of whom 21 were full surgeons. The debts to the foregoing must have been incurred during the palmy days, when medical contracts existed and pluralities of medical charges were held: these are now done away, and their allowances must have suffered a great reduction.

The period of promotion to a superintending surgeoncy, from the time the medical man enters the service, is now upwards of thirty years.

The rank of superintending surgeon is not granted as a matter of right, for length of service, nor in the order of regular succession; but depends on physical fitness, or the discretionary power of the Local Government. Few men can realize the hope of living thirty years in an uncongenial climate, or, if they live so long, of retaining their bodily and mental energies, on which, according to the following order, their prospect of promotion depends.

"The Governor General in Council farther deems it proper to declare, with reference to the principles established by the existing regulations of Government on this subject, and the great importance of duties to be performed by the superintending surgeons, that the succession to such appointment will not depend upon seniority alone; but that the selection will be made with reference to established character for distinguished zeal, strict assiduity, and professional ability, due regard being, however, had to seniority, when not opposed by considerations of a still more powerful nature."—

Yet the attainment of this grade, which happens not before he has past the 50th year of his age, affords the only prospect he has of extricating himself from his pecuniary difficulties. We extract the following from the general gradation list of the Bengal military establishment, compiled in the adjutant general's office, Fort William.

From 1795 to 1810, the number of medical men were	336
Retired	33
Died	71

For fifteen years, this is a most awful mortality. It is 17 to 1 against an assistant surgeon's obtaining the step of superintending surgeon from the period of his entering the service. Captain Badenack, in his work on the Bengal army, states on the unquestionable faith of public returns, that in twenty-five years out of every hundred officers who had entered the service in their boyhood, ninety-five died by a premature death, or remained in exile. This result, says the author just quoted,—

"Is not to be wondered at when we consider the great variety of climate to which our officers are exposed, in consequence of the great increase of territory during the last thirty years; when, for instance in the course of a few months, a man may be called on to serve in a flat and burning desert, exposed to hot and pestilential winds; then amid frost and snow, on the elevated ranges of the highest mountains in the world; and afterwards in the dismal swamps of Arracan."

It will be observed, that in specifying the period for retirement and pensions thereon, in regard to members of the Medical Board and superintending surgeons, the term of twenty years is mentioned. This specification, with the knowledge that no superintending surgeon can retire under thirty years' service, nor member of the Board under thirty-five to forty, is irreconcilable with the accuracy of calculation which ought to mark the adjustment of pensions. Nor is it to be accounted for, why this class of the Honourable Company's servants should alone be debarred the privilege of receiving their pensions, immediately on promotion to the higher grades in their department. Surely not from the circumstance of the short period of servitude, or because there was an apprehension of a surgeon becoming a member of the board, before he had been twenty years in the service, including three for furlough. Such an instance is not on record, and, indeed, under the present system it never can. Promotion must be slower now, since the numerical list has increased with the augmentation in the Honourable Company's military establishments and territorial possessions.

Hence is exhibited that on the present system the exactions of the service are grievous, and its rewards indisputably nominal.

The pensions of surgeons are as follows:—A member of the medical board, having been in that situation not less than two years, gets £500 per annum, or £700 per annum after five years; a superintending surgeon, having been in that situation not less than two years, is permitted to retire from the service, and allowed £300 per annum, or after serving in that situation for five years, £365. A surgeon is permitted to retire after twenty years service, on £192. From which it appears that after thirty-two years' service, and when about fifty-seven years of age, a superintending surgeon may be entitled to £300, or after being five years in that situation, or sixty years of age, to £365; and a member of the medical board, at the age of sixty-four, is allowed £500 a year, or after being five years in that situation £700. Thus, it is, that in the evening of life, a valuable and laborious servant, having received barely a comfortable subsistence during the period of his employment, is suffered to pass away almost unheeded and unrewarded.

When it is considered, how much a surgeon must necessarily be exposed to the climate; how many comforts he is compelled to renounce; how many dangers, both by night and day, he must encounter; how many hardships he must endure; how soon his constitution is liable to be impaired, by the fatigue and sudden changes which are inseparably connected with his employment; it must be confessed, that few situations can be inferior to that which he fills.

We now arrive at the prize. The staff pay of the superintending surgeon above Benares is 1600 rupees or £160 per mensem, below it 1266 or £126 12s.; allowing he has had bodily health and strength to attain this rank.

The age of 70 is the stated limit of man's existence, he had fifteen years then to live on his superior allowances, but if circumstances be such as to compel him to remain for the next step, the medical board, his span is contracted indeed. The senior superintending surgeon now on the list was promoted to that step in March 1827, he has already been upwards of nine years a superintending surgeon, at the average age he should be 59 years of age. The staff allowance to a member of the board is 2409 per mensem. As to the value of the allowances at such a time of life, on such a constitution, and after a lengthened residence in a tropical climate, we leave it to the actuaries of insurance societies to decide.

Having now considered fully the constitution of the department in His Majesty's and the Honourable Company's Services, we proceed to contrast them as regards pay, rank, and pension. We beg the attention of our readers to that part of our subject wherein is fully shewn the deep interest His Royal Highness the late Duke of York took in improving the condition of medical officers in the King's army. It had been found that the pay had been such that properly educated men would not enter it, a warrant was accordingly issued by order of His Majesty approving of an arrangement for increasing the advantages and improving the situation of medical officers, with the view of "*encouraging able and well educated persons* to enter *and continue* in *that line*," of His Majesty's Service. Now we have maintained, from the tenor of that warrant, that it is evident His Majesty would never have issued it if the evil effects arising from smallness of pay and inferiority of rank, had not deterred well educated persons from entering into and continuing in His Majesty's medical department. We conclude from the word to continue, that the respectable portion had quitted, and left Smollett's Morgans alone to discharge the important duties. The result as shewn by us was that so far back as 1805, the position of medical men was put altogether on a new and respectable footing as regarded pay; in comparison with that before allowed. What was the further result? A decidedly beneficial change, and hence a manifest improvement in the health of the troops; proving that to the Government it was unquestionably a most economical arrangement. It now secured the services of men who had incurred the expence and labour necessary for the acquisition of that correct and systematic education which alone can qualify gentlemen for the proper discharge of the important and sacred duties of the physician and surgeon, who were willing to devote their talents to the investigation of the causes upon which the preservation of health depended. It was an imperative duty of the state to require such efficiency, although it involved the apparent additional expence of remunerating men capable of the task, as an inducement for them to accept commissions and to continue in the service. The soundness of the reasoning is incontestibly proved by experience. The pay was therefore again increased, and in 1829 other improvements were made as regarded mess, board, servants' allowances, passage allowances to foreign stations, compassionate allowances to widows, orphans, and even mothers and sisters, when left destitute, under peculiar circumstances. In 1830, another warrant was issued by His Majesty's command still further improving the rate of pay, with additional allowances for servants in hot climates. Thus shewing, beyond doubt, that in the King's Service, as regards pay, it has progressively increased.

How has it been in the service of the Honourable Company? In considering what the pay of highly qualified medical officers in India should be, we have maintained that it was reasonable to expect that their services should be better remunerated here than in any other part of the world; because being mere sojourners, that is to say not permanent inhabitants of the country, their only object in coming to it would be to secure an independence, and to quit it again as soon as possible. No professional man ever came to this country, we will venture to prove, under the impression that he would not be able to secure something beyond a bare subsistence to enable him to retire long before a service from thirty-five to forty years. We need not tire the patience of our readers by going over the grounds on which we have so fully established the fact, that this, notwithstanding, has never been the medical officer's reward in the Honourable Company's Service. The history of this department shews the reverse.

In the King's Service there has been progressive improvement as regards pay, while in the Honourable Company's there has been progressive and considerable reductions. That at this moment the circumstances of its members are such as to excite universal alarm, that unless some favourable modifications be speedily made, the medical service will deteriorate. But before quitting the subject of pay, there is some points we feel ourselves called upon to advert to, and earnestly, but respectfully, to urge on the serious attention of the Government and the Honourable Court of Directors.

In addition to other grievances of their medical department, we beg to state that a memorial on the subject of pay to the home authorities has not been replied to or even so much has the receipt of it been acknowledged. Simultaneously with the half batta order, in 1828, the compensation for the medicine allowance was directed to be paid under the designation of majors' batta; surgeons at half batta stations, however, lost half their compensation instead of half their batta, i. e. of the captain. Although the mistake was eventually rectified, yet it existed for three years. Several surgeons suffered the loss during that time who never had their arrears paid up. They sent a memorial to the Honourable Court; but it has not to this day been acknowledged. The members of this service can never cease to look to the Honourable Court and the Government of this country as their only patrons and friends, and it is an aggravation of their depressed condition when they find their respectful and humble appeal overlooked, and we are sure the Court and the Government will be glad that we have brought this oversight to their notice.

On comparing the pay and allowances, as described in our several articles, it will be found that they do not cover the expenditure of the medical officer.

V.

The Court of Directors require of every gentleman appointed Chaplain, a Testimonial in the form subjoined, and his Letters of Orders, Deacon, and Priest.

> " We whose names are hereunder written, declare, " and testify from our personal knowledge of the life and " behaviour of ——— for the space of three years last " past, that he hath during that time lived piously, soberly, " and honestly, nor hath he at any time (as far as we " know or believe) written, taught, or held anything " contrary to the doctrine or discipline of the Church of " England.
>
> " In Witness whereof we have hereunto set our " hands the ———"

This Testimonial must be signed by three beneficed Clergymen.

Chaplains must attend the Political and Military Committee with their Letters of Ordination as Deacon and Priest, and Testimonials as above, previous to Appointment.

The Bishop of London requires a Testimonial in a form differing somewhat from the above; which form may be obtained upon application to the Bishop's Secretary.

When Sworn, the sum of £150 is paid to them to defray the Expences of their Passage and Outfit.

Chaplains must proceed to their destination within six months from the date of the Court's resolution by which they were nominated (unless with Court's leave) otherwise their Appointments will lapse.

SALARIES OF THE CHAPLAINS IN INDIA, TOGETHER WITH THEIR PAY ON RETIREMENT FROM THE SERVICE.

	No. of Chaplains.	Per Month Company's Rupee.			Per Annum @ 1s. 10½d. per Rupee £ Sterling		
BENGAL.							
Senior Presidency Chaplain	1	1226	1	0	1379	6	6
Junior ditto ditto . . .	1	1149	7	0	1293	2	0
Chaplains	17	800	0	0	900	0	0
Factory Chaplains . . .	30	500	0	0	562	10	0
	49						
MADRAS.							
Senior Presidency Chaplain	1	1200	0	0	1350	0	0
Junior ditto ditto . . .	1	980	0	0	1102	10	0
Chaplains	9	700	0	0	787	10	0
Factory Chaplains . . .	18	500	0	0	562	10	0
	29						
BOMBAY.							
Senior Presidency Chaplain	1	1200	0	0	1350	0	0
Junior ditto ditto . . .	1	980	0	0	1102	10	0
Chaplains	5	670	0	0	753	15	0
Factory Chaplains . . .	10	500	0	0	562	10	0
	17						

RETIRING PAY.

	PER ANNUM.		
After 18 Years Service, including 3 Years on Furlough	£292	0	0
If compelled through ill-health to retire after 10 Years	173	7	6
——— 7 Years	127	15	0

FURLOUGH.

After 7 Years Service	£191	12	6
Before 7 Years Service, if compelled by ill-health to come to Europe, he is entitled to	127	15	0

CLERGY (EAST INDIA.)

RETURN TO AN ORDER OF THE HONOURABLE THE HOUSE OF COMMONS,

Dated July 5, 1836; for

A Return of the number of Persons on the Ecclesiastical Establishment of the Church of England, and of the Presbyterian Church, and other Religious Denominations, in the Territories of the East India Company; stating the Rank of each, where stationed, the Expences of fixed Salary and of Allowances of each, and the total expences of each Presidency and Dependency for such Establishments, in Rupees and in Sterling Money, for the last Year the Account can be made up, so as to exhibit the whole Amount paid from the Revenues of *India* for the support of Religion of every Denomination.

A Return of the Ecclesiastical Establishment of the Church of England, and of the Presbyterian Church, also of Allowances to Roman Catholic Priests, in the Territories of the East India Company, in the Year 1834 (the latest Accounts received); shewing the Station of each Minister, and the Amount of his Salary and Allowances; together with the Total Expence of each Presidency and the aggregate Amount of the whole.

BENGAL.	Salary and Allowances of the Lord Bishop and Clergy.	Allowances and Contingencies of the Subordinate Establishments.
	Sa. Rupees.	Sa. Rupees.
The Lord Bishop of Calcutta..............	50,303	——
The Venerable the Archdeacon............	17,241	10,800
Domestic Chaplain to the Bishop..........	8,621	——
Senior Presidency Chaplain } Officiate at the Cathedral	14,993	12,310
Junior ditto }	12,931	

BENGAL—continued.	Salary and Allowances of the Lord Bishop and Clergy.	Allowances and Contingencies of the Subordinate Establishments.
	Sa. Rupees.	Sa. Rupees.
Chaplain at Nusseerabad	10,345	355
" Agra	10,345	276
" Bareilly	10,345	283
" Dacca and Chittagong	9,193	810
" Kurnaul	10,345	522
" Barrackpore.....................	10,345	220
" Meerut	10,345	2,100
" Ditto	10,345	
" Cawnpore.......................	10,345	727
" Ditto	10,345	
" Futtehgur.......................	10,345	96
" Delhi	10,345	80
" Neemuch	10,345	138
" Saugor	10,345	1,121
" Mhow	10,345	207
" Dum Dum	10,061	1,808
Chaplain to the Garrison at Fort William ..	9,777	——
Senior Chaplain at the old Church, Calcutta	8,621	5,658
Junior ditto ditto	8,621	
Chaplain at St. James's Church, ditto	8,621	3,276
" St. Peter's Church, ditto	8,621	1,962
" Dinagepore and Gazeepore	8,621	815
" Benares	8,621	138
" Dinapore and Patna	8,621	936
" Berhampore	8,621	367
" Allahabad	8,621	689
" Chinsurah	8,621	714
" Cuttack	8,621	270
" Hazareebaug	8,621	——
" Moulmein	8,621	150
Officiating Minister at Howrah	1,200	762
" " Lucknow	4,593	——
" " Chunar	4,593	494
	4,00,409	48,084

	Sicca Rupees.
Travelling Allowances to Archdeacon and Chaplains, and other Expences	8,623
Expence of the Church Establishment in Bengal	457,116

BENGAL.—continued.	
	Sa. Rupees.
Senior Minister of the Scotch Church	12,931
Junior ditto ditto	9,483
Expence of the Scotch Church in Bengal	22,414
Allowance to a Roman Catholic Priest at the Presidency and Dum Dum	2,400
" " Cawnpore	600
" " Dinapore	600
" " Berhampore	600
" " Meerut	600
Allowances to Roman Catholic Priests in Bengal	4,800
Total Expence	484,330
At 2s. the Sicca Rupee	48,433

	Salary and Allowances of the Clergy.	Allowances and Contingencies of the Subordinate Establishments.
	Sa. Rupees.	Sa. Rupees.
Chaplain at Singapore	9,186	689
" Prince of Wales' Island	9,186	1,000
Officiating Chaplain at Malacca	2,871	——
Allowances to Roman Catholic Priests at ditto	1,895	——
	23,138	1,689

At 2s. the Sicca Rupee . . . £2,483

MADRAS.	Salary and Allowances of the Archdeacon and Clergy.	Allowances and Contingencies of the Subordinate Establishments.
	Rupees.	Rupees.
The Venerable the Archdeacon......... ...	19,091	7,618
Senior Presidency Chaplain	14,400	——
Junior ditto	11,760	——

MADRAS.—continued.	Salary and Allowances of the Archdeacon and Clergy.	Allowances and Contingencies of the Subordinate Establishments.
	Rupees.	Rupees.
Chaplain at Black Town	8,643	906
" Vepery	7,875	1,728
" the Garrison	8,715	2,967
" St. Thomas's Mount	8,643	1,650
" Arcot	7,875	1,470
" Cuddalore	8,559	543
" Trichinopoly	7,875	819
" Ootacamund	7,875	588
" Masulipatam	8,463	882
" Bellary	7,875	588
" Vizagapatam	8,127	459
" Cannanore	7,875	861
1st " Bangalore	8,559	639
2d " "	7,875	
" Secunderabad	9,759	702
" Nagpore	9,639	639
Officiating Minister at Black Town	1,050	—
" " Cuddalore	420	—
" " Negapatam	1,050	78
" " Tanjore	960	—
Establishment at Sadras and Madura	- - -	462
	182,963	23,599
Expence of the Church Establisment at Madras	Rupees 206,562	

	Salary and Allowances of the Clergy.	Allowances and Contingencies of the Subordinate Establishments.
	Rupees.	Rupees.
Senior Minister of the Scotch Church	11,760	1,050
Junior ditto ditto	7,875	
	19,635	1,050

Expence of the Scotch Church at Madras... Rupees 20,685

MADRAS.—continued	
	Rupees.
Allowance to a Roman Catholic Priest at the Garrison	420
" " St. Thomas's Mount	1,050
" " Poonamallee	360
" " Cuddalore	420
" " Trichinopoly	360
" " Masulipatam	600
" " Bellary	360
" " Vizagapatam	240
" " Cannanore	756
" " Bangalore	756
" " Secunderabad	600
Allowances to Roman Catholic Priests at Madras	5,922
Total.—Madras Rupees	233,169
or Sicca Rupees	218,938
At 2s. each	£21,894

BOMBAY.	Salary and Allowances of the Archdeacon and Clergy.	Allowances and Contingencies of the Subordinate Establishments.
	Rupees.	Rupees.
The Venerable the Archdeacon	17,778	2,664
Senior Chaplain at the Presidency	14,400	6,086 (Senior and Junior Chaplains)
Junior ditto and Garrison Chaplain	15,060	
Chaplain at Byeullah and Tannah	9,200	1,308
" Surat	9,080	1,526
" Poonah	9,800	
" Ahmedabad, &c.	10,400	10,695 (Ahmedabad to Dapoolee)
" Kirkee, &c.	11,000	
" Belgaum	8,000	
" Ahmednuggur, &c.	10,400	
" Deesa	8,000	
" Dapoolee	9,608	
	132,726	22,279

Expence of the Church Establishment at Bombay Rupees 155,005

BOMBAY.—continued.	Salary and Allowances of the Archdeacon and Clergy.	Allowances and Contingencies of the Subordinate Establishments.
	Rupees.	Rupees.
Senior Minister of the Scotch Church	11,760	} 984
Junior ditto ditto	9,200	
	20,960	984

Expence of the Scotch Church at Bombay . Rupees 21,944

	Rupees.
Allowance to a Roman Catholic Priest at Bombay..	720
" " Colabah	1,140
" " Poonah	600
" " Surat	600
" " Ahmednuggur	540
" " Deesa	360
" " Scholapoore	120
Allowances to Roman Catholic Priests at Bombay .	4,080
Total.—Bombay Rupees ..	181,029
or Sicca Rupees ..	169,980
At 2s. each	16,998

Bengal Presidency	£48,433	
Singapore, P. W. Island, Malacca	2,483	
		50,916
Madras Presidency		21,894
Bombay "		16,998
		£89,808

Note.—In addition to the above sum of £89,808 incurred in India, there was also defrayed at home in the same year for Pensions and Furlough Allowances to Chaplains, &c., the sum of £7,785, making together £97,593.

(Errors excepted.)

JAMES C. MELVILL, Secretary.

East India House, August 1, 1236.

CLERGY (EAST INDIA.)

A Return of Persons on the Ecclesiastical Establishment of the Church of England, and of the Presbyterian Church, and other Religious Denominations, in the Territories of the East India Company.

(Mr. Hume.)

Ordered, by The House of Commons, to be Printed, August 4, 1836.

Table showing the Organization of Steam Packets, the

Stations. Points of Departure.	Stations. Places of Destination.	Rates of postage for a single letter weighing one quarter of an ounce.	Distance in miles.	Fares of Passengers in the Packets: for Places of the 1st class.			Places of the 2nd class.			Places of the 3rd class.		
		d.		£.	s.	d.	£.	s.	d.	£.	s.	d.
MARSEILLES	To Alexandria -	10	1943	17	12	0	10	8	0	5	12	0
	Civita Vecchia	5	380	4	0	0	2	16	0	1	4	0
	Constantinople	9	1921	17	4	0	10	0	0	5	4	0
	Dardanelles	9	1771	16	9	0	9	4	0	4	16	0
	Leghorn -	5	257	2	16	0	1	16	0	0	16	0
	Malta -	7	897	9	4	0	5	12	0	2	8	0
	Naples -	6	543	4	16	0	3	12	0	1	12	0
	Athens -	8	1531	14	8	0	8	0	0	3	12	0
	Smyrna -	9	1618	15	4	0	8	16	0	4	8	0
	Syra -	9	1456	13	12	0	7	4	0	3	4	0
LEGHORN	To Alexandria -	10	1687	15	12	0	9	4	0	4	16	0
	Civita Vecchia	4	123	1	0	0	0	12	0	0	8	0
	Constantinople	8	1664	15	12	0	9	4	0	4	16	0
	Dardanelles	8	1514	14	8	0	8	0	0	3	12	0
	Malta -	7	640	6	0	0	3	12	0	1	16	0
	Marseilles -	5	257	2	16	0	1	16	0	0	16	0
	Naples -	5	286	2	16	0	1	12	0	0	16	0
	Athens -	8	1274	12	0	0	6	16	0	2	16	0
	Smyrna -	8	1362	13	4	0	7	4	0	3	4	0
	Syra -	8	1199	11	12	0	6	0	0	2	16	0
CIVITA VECCHIA	To Alexandria -	9	1563	14	16	0	8	8	0	4	0	0
	Constantinople	8	1540	14	8	0	8	0	0	3	12	0
	Dardanelles	8	1391	14	0	0	7	12	0	3	4	0
	Leghorn -	4	123	1	0	0	0	12	0	0	8	0
	Malta -	6	517	4	8	0	3	4	0	1	4	0
	Marseilles -	5	380	4	0	0	2	16	0	1	4	0
	Naples -	4	162	1	4	0	0	16	0	0	12	0
	Athens -	8	1150	11	4	0	7	0	0	2	8	0
	Smyrna -	8	1238	12	0	0	6	8	0	2	16	0
	Syra -	8	1076	10	8	0	5	12	0	2	8	0
MALTA	To Alexandria -	8	1046	10	0	0	6	0	0	2	16	0
	Civita Vecchia	6	517	4	8	0	3	4	0	1	4	0
	Constantinople	8	1024	10	0	0	6	0	0	2	16	0
	Dardanelles	8	874	9	0	0	5	8	0	2	4	0
	Leghorn -	7	640	6	0	0	3	12	0	1	16	0
	Marseilles -	7	897	9	4	0	5	12	0	2	8	0
	Naples -	5	354	3	4	0	2	8	0	0	16	0
	Athens -	7	634	6	0	0	3	12	0	1	12	0
	Smyrna -	8	721	6	16	0	4	0	0	2	0	0
	Syra -	7	559	4	12	0	3	8	0	1	8	0

Rates of Postage for Letters, and Fares of Passengers.

ARRIVAL AND DEPARTURE OF PACKETS IN EACH SEA-PORT.

Packet coming from MALTA	Arrives at MARSEILLES	On the 1st, 11th, and 21st of each month, at 6 o'clock P. M.
	Departs from MARSEILLES	On the 1st, 11th, and 21st of each month, at 5 o'clock P. M.
Packet coming from FRANCE	Arrives at LEGHORN	On the 3d, 13th, and 23d of each month, at 6 o'clock, A. M.
	Departs from LEGHORN	On the 3d, 13th, and 23d of each month, at noon.
Packet coming from MALTA	Arrives at LEGHORN	On the 10th, 20th, and 30th of each month, at 2 o'clock P. M.
	Departs from LEGHORN	On the 10th, 20th, and 30th of each month, at 8 o'clock P. M.
Packet coming from FRANCE	Arrives at CIVITA VECCHIA	On the 4th, 14th, and 24th of each month, at 6 o'clock A. M.
	Departs from CIVITA VECCHIA	On the 4th, 14th, and 24th of each month, at 2 o'clock P. M.
Packet coming from MALTA	Arrives at CIVITA VECCHIA	On the 9th, 19th, and 29th of each month, at 6 o'clock A. M.
	Departs from CIVITA VECCHIA	On the 9th, 19th, and 29th of each month, at 2 o'clock P. M.
Packet coming from FRANCE	Arrives at MALTA	On the 7th, 17th, and 27th of each month, at 8 o'clock A. M.
	Departs from MALTA	On the 6th, 16th, and 26th of each month, at 10 o'clock A. M.
Packet coming from CONSTANTINOPLE	Arrives at MALTA	On the 4th, 14th, and 24th of each month, at 3 o'clock, P. M.
	Departs from MALTA	On the 8th, 18th, and 28th of each month, at 6 o'clock, A. M.

Points of Departure.	Places of Destination.	Rates of postage for a single letter weighing ¼ of an ounce.	Distance in miles.	Fares of Passengers in the Packets: for Places of the 1st class.			Places of the 2nd class.			Places of the 3rd class.		
		d.		£	s.	d.	£.	s.	d.	£.	s.	d.
SYRA	To Alexandria -	7	487	4	0	0	2	16	0	1	4	0
	Civita Vecchia	8	1076	10	8	0	5	12	0	2	8	0
	Constantinople	5	432	3	16	0	2	12	0	1	0	0
	Dardanelles	5	283	2	16	0	1	12	0	0	16	0
	Leghorn -	8	1199	11	12	0	6	0	0	2	16	0
	Malta -	7	559	4	12	0	3	8	0	1	8	0
	Marseilles -	9	1456	13	12	0	7	4	0	3	4	0
	Naples -	7	913	8	0	0	5	4	0	2	0	0
	Athens -	7	75	0	12	0	0	8	0	0	4	0
	Smyrna -	4	162	1	12	0	1	0	0	0	8	0
ATHENS	To Alexandria -	7	487	4	12	0	3	8	0	1	12	0
	Civita Vecchia	8	1076	11	4	0	7	0	0	2	8	0
	Constantinople	5	432	4	8	0	3	0	0	1	8	0
	Dardanelles	5	283	4	0	0	2	16	0	1	4	0
	Leghorn -	8	1199	12	0	0	6	16	0	2	16	0
	Malta -	7	634	6	0	0	3	12	0	1	12	0
	Marseilles -	8	1531	14	8	0	8	0	0	3	12	0
	Naples -	7	988	9	16	0	5	16	0	2	4	0
	Smyrna -	5	237	2	0	0	1	4	0	0	16	0
	Syra -	4	75	0	12	0	0	8	0	0	4	0
SMYRNA	To Alexandria -	7	650	6	0	0	3	12	0	1	16	0
	Civita Vecchia	8	1238	12	0	0	6	8	0	2	16	0
	Constantinople	5	310	3	4	0	2	0	0	0	16	0
	Dardanelles	4	160	1	12	0	1	0	0	0	8	0
	Leghorn -	8	1362	13	4	0	7	4	0	3	4	0
	Malta -	8	721	6	16	0	4	0	0	2	0	0
	Marseilles -	9	1618	15	4	0	8	16	0	4	8	0
	Naples -	8	1076	10	8	0	5	12	0	2	8	0
	Athens -	5	236	2	0	0	1	4	0	0	16	0
	Syra -	4	163	1	12	0	1	0	0	0	8	0
DARDANELLES	To Alexandria -	7	770	6	16	0	4	8	0	2	0	0
	Civita Vecchia	8	1387	14	0	0	7	12	0	3	4	0
	Constantinople	4	150	1	12	0	1	0	0	0	8	0
	Leghorn -	8	1512	14	8	0	8	0	0	3	12	0
	Malta -	8	870	9	0	0	5	8	0	2	4	0
	Marseilles -	9	1767	16	0	0	9	4	0	4	16	0
	Naples -	7	1225	11	12	0	6	0	0	2	16	0
	Athens -	5	356	4	0	0	2	16	0	1	4	0
	Smyrna -	4	160	1	12	0	1	0	0	0	8	0
	Syra -	5	283	2	16	0	1	12	0	0	16	0

ARRIVAL AND DEPARTURE OF PACKETS IN EACH SEA-PORT.—*continued.*

Packet coming from FRANCE	Arrives at SYRA	On the 1st, 11th, and 21st, at 8 o'clock A. M.
	Departs from SYRA	On the 1st, 11th, and 21st, at 2 o'clock P. M.
Packet coming from CONSTANTINOPLE	Arrives at SYRA	On the 1st, 11th, and 21st, at 5 o'clock, A. M.
	Departs from SYRA	On the 1st, 11th, and 21st, at 1 o'clock, P. M.
Packet coming from ATHENS	Arrives at SYRA	On the 10th, 20th, and 30th, at 5 o'clock, A. M.
	Departs from SYRA	On the 1st, 11th, and 21st, at 1 o'clock, P. M.
Packet coming from ALEXANDRIA	Arrives at SYRA	On the 10th, 20th, and 30th, at noon.
	Departs from SYRA	On the 1st, 11th, and 21st, at 6 o'clock A. M.
Packet coming from ALEXANDRIA	Arrives at ATHENS	On the 2nd, 12th, and 22nd of each month, at 6 o'clock A. M.
	Departs from ATHENS	On the 9th, 19th, and 29th of each month, at 5 o'clock P. M.
Packet coming from FRANCE	Arrives at SMYRNA	On the 2d, 12th, and 22d of each month, at 11 o'clock A. M.
	Departs from SMYRNA	On the 2d, 12th, and 22d of each month, at 5 o'clock P. M.
Packet coming from CONSTANTINOPLE	Arrives at SMYRNA	On the 9th, 19th, and 29th of each month, at 8 o'clock A. M.
	Departs from SMYRNA	On the 10th, 20th, and 30th of each month, at 8 o'clock A. M.
Packet coming from FRANCE	Arrrives at the DARDANELLES	On the 3rd, 13th, and 23rd of each month, at 10 o'clock, A. M.
	Departs from the DARDANELLES	On the 3rd, 13th, and 23rd of each month, at noon.
Packet coming from CONSTANTINOPLE	Arrives at the DARDANELLES	On the 8th, 18th, and 28th of each month, at 7 o'clock A. M.
	Departs from the DARDANELLES	On the 8th, 18th, and 28th of each month, at 9 o'clock A. M.

Points of Departure.	Places of Destination.	Rates of postage for a single letter weighing one quarter of an ounce.	Distance in miles.	Fares of Passengers in the Packets: for Places of the 1st class. £. s. d.	Places of the 2nd class. £. s. d.	Places of the 3rd class. £. s. d.
CONSTANTINOPLE	To Alexandria -	8	920	8 0 0	5 4 0	2 8 0
	Civita Vecchia	8	1537	14 8 0	8 0 0	3 12 0
	Dardanelles	4	150	1 12 0	1 0 0	0 8 0
	Leghorn -	8	1661	15 12 0	9 4 0	4 16 0
	Malta -	8	1020	10 0 0	6 0 0	2 16 0
	Marseilles -	9	1917	17 4 0	10 0 0	5 4 0
	Naples -	8	1375	13 4 0	7 4 0	3 4 0
	Athens -	5	506	4 8 0	3 0 0	1 8 0
	Smyrna -	5	310	3 4 0	2 0 0	0 16 0
	Syra -	5	433	3 16 0	2 12 0	1 0 0
ALEXANDRIA	To Civita Vecchia	9	1562	14 16 0	8 8 0	4 0 0
	Constantinople	8	920	8 0 0	5 4 0	2 8 0
	Dardanelles	7	770	6 16 0	4 8 0	2 0 0
	Leghorn -	10	1686	15 12 0	9 4 0	4 16 0
	Malta -	8	1045	10 0 0	6 0 0	2 16 0
	Marseilles -	10	1942	17 12 0	10 8 0	5 12 0
	Naples -	9	1430	13 4 0	7 12 0	3 4 0
	Athens -	7	502	4 12 0	3 8 0	1 12 0
	Smyrna -	7	650	6 0 0	3 12 0	1 16 0
	Syra -	7	490	4 0 0	2 16 0	1 4 0

ARRIVAL AND DEPARTURE OF PACKETS IN EACH SEA-PORT.—*continued.*

Packet coming from FRANCE	Arrives at CONSTANTINOPLE	On the 4th, 14th and 24th of each month, at 9 o'clock A. M.
	Departs from CONSTANTINOPLE	On the 7th, 17th, and 27th of each month, at 4 o'clock P. M.
Packet coming from ATHENS	Arrives at ALEXANDRIA	On the 4th, 14th, and 24th of each month, at 5 o'clock A. M.
	Departs from ALEXANDRIA	On the 7th, 17th, and 27th of each month, at 9 o'clock A. M.

REGULATIONS RESPECTING PASSENGERS

IN THF

FRENCH STEAM PACKETS.

PASSENGERS' LUGGAGE.—Each Passenger is allowed as luggage a weight determinable in the following proportions; viz.

Within the Stations between Marseilles and Malta.

200 lbs. for places of the 1st class.
120 lbs. for places of the 2d class.
60 lbs. for places of the 3d class.

And from any one of the Stations in the Levant to another in the same Sea, of which Malta forms the intermediate point.

400 lbs.	for places of the	1st class.
200	ditto	2nd class.
100	ditto	3rd class.

When the weight of luggage exceeds the weights mentioned above, each 20 lbs. or less above such weight will be liable to the payment of one centime (about the tenth of a penny) per marine league.

CHILDREN under 10 years of age to pay half the fare of the person in charge of them. For children above 10 years of age the whole fare is demanded.

CARRIAGES.—Eighty centimes per marine league for the transport of a four-wheeled carriage, and fifty centimes per marine league for a carriage on two wheels.

DOGS.—Dogs will be admitted on payment of two francs for a distance of less than one hundred marine leagues, and five francs for that distance and upwards.

A Restaurateur will be found on board each packet, who provides two meals daily for first and second class passengers, payment from whom is compulsory, whether partaken of or not. Passengers of the first class are charged six francs each, daily, for breakfast and dinner, for which tea also is provided if asked for. Passengers of the second class are charged four francs, viz.:—one franc fifty centimes for breakfast, and two francs 50 centimes for dinner. Prices of the articles furnished to third-class passengers, are indicated on a card on board. These pay for what they make use of only. Passengers of the first and second classes, who may be ill and unable to partake of the ordinary, will have soup, tea, or refreshing drinks given them, free of charge; but in every other instance, whatever passengers may require between meals, will be charged against them.

THE END.